Word 2019

by Dan Gookin

A Wiley Brand

Word 2019 For Dummies®

Published by: **John Wiley & Sons, Inc.**, 111 River Street, Hoboken, NJ 07030-5774, www.wiley.com

Copyright © 2019 by John Wiley & Sons, Inc., Hoboken, New Jersey

Published simultaneously in Canada

For general information on our other products and services, please contact our Customer Care Department within the U.S. at 877-762-2974, outside the U.S. at 317-572-3993, or fax 317-572-4002. For technical support, please visit https://hub.wiley.com/community/support/dummies.

Wiley publishes in a variety of print and electronic formats and by print-on-demand. Some material included with standard print versions of this book may not be included in e-books or in print-on-demand. If this book refers to media such as a CD or DVD that is not included in the version you purchased, you may download this material at http://booksupport.wiley.com. For more information about Wiley products, visit www.wiley.com.

Library of Congress Control Number: 2018956415

ISBN: 978-1-119-51406-0; ISBN: 978-1-119-51405-3 (ebk); ISBN: 978-1-119-51408-4 (ebk)

Manufactured in the United States of America

C10004687_092018

Contents at a Glance

Table of Contents

Introduction

The only thing standing between you and your writing is your word processor. Yeah, I know: It's supposed to be helpful. Well, it tries. Computers can do only so much. But you, as a smart person, are capable of so much more, which is why I'm guessing you opened this book.

Welcome to *Word 2019 For Dummies,* which removes the pain from using Microsoft's latest, greatest, most confusing word processing software ever! This book is your friendly, informative, and entertaining guide to getting the most from Word 2019.

Be warned: I'm not out to force you to love Word. This book won't make you enjoy the program. Use it, yes. Tolerate it, of course. The only promise I'm offering is to ease the pain that most people feel from using Microsoft Word. Along the way, I kick Word in the butt, and I hope you enjoy reading about it.

About This Book

I don't intend for you to read this book from cover to cover. It's not a novel, and if it were, it would be a political space opera with an antihero and a princess fighting corrupt elected officials who are in cahoots with an evil intergalactic urban renewal development corporation. The ending would be extremely satisfying.

This book is a reference. Each chapter covers a specific topic or task you can accomplish by using Word 2019. Within each chapter, you find self-contained sections, each of which describes how to perform a specific task or get something done. Sample topics you encounter in this book include

>> Moving a block

>> Check your spelling

>> Save your stuff!

>> Text-formatting techniques

>> Working with tables in Word

>> Plopping down a picture

>> Mail merge, ho!

I give you no codes to memorize, no secret incantations, no tricks, no presentations to sleep through, and no wall charts. Instead, each section explains a topic as though it's the first thing you read in this book. Nothing is assumed, and everything is cross-referenced. Technical terms and topics, when they come up, are neatly shoved to the side, where you can easily avoid reading them. The idea here isn't for you to master anything. This book's philosophy is to help you look it up, figure it out, and get back to work.

How to Use This Book

You hold in your hands an active book. The topics between this book's yellow-and-black covers are all geared toward getting things done in Word 2019. All you need to do is find the topic that interests you and then read.

Word uses the mouse and keyboard to get things done, but mostly the keyboard.

I use the word *click* to describe the action of clicking the mouse's main (left) button.

This is a keyboard shortcut: Ctrl+P. Press and hold down the Ctrl (Control) key and type the letter *P*, just as you would press Shift+P to create a capital *P.*

Sometimes, you must press more than two keys at the same time, such as Ctrl+Shift+T. Press Ctrl and Shift together and then press the T key. Release all three keys.

Commands in Word 2019 exist as *command buttons* on the Ribbon interface. I may refer to the tab, the command group, and then the button itself to help you locate that command button.

Menu commands are listed like this: Table⇨Insert Table. This direction tells you to click the Table command button and then choose the Insert Table item from the menu that appears.

Some of Word's key commands are kept on the File screen. To access that screen, click the File tab on the Ribbon. To return to the document, click the Back button, found in the upper left corner of the File screen and shown in the margin. Or you can press the Esc key.

When I describe a message or something else you see onscreen, it looks like this:

```
Why should I bother to love Evelyn when robots will
eventually destroy the human race?
```

If you need further help with operating your computer, I can recommend my book *PCs For Dummies,* 14th Edition (Wiley). It contains lots of useful information to supplement what you find in this book.

Foolish Assumptions

This book was written with the beginner in mind, but I still make a few assumptions. Foremost, I assume that you're a human being, though you might also be an alien from another planet. If so, welcome to Earth. When you conquer our planet, please do Idaho last. Thanks.

Another foolish assumption I make is that you use Windows as the computer's operating system. For Word 2019, you must use Windows 10. The Office 365 version of Word is similar to Word 2019 and it runs on older versions of Windows, though it's not the same. Differences between Word 2019 and Office 265 Word are mentioned in the text. This book doesn't specifically address the Macintosh version of Word, which is different.

This book doesn't cover using Windows. Word is a program (software) that runs under the Windows operating system. You must understand both to get the most from your PC.

Throughout this book, I use the term *Word* to refer to the Microsoft Word program. The program may also be called Word 2019 or even Microsoft Office Word 2019. It's all Word as far as this book is concerned. Word 2019 is part of the Microsoft Office 2019 suite of programs. This book doesn't cover any other part of Microsoft Office, though I mention Excel and Outlook wherever they encroach on Word's turf.

What's Not Here

This book covers using Word for anyone from a bare beginner to a modestly sophisticated scrivener. More advanced material is covered in its companion book, *Word 2016 For Professionals For Dummies.* I recommend that book if you really want to dig into advanced topics such as manuscript preparation, using Word in a legal office, programming macros, and other "professional" word processing duties. The title covers Word 2016 specifically, but nearly all of it also applies to Word 2019.

Icons Used in This Book

TIP

This icon flags useful, helpful tips or shortcuts.

REMEMBER

This icon marks a friendly reminder to do something.

WARNING

This icon marks a friendly reminder *not* to do something.

TECHNICAL STUFF

This icon alerts you to overly nerdy information and technical discussions of the topic at hand. The information is optional reading, but it may enhance your reputation at cocktail parties if you repeat it.

Where to Go from Here

Start reading! Behold the table of contents and find something that interests you. Or look up your puzzle in the index.

Read! Write! Let your brilliance shine!

My email address is dgookin@wambooli.com. Yes, that's my real address. I reply to all email I receive, and you'll get a quick reply if you keep your question short and specific to this book or to Word itself. Although I enjoy saying "Hi," I cannot answer technical support questions or help you troubleshoot your computer. Thanks for understanding.

You can also visit my web page for more information or as a diversion: www.wambooli.com. This book's specific support page can be found at www.wambooli.com/help/word. I place errata and updates on that page, as well as write frequent blog posts with Word information, tips, and tricks.

To find this book's online Cheat Sheet, simply go to www.dummies.com and search for *Word 2019 Cheat Sheet* in the Search box.

Enjoy this book. And enjoy Word. Or at least tolerate it.

1

Your Introduction to Word

Chapter **1**

Hello, Word!

A ccording to the popular book *Pencils For Dummies*, the pencil is the ultimate word processing tool. It's easy to use, it's wireless, and it features the original Undo command, in the form of an eraser. And that's about as funny as *Pencils For Dummies* gets.

As a writing tool, the pencil remains popular and easy to figure out, but it's not that technologically advanced. Your typical Ticonderoga #2 lacks many of the powerful capabilities you find in a sophisticated application like Microsoft Word, which is why Word requires a more formal introduction.

Start Your Word Day

As a digital resident of your PC, Microsoft Word serves as a loyal subject to the king of computer realm, Windows. To get work done in Word, you must contend with the multitudinous ways available in Windows to start the Word program. These methods can vary from the obvious to the obnoxiously cryptic, so instead I present you with the three most common ways to start your Word day:

>> Before you can use Word, your computer must be on and ready to work. So turn on your PC, laptop, or tablet if it's not already on and toasty. Log in to Windows.

REMEMBER

TECHNICAL STUFF

>> Do not attempt to make toast in your computer.

>> Ensure that you sport a proper posture as you write. Your wrists should be even with your elbows. Your head should tilt down only slightly, though it's best to look straight ahead. Keep your shoulders back and relaxed. Have a minion gently massage your feet.

>> Other nerdy terms for starting a program: Run. Launch. Open. Fire up. Beg. Thrash. Whimper.

Starting Word the traditional way

Propriety demands that I show the traditional, boring way to start Word. I'll be quick:

1. Press the Windows key on the keyboard.

The Windows key is adorned with the Windows logo icon, which I won't illustrate here because it changes more frequently than teenage fashion. The key is nestled between the Ctrl and Alt keys to the left of the spacebar. A duplicate is found on the right side of the spacebar on desktop computers. Use either key.

2. Look for Microsoft Word on the Start menu.

The item might be titled Word or Word 2019 or something similar.

If you don't find Word right away in Windows 10, click the All Apps button to hunt it down. In Windows 7, click the All Programs button.

Sometimes Word is found on a Microsoft Office or Office 2019 folder or submenu.

3. Click the Word icon or button to start the program.

Watch in amazement as the program unfurls on the screen.

Starting Word the best way

The *best* way to start Word, and the way I do it every day, is to click the Word icon on the taskbar. Word starts simply and quickly.

The issue, of course, is how to get the Word icon on the taskbar. If the icon doesn't appear on the taskbar, follow these steps to add it:

1. Find the Word icon on the Start menu.

See the preceding section, Steps 1 and 2.

2. **Right-click the Word icon.**

3. **Choose the command More, Pin to Taskbar.**

   The Pin to Taskbar command might appear directly on the right-click menu; otherwise, you find it on the More submenu.

The Word icon is *pinned* (permanently added) to the taskbar. From there you need click it only once to start the program.

Opening a document to start Word

You use the Word program to create *documents*, which are stored on your computer in much the same way as people pile junk into boxes and store them in their garages. To start Word, open a Word document. Follow these steps:

1. **Locate the Document icon.**

   Use your Windows kung fu to open the proper folders and hunt down a Word document icon, similar to the one shown in the margin.

2. **Double-click the icon.**

   This step is a standard Windows operation: Double-click an icon to open a program. In this case, opening a Word document starts the Word program.

The document is opened and presented on the screen, ready for whatever.

TECHNICAL STUFF

>> You use Word to create documents. They're saved to storage on your computer or in the cloud. Details are offered in Chapter 8.

>> The document name is assigned when it's originally saved. Use the name to determine the document's contents — providing that it was properly named when first saved.

>> Documents are files. As such, they are managed by Windows. If you need to find a lost document or rename it or organize your documents into a folder, you use Windows, not Word.

Behold the Word Program

Like all programs in Windows, Word offers its visage in a program window. It's the place where you get your word processing work done.

Working the Word Start screen

After starting Word, you may first see something called the Word Start screen, as shown in Figure 1-1. It's friendlier than that ominous empty page that has intimidated writers since the dawn of paper.

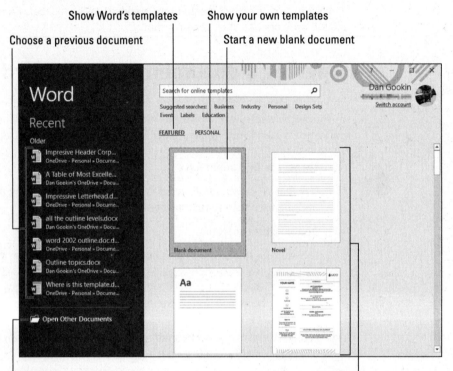

Show Word's templates

Show your own templates

Choose a previous document

Start a new blank document

Browse for a document

Select a template

FIGURE 1-1: The Word Start screen.

You can use the Start screen to open a previously opened document, start a new document based on a template, or start with a blank document.

Previously opened documents are listed on the left side of the window, as illustrated in Figure 1-1. Word's templates are found under the Featured heading. Templates you've created appear under the Personal heading. Click a template thumbnail to create a new document based on that template.

To start on a blank document, click the Blank Document template. Then you see the ominous empty page, which I wrote about earlier.

Once you've made your choice, Word is ready for you to start writing. Word is also equally content if you just stare at the screen and await inspiration.

>> The Word Start screen doesn't appear when you open a document to start Word. Refer to the earlier section "Opening a document to start Word."

>> You can disable the Start screen so that Word always opens with a blank document. See Chapter 33.

>> A *template* is a document that contains preset elements, such as formatting, styles, text, and possibly graphics. You use a template to help you start a common type of document, such as a résumé, a report, or an angry letter to the editor.

>> The Word Start screen appears only when you first start the Word program. It doesn't appear when you start a new document while the Word program window is already open.

Examining Word's main screen

Writing is scary enough when you first see that blank page. With a computer, the level of terror increases because Word festoons its program window with all kinds of controls and doodads. I recommend that you refer to Figure 1-2 to get an idea of some basic terms. Ignore them at your peril.

The details of how all these gizmos work, and the terms to describe them, are covered throughout this book. The good news is that the basic task of typing text is straightforward. See Chapter 2 to get started.

>> To get the most from Word's window, adjust its size: Use the mouse to drag the window's edges outward. You can also click the window's Maximize button (refer to Figure 1-2) to have the window fill the screen.

>> The largest portion of Word's screen is used for composing text. It looks like a fresh sheet of paper. If you choose to use a template to start a new document, this area may contain some preset text.

Working the Ribbon

An important part of Word's interface is the Ribbon. It's where a majority of Word's commands dwell and where settings are made. These items appear as buttons, input boxes, and menus.

The Ribbon is divided into tabs, as shown in Figure 1-3. Each tab holds separate groups. Within the groups, you find the command buttons and doodads that carry out various word processing duties.

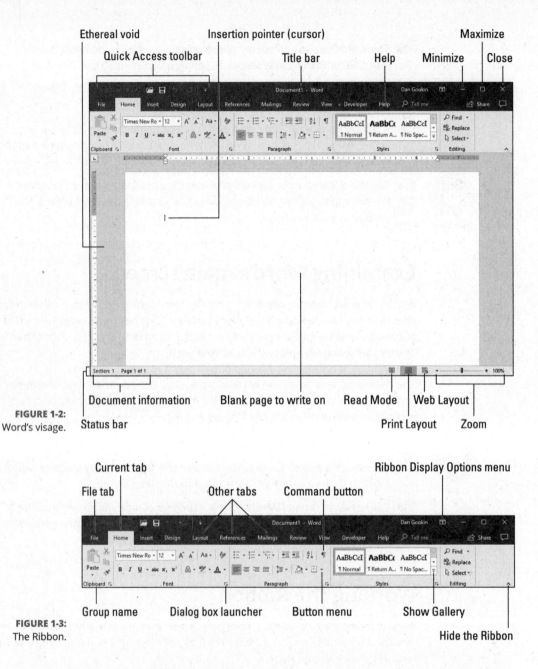

FIGURE 1-2:
Word's visage.

Labels (Figure 1-2): Ethereal void, Quick Access toolbar, Insertion pointer (cursor), Title bar, Help, Maximize, Minimize, Close, Document information, Status bar, Blank page to write on, Read Mode, Web Layout, Print Layout, Zoom

FIGURE 1-3:
The Ribbon.

Labels (Figure 1-3): Current tab, File tab, Other tabs, Command button, Ribbon Display Options menu, Group name, Dialog box launcher, Button menu, Show Gallery, Hide the Ribbon

To use the Ribbon, first click a tab. Then scan the group names to locate the command you need. Finally, click the button to activate the command or to display a menu from which you can choose a command. This book describes finding commands on the Ribbon in exactly this manner: *tab, group, command button.*

- » Some items on the Ribbon are controls that let you input text or values or adjust other settings.

- » Buttons with menus attached appear with a downward-pointing triangle to the right of the icon, as illustrated in Figure 1-3.

- » Galleries on the Ribbon display a smattering of tiles. To see them all, click the Show Gallery button in the gallery's lower right corner, also shown in Figure 1-3.

- » Use the Dialog Box Launcher icon in the lower right corner of a group to open a dialog box that's relevant to the group's function. Not every group features a dialog box launcher.

- » The amazingly frustrating thing about the Ribbon is that it can change. Some tabs may appear and disappear, depending on what you're doing in Word.

TIP

- » To ensure that you always see all the command buttons, adjust the program's window as wide as is practical.

- » Clicking the File tab replaces the contents of the Word window with a screen full of commands and other information. To return to the Word window, click the Back button (shown in the margin) or press the Esc key.

Showing and hiding the Ribbon

Microsoft may believe that showing and hiding the Ribbon is a feature, one that you control according to your preferences. I find that this option frustrates most people, especially when you unintentionally hide the Ribbon.

To resolve Ribbon frustrations, use the Ribbon Display Options menu, located in the upper right area of the Word window and illustrated in Figure 1-3. Choose an item to determine how to display the Ribbon. Your choices are

Auto-Hide Ribbon: The most annoying choice, the Ribbon appears only when you hover the mouse pointer near the top of the document.

Show Tabs: With this choice, only the Ribbon's tabs appear. Click a tab to show the bulk of the Ribbon, which disappears again after you've chosen a command.

Show Tabs and Commands: This option shows the entire Ribbon — tabs and commands — as illustrated in Figures 1-2 and 1-3. This is the choice you probably want.

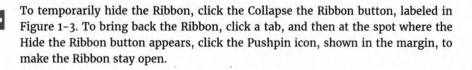

To temporarily hide the Ribbon, click the Collapse the Ribbon button, labeled in Figure 1-3. To bring back the Ribbon, click a tab, and then at the spot where the Hide the Ribbon button appears, click the Pushpin icon, shown in the margin, to make the Ribbon stay open.

TIP

» I recommend that you keep the Ribbon visible as you discover the wonders of Word.

» The online version of Word shows a different Ribbon than the Windows program does. This book doesn't cover the online version specifically, though I recommend that you learn to use the Word program first, and then go online and enjoy (or not) that version of Word.

Working with Word on a tablet

If you're using Word on a tablet, you can adjust the spacing between buttons on the Ribbon by activating Touch mode. This spacing feature makes the Ribbon more useful in Touch mode. Follow these steps:

1. **Click or touch the Customize Quick Access Toolbar button.**

   The button appears to the right of the Quick Access toolbar buttons. (Refer to Figure 1-2.)

2. **Choose Touch/Mouse Mode.**

   The Touch Mode button appears on the Quick Access toolbar, shown in the margin.

Tap the button to switch the Ribbon between Mouse and Touch modes. In Mouse mode, the buttons on the Ribbon appear closer together. In Touch mode, more space is added between the buttons, which makes it easier for your stubby fingers to tap the proper command.

Changing the document view

Just to keep you on your toes, Word offers multiple ways to view your document in its window. The blank area where you write, which should be full of text by now, can be altered to present information in different ways. Why would you want to do that? You don't! But it helps to know about the different ways so that you can change them back.

The standard way to view a document is called Print Layout view. It's the view shown in this book, and it's how Word typically presents a document. A virtual page appears on the screen, with four sides, like a sheet of paper with text in the middle. What you see on the screen is pretty much what you'll see in the final results, whether printed or published as an electronic document.

The other views are

> **Read Mode:** Use this view to read a document like an eBook. The Ribbon and pretty much the rest of Word is hidden while in Read mode.

> **Web Layout:** This view presents your document as a web page. It's available should you use Word's dubious potential as a web page editor.

> **Outline:** This mode helps you organize your thoughts, as covered in Chapter 25.

> **Draft:** Draft view presents only basic text, not all the formatting and fancy features, such as graphics.

To switch between Read Mode, Print Layout, and Web Layout views, click one of the View buttons, found in the lower right corner of the Word program window. (Refer to Figure 1-2.)

To get to Outline and Draft views, as well as to see all View modes in one location, click the View tab and choose the appropriate command button from the Views group.

REMEMBER

When your document looks weird in the Word program window, switch back to Print Layout view to fix the problem. Click the Print Layout button on the status bar, or click the View tab and choose Print Layout in the Views group.

Making text look larger or smaller

When the information in Word's window just isn't big enough, don't increase the font size! Instead, whip out the equivalent of a digital magnifying glass, the Zoom command. It helps you enlarge or reduce your document's presentation, making it easier to see or giving you the Big Picture look.

Several methods are available to zoom text in Word. The most obvious is to use the Zoom control found in the lower right corner of the Word window, on the status bar. Adjust the slider right or left to make the text larger or smaller, respectively.

To set specific zoom sizes, click the 100% button on the status bar. Use the Zoom dialog box to set a size based on percentage, page width, or even multiple pages.

REMEMBER

>> Zooming doesn't affect how a document prints — only how it looks on the screen.

>> For more specific zoom control, click the View tab and use the commands found in the Zoom group.

CAJOLING WORD TO HELP YOU

Like most Windows programs, a Help system is available in Word. Press the F1 key to summon this support, which displays the Word Help pane on the side of the document window. There you can type a topic, a command name, or even a question in the box to search for help.

The F1 key also works any time, and the information displayed tends to be specific to whatever you're doing in Word.

Little buttons that look like question marks appear in various places in the program. Click one of these buttons to also summon Word Help.

In the age of Google, Word also offers a Tell Me What You Want to Do help box on the Ribbon. Type a topic or question in the box and press the Enter key to see a quick list of commands or suggestions, or to obtain online help. Oh, and yes: Word's Help works best when your computer has an Internet connection.

TIP

>> If the computer's mouse has a wheel button, you can zoom by holding the Ctrl key on your keyboard and rolling the mouse wheel up or down. Rolling up zooms in; rolling down zooms out.

>> If you find that the document zoom has changed accidentally, it's probably because of the Ctrl+mouse wheel trick described in the preceding bullet.

>> Word has plenty of document-viewing tools that work similarly to the Zoom command, including side-by-side page presentation and tools for viewing multiple documents. See Chapter 24 for details.

End Your Word Day

It's the pinnacle of etiquette to know when and how to excuse oneself. For example, the phrase "Well, I must be off" works a lot better than growling, "I wish you all would rot" before leaving a family dinner. The good news for Word is that's completely acceptable to quit the program without hurting its feelings.

Quitting Word

When you've finished word processing and you don't expect to return to it any time soon, quit the Word program. Click the X button in the upper right corner of the Word program window. (Refer to Figure 1-2.)

The catch? You have to close each and every Word document window that's open before you can proclaim that you've completely quit Word.

The other catch? Word won't quit during that shameful circumstance when you've neglected to save a document. If so, you're urged to save, as shown in Figure 1-4. My advice is to click the Save button to save your work; see Chapter 8 for specific document-saving directions.

Microsoft Word   ✕

⚠   Want to save your changes to Document1?

If you click "Don't Save", a recent copy of this file will be temporarily available.
Learn more

[Save]   [Don't Save]   [Cancel]

If you click the Don't Save button, your work isn't saved and Word quits. If you click the Cancel button, Word doesn't quit and you can continue working.

» You don't have to quit Word just to start editing another document. Refer to the next couple of sections for helpful, time-saving information.

» After quitting Word, you can continue to use Windows to accomplish whatever task comes next. Or you can choose to do something relaxing, like playing *Baby Vampire Killer IV*.

Closing a document without quitting Word

You don't always have to quit Word. For example, if you're merely stopping work on one document to work on another, quitting Word is a waste of time. Instead, you *close* the first document. Follow these steps:

1. **Click the File tab.**

   The File screen appears. Commands line the left side of the screen, as shown in Figure 1-5.

2. **Choose the Close command.**

3. **Save the document, if you're prompted to do so.**

The shame! Always save before closing. Tsk-tsk.

Commands

Return to document

FIGURE 1-5:
The File tab
screen.

Info

Protect Document
Control what types of changes people can make to this document.

Inspect Document
Before publishing this file, be aware that it contains:
▪ Document properties and author's name

Manage Document
There are no unsaved changes.

Properties ▾
Size   Not saved yet
Pages   1
Words   1
Total Editing Time   56 Minutes
Title   Add a title
Tags   Add a tag
Comments   Add comments

Related Dates
Last Modified
Created   Today, 3:35 PM
Last Printed

Related People
Author   DG Dan Gookin
              Add an author
Last Modified By   Not saved yet
Show All Properties

After the document has closed, you return to the main Word window. You don't see a document in the window, and many command buttons are dimmed (unavailable). At this point, you can create a new document or open a document you previously saved.

Bottom line: There's no point in quitting Word when all you want to do is start editing a new document.

>> There's no urgency to close a document. I keep mine open all day, saving frequently. Occasionally, I wander off to do something not work related, like play a game or see who's being obnoxious on Facebook. To return to the document at any time, click its button on the Windows taskbar.

REMEMBER

» The keyboard shortcut for the Close command is Ctrl+W. This command may seem weird, but it's a standard keyboard shortcut used to close documents in many programs.

» To swiftly start a new, blank document in Word, press Ctrl+N.

Setting Word aside

Don't quit Word when you know that you'll use it again soon. In fact, I've been known to keep Word open and running on my computer for *weeks* at a time. The secret is to use the Minimize button, found in the upper right corner of the screen. (Refer to Figure 1-2.)

Click the Minimize button to shrink the Word window to a button on the taskbar. With the Word window out of the way, you can do other things with your computer. Then when you're ready to word-process again, click the Word button on the taskbar to restore the Word window to the desktop.

Chapter **2**

The Typing Chapter

Word processing is about using a keyboard. It's typing. That's the way computers were used for years, long before the mouse and all the fancy graphics became popular. Yep — ask a grizzled old-timer and you'll hear tales of unpleasant text screens and mysterious keyboard commands that would tie your fingers in knots. Things today aren't that bad.

Input Devices Galore

When you process words, you type: clickity-clack-clack. You use your fingers and one thumb to manipulate the computer keyboard. It's an important part of getting text on a page, but also important is the mouse. No, you don't type with the mouse, but you do some pointing and clicking in addition to clickity-clack-clacking.

Using the PC keyboard

I'm sure you can easily recognize a computer keyboard, but do you know the technical terms that refer to its various keys?

Relax: No one does.

Rather than look at all 100+ keys as a single, marauding horde, consider how the keys are clustered into groups, as illustrated in Figure 2-1. To best use Word and understand how the keyboard is referenced in this book, it helps to know the general keyboard areas illustrated in the figure.

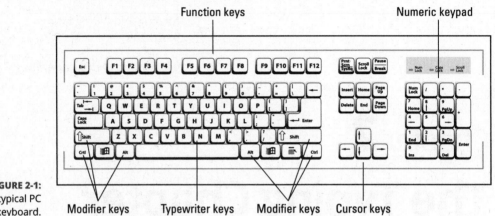

Function keys   Numeric keypad

FIGURE 2-1:
A typical PC
keyboard.

Modifier keys   Typewriter keys   Modifier keys   Cursor keys

Of all the keys, a few play important roles in the word processing task. They are

> **Enter:** Marked with the word *Enter* and sometimes a cryptic, bent-arrow thing, use this key to end a paragraph of text. See the later section "Pressing the Enter key."
>
> **Spacebar:** The only key with no symbol, it inserts a space between words and sentences. Yes, just one space. See the later section "Whacking the spacebar."
>
> **Tab:** This key inserts the Tab character, which shoves the next text you type over to the next tab stop. Using this key properly is an art form. Chapter 12 is dedicated to typing tabs and setting tab stops.
>
> **Backspace and Delete:** Use these keys to back up and erase text. Read more about these keys in Chapter 4.

Every character key you press on the keyboard produces a character in your Word document, on the blank part where you write. Typing those character keys over and over is how you create text in a word processor.

>> A laptop keyboard's layout is different from the desktop keyboard layout, as shown in Figure 2-1. Typically, laptop keyboards lack a numeric keypad. The cursor keys are clustered tightly around the typewriter keys in unusual and creative patterns. The function keys might be accessed by pressing special key combinations.

» Keys on the numeric keypad can be number keys or cursor keys. The split personality is evident on each key cap, which displays two symbols. When the Num Lock key's lamp is on, the keys generate numbers. When the lamp is off, the keys serve as duplicate cursor keys.

» Cursor keys control the cursor, which is officially known as the *insertion pointer* in Microsoft Word. The cursor keys include the four arrow keys (up, down, left, right) and also the keys Home, End, PgUp (or Page Up), PgDn (or Page Down), Insert, and Delete.

» Ctrl is pronounced "control." It's the control key.

» The Delete key may also be labeled Del on the keyboard.

» The modifier keys — Shift, Ctrl, and Alt — work in combination with other keys.

Working an onscreen keyboard

Two-in-one laptops and tablets sport an onscreen keyboard, which you can use to type text in Word. You can also draw text, scribble, and perform a host of other options. For email or short missives, the onscreen keyboard is great! For true word processing, however, attach the keyboard.

When it's not possible to use a real keyboard, here are my onscreen keyboard thoughts and suggestions:

» The onscreen keyboard's operation works basically the same as a real keyboard: You type text using your fingers, albeit probably not as fast as on a physical keyboard.

» Accessing some of the specialized keys (function keys, cursor keys, and so on) is problematic. Sometimes they're available by choosing a different touch-screen keyboard layout, but often they're not available at all.

» Using the Ctrl key on the onscreen keyboard is a two-step process: Tap the Ctrl key, and then touch another key — for example, Ctrl and then the S key for Ctrl+S.

» Not all Ctrl-key combinations in Word can be produced by using the onscreen keyboard.

» Refer to Chapter 1 for information on activating Touch mode, which makes it easier to use Word on a tablet.

Understanding the mouse pointer

Though word processing is a keyboard thing, you inevitably lift your hand from the keyboard to fondle the computer mouse. Use the mouse to choose commands, move around the document, and select text. Specific information on these tasks is found throughout this book. For now, it helps to understand how the mouse pointer changes its appearance as you work in Word:

For editing text, the mouse pointer becomes the I-beam.

For choosing items, the standard 11 o'clock mouse pointer is used.

For selecting lines of text, a 1 o'clock mouse pointer is used.

The mouse pointer changes its appearance when the *click-and-type* feature is active: Teensy lines appear below and to the left and right of the I-beam mouse pointer. Refer to Chapter 32 for information on click-and-type.

TIP

When you point the mouse at a command button or any icon on the Word screen, you see a pop-up information bubble. The text in the bubble describes the command and perhaps offers a hint on how the command is used.

Keyboard Do's and Don'ts

You don't need to be a 70-words-per-minute touch typist to use a word processor. And if you don't know how to type, see the nearby sidebar, "Do I need to learn to type?" — although I can tell you that the answer is "Yes, you need to learn to type." It also helps to know a few typing do's and don'ts that are particular to word processing.

Following the insertion pointer

Text you compose in Word appears at the *insertion pointer*'s location. The insertion pointer looks like a flashing vertical bar:

|

Characters appear *before* the insertion pointer, one at a time. After a character appears, the insertion pointer hops to the right, making room for more text.

TIP

"DO I NEED TO LEARN TO TYPE?"

No one needs to learn to type to use a word processor, but you do yourself a favor when you learn. My advice is to get a computer program that teaches you to type. I can recommend the *Mavis Beacon Teaches Typing* program, even though I don't get any money from her and none of her children resembles me. I just like the name Mavis, I suppose.

The program *Typing Instructor Platinum* is also recommended.

No matter which software you choose, knowing how to type makes the word processing chore a wee bit more enjoyable.

TECHNICAL STUFF

>> The insertion pointer moves as you type, but its location can be set to any position in the document's text. Chapter 3 covers moving the insertion pointer around in more detail.

>> Some documentation refers to the insertion pointer as a cursor. The mouse pointer might also be referred to as a cursor. For clarity, this book refers to the insertion pointer and mouse pointer without using the term *cursor*.

Whacking the spacebar

Pressing the spacebar inserts a *space character* into the text. Spaces are important between words and sentences. Withoutthemreadingwouldbedifficult.

REMEMBER

The most important thing to remember about the spacebar is that you need to whack it only once when word processing. Only *one* space appears between words and after punctuation. That's it!

>> I'm serious! Back in the dark ages, typing instructors directed students to use two spaces between sentences. That extra space was necessary for readability because typewriters used monospaced characters. On a computer, however, the extra space does nothing and potentially leads to formatting woes down the road.

>> Anytime you feel like using two or more spaces in a document, use a tab instead. Tabs are best for indenting text as well as for lining up text in columns. See Chapter 12 for details.

Backing up and erasing

When you make a typo or another type of typing error, press the Backspace key on the keyboard. The Backspace key moves the insertion pointer back one character and erases that character. The Delete key also erases text, though it gobbles up characters to the *right* of the insertion pointer.

See Chapter 4 for more information on deleting text.

Pressing the Enter key

In word processing, you press the Enter key only when you reach the end of a paragraph. Do not press the Enter key at the end of a line.

When your text wanders precariously close to the right margin, Word automatically wraps the last word on the line down to the next line. This *word wrap* feature eliminates the need to press Enter at the end of a line.

>> Don't use the Enter key to double-space your text. Double-spacing is a paragraph format in Word. See Chapter 11 for more information.

>> Don't press the Enter key twice to add extra space between your paragraphs. That extra space is added automatically, provided it's part of the paragraph format, also covered in Chapter 11.

>> If you want to indent a paragraph, press the Tab key after pressing Enter. As with other word processing rules and regulations, paragraphs can be indented automatically, provided that format is applied, as covered in (you guessed it) Chapter 11.

Stuff That Happens While You Type

As you madly compose your text, fingers energetically jabbing the buttons on the keyboard, you may notice a few things happening on the screen. You might see spots. You might see lines and boxes. You may even see lightning! All are side effects of typing in Word. They're normal, and they're presented to help you.

Watching the status bar

The reason it's called the *status* bar is that it shows you the status of your document, updating information as you type. A collection of information appears, starting at the left end of the status bar and marching right, as shown in Figure 2-2.

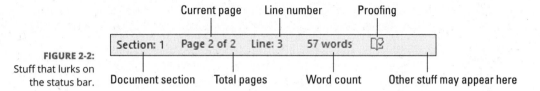

FIGURE 2-2:
Stuff that lurks on the status bar.

Use the status bar's information to see which page and line you're editing, the word count, and so on.

The details that appear on the status bar are customizable. Chapter 29 explains how to control what shows up and how to hide items on the status bar.

Observing page breaks

As your document gains length, Word shows you where one page ends and another page begins. This visual assistance helps you keep elements on the same page, but also shows you how text flows between pages.

The visual clue for a new page is shown in Figure 2-3. In Print Layout view, the page break appears graphically. Text above the ethereal void is on one page, and text below the void is on the next page.

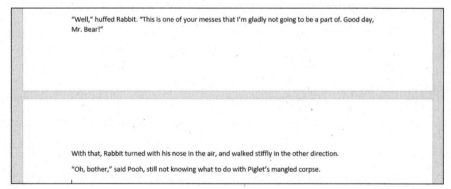

FIGURE 2-3:
The page break in Print Layout view.

In Draft view, the page break appears as a line of dots marching from left to right across the document. In other views, the page break may not show up at all, in which case you use the status bar to determine the current page. For example, when the page-number indicator changes from 6 to 7, you've started a new page.

>> You can change the gap between pages in Print Layout view. Point the mouse at the gap. When the mouse pointer changes, as shown in the margin, double-click to either close or open the gap.

>> Don't force a page break by pressing the Enter key a gazillion times! Instead, see Chapter 13 for information on inserting page breaks (new pages) in Word.

>> The topic of page breaks brings up the concept of widows and orphans, which refer to a single line of text at the page's top or bottom, respectively. Word automatically moves such text to the next or previous page to prevent widows and orphans from happening.

TECHNICAL STUFF

Working collapsible headers

You may see a tiny triangle to the left of various headings in your documents, as shown in the margin. These triangles allow you to expand or collapse all text in the header's section. Click once to collapse the text; click again to expand it.

See Chapter 25 for a longer discussion of collapsible headers, as well as information on Word's Outline view.

Dealing with spots and clutter in the text

There's no cause for alarm if you see spots — or dots — amid the text you type, such as

```
This•can•be•very•annoying.¶
```

What you're seeing are *nonprinting characters*. Word uses various symbols to represent things you normally don't see: spaces, tabs, the Enter key, and more. These jots and tittles appear when the Show/Hide feature is activated:

1. **Click the Home tab.**

¶

2. **In the Paragraph group, click the Show/Hide command button.**

   The button features the Paragraph symbol as its icon, shown in the margin.

To hide the symbols again, click the Show/Hide command button a second time.

>> Why bother with showing the goobers? Sometimes, it's useful to check out what's up with formatting, find stray tabs visually, or locate missing paragraphs, for example.

TECHNICAL STUFF

- >> WordPerfect users: The Show/Hide command is as close as you can get to your beloved Reveal Codes command.

- >> The keyboard shortcut for the Show/Hide command is Ctrl+Shift+8. Use the 8 on the typewriter area of the keyboard, not the numeric keypad.

- >> The Paragraph symbol is called the *pilcrow*.

Understanding colorful underlines

When Word underlines your text without permission, it's drawing your attention to something amiss. These special underlines are not text formats. Here are a few of the underlines you may witness from time to time:

Red zigzag: Spelling errors in Word are underlined with red zigzags. See Chapter 7.

Blue zigzag: Grammatical and word choice errors are flagged with a blue zigzag underline. Again, see Chapter 7.

DICTATE THY PROSE

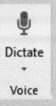

An option for some versions of Word is using dictation instead of typing to generate text. To confirm that your edition of Word sports this feature, look for the Voice group on the Home tab, which features the Dictation button, shown nearby. If you're prompted, activate the feature, which requires your computer to have a microphone attached and configured.

To dictate text, click the Dictate button. A red "Record" icon appears on the button, indicating that Word is ready to translate your utterances into text. Whatever you say appears in the document, almost immediately and with fair accuracy. You can dictate some punctuation, such as *period*, *comma*, and *new line* to start a new paragraph.

Click the Dictate button again to disable this feature.

Blue underlines: Word courteously highlights web page addresses by using blue underlined text in your document. You can Ctrl+click the blue underlined text to visit the web page.

Red lines: You may see red lines in the margin, underneath text, or through text. If so, it means that you're using Word's Track Changes feature. See Chapter 26.

Beyond these automatic underlines, you can apply the underline format to your text, choosing the type of underline and its color. See Chapter 10.

2

Your Basic Word

Discover how to use the scroll bars, move the insertion pointer, and get around with keyboard shortcuts.

Find out how to delete characters, lines, sentences, paragraphs, and pages. You'll also be introduced to the lifesaving Undo command.

Learn how to find and replace text in your documents.

Work with blocks of text and see how you can mark, select, copy, move, and paste blocks.

Customize the spell checker and AutoCorrect settings.

Get familiar with how to preview and print your documents, both on paper and electronically.

IN THIS CHAPTER

» **Using the scroll bars**

» **Moving the insertion pointer**

» **Getting around with keyboard shortcuts**

» **Getting lost and getting back**

» **Using the Go To command**

Chapter **3**

To and Fro in a Document

A computer screen is only so big. Your Word document can be much larger, perhaps requiring several monitors all stacked atop each other so that you could view it all at once. That somehow seems impractical. Therefore, Word offers techniques to let you hop, skip, and jump around your document hither, thither, and yon.

Document Scrolling

It's ironic that the word *scroll* is used when referring to an electronic document. The scroll was the first form of portable recorded text, existing long before bound books. On a computer, scrolling is the process by which you view a little bit of a big document in a tiny window.

Working the vertical scroll bar

The document portion of the Word program window features a vertical scroll bar, illustrated in Figure 3-1. The scroll bar's operation is similar to the scroll bar in any Windows program. As a review, the figure illustrates the mouse's effect on parts of the scroll bar.

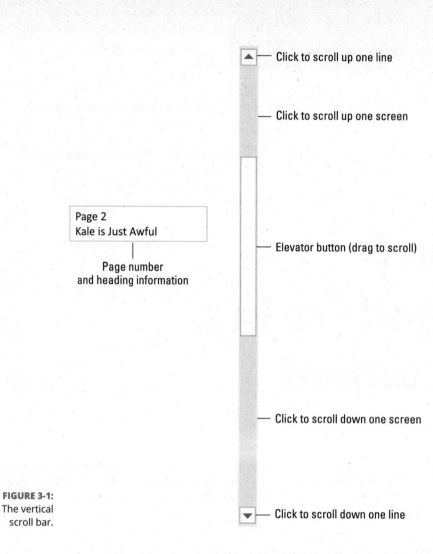

Click to scroll up one line

Click to scroll up one screen

Page 2
Kale is Just Awful

Page number
and heading information

Elevator button (drag to scroll)

Click to scroll down one screen

FIGURE 3-1:
The vertical
scroll bar.

Click to scroll down one line

A key feature in the scroll bar is the elevator button. (Refer to Figure 3-1.) Use the mouse to drag this button up or down to scroll the document. Its position on the scroll bar reflects the location of the text you see. For example, when the elevator button is at the top of the scroll bar, the window shows text at the start of the document.

>> As you drag the elevator button up or down, you see a page number displayed, as shown in Figure 3-1. When a document is formatted with heading styles, you also see the heading title below the page number, as shown in the figure.

>> The vertical scroll bar may disappear at times; move the mouse pointer over your text, and it shows up again.

- » When the elevator button doesn't show up, or is dimmed, the whole document appears in the window.

- » Because the elevator button's size reflects how much of the document appears in the window, the button grows smaller as your document grows longer.

REMEMBER

- » Using the scroll bar to scroll through your document doesn't move the insertion pointer. If you start typing, don't be surprised when Word jumps back to where the insertion pointer lurks.

Using the horizontal scroll bar

When your document is wider than can be displayed in the window, a horizontal scroll bar appears. It shows up at the bottom of the document part of the window, just above the status bar. Use the horizontal scroll bar to shift the page back and forth, left and right.

- » Word automatically slides the document left and right as you type, but that action can be jarring. Instead, try to adjust the horizontal scroll bar to display as much of the text as possible. Or, if you can, enlarge the document window to make it wider.

TIP

- » When the horizontal (left-to-right) shifting bugs you, consider using Word's Zoom tool to adjust the size of your document on the screen. See Chapter 1.

Using the mouse wheel to scroll

The computer mouse's wheel button scrolls your Word document as it scrolls any other window, such as a web page. Roll the wheel to scroll up or down; the direction is set in Windows, so I can't for certain tell you whether rolling the wheel up scrolls your document up or down. Just try it to see how it works.

Some mice let you press the wheel button or tilt it from side to side. If so, press and hold down the wheel button and drag the mouse forward or backward to slowly pan the document up or down. Tilt the wheel button from side to side to pan the document left and right.

REMEMBER

Unlike using the scroll bars, when you use the mouse wheel to scroll the document, the insertion pointer moves with your view. Use the Shift+F5 keyboard shortcut to return the insertion pointer to the spot where you last edited text. See the later section "Return to the Previous Edit."

Move the Insertion Pointer

In Word, you can edit any part of your document; you don't always have to work at "the end." The key to pulling off this trick is to know how to move the insertion pointer to the exact spot you want.

>> Moving the insertion pointer is important! Scientific studies have shown that merely looking at the computer screen does no good.

>> New text appears only at the insertion pointer. Text is deleted at the insertion pointer's location. Text is pasted at the insertion pointer. Formatting commands affect text where the insertion pointer lies blinking.

Commanding the insertion pointer

The easiest way to put the insertion pointer exactly where you want it is to click the mouse at that spot in the text. Point. Click. The insertion pointer moves.

If your computer or laptop features a touchscreen, tap the screen with your finger to relocate the insertion pointer.

Moving in small increments

For short hops, nothing beats using the keyboard's cursor keys to quickly move the insertion pointer around a document. The four arrow keys move the insertion pointer up, down, right, and left:

Press This Key	To Move the Insertion Pointer
↑	Up to the preceding line of text
↓	Down to the next line of text
→	Right to the next character
←	Left to the preceding character

Moving the cursor doesn't erase characters. See Chapter 4 for information on deleting stuff.

REMEMBER

If you press and hold down the Ctrl (Control) key and then press an arrow key, the insertion pointer moves in larger increments. The invigorated insertion pointer leaps desperately in all four directions:

Press This Key Combo	To Move the Insertion Pointer
Ctrl+↑	Up to the start of the previous paragraph
Ctrl+↓	Down to the start of the next paragraph
Ctrl+→	Right to the start (first letter) of the next word
Ctrl+←	Left to the start (first letter) of the previous word

WARNING

You can use either set of arrow keys on the computer keyboard, but when using the numeric keypad, ensure that the Num Lock light is off, (If it's on, press the Num Lock key.) If you don't, you see numbers in the text rather than the insertion pointer dancing all over — like444this.

Moving from beginning to end

The insertion pointer also bows to pressure from those cursor keys without arrows on them. The first couple consists of End and Home, which move the insertion pointer to the start or end of something, depending on how End and Home are used:

Press This Key or Combination	To Whisk the Insertion Pointer
End	To the end of a line of text
Home	To the start of a line of text
Ctrl+End	To the end of the document
Ctrl+Home	To the tippy-top of the document

The remaining cursor keys are the Page Up, or PgUp, key and the Page Down, or PgDn, key. As you might suspect, using these keys doesn't move up or down a page in the document. Nope. Instead, they slide through the document based on the amount of text visible in the window. Here's the round-up:

Press This Key or Combination	To Whisk the Insertion Pointer
PgUp	Up one window full of text or to the tippy-top of the document if you're near there
PgDn	Down one window full of text or to the end of the document if you're near there
Ctrl+Alt+PgUp	To the top of the current window's text
Ctrl+Alt+PgDn	To the bottom of the current window's text

WHAT ABOUT CTRL+PgUp AND CTRL+PgDn?

The Ctrl+PgUp and Ctrl+PgDn keyboard shortcuts are the Browse Previous and Browse Next commands, respectively. Their function changes based on what you've recently done in Word.

For example, the Ctrl+PgDn keyboard shortcut repeats the Find Next command. It might also repeat the Go To command, or a number of other Word commands that move the insertion pointer.

Because of their changing behavior, I don't recommend using Ctrl+PgUp or Ctrl+PgDn as a consistent way to move the insertion pointer.

REMEMBER

The key combinations to move to the top or bottom of the current window's text are Ctrl+Alt+PgUp and Ctrl+Alt+PgDn, respectively. That's Ctrl+Alt, not just the Ctrl key. And yes, few people know or use these commands.

Return to the Previous Edit

Considering all the various commands for moving the insertion pointer, it's quite possible to make a mistake and not know where you are in a document. Yea, verily, the insertion pointer has gone where no insertion pointer has gone before.

TIP

Rather than click your heels together three times and try to get back the wishful way, just remember this keyboard combination:

Shift+F5

Pressing the Shift+F5 keyboard shortcut forces Word to return you to the last spot you edited. You can use this keyboard shortcut three times before the cycle repeats. The first time should get you back to where you were before you got lost.

REMEMBER

Sadly, the Shift+F5 keyboard shortcut works only in Word; you can't use this command in real life.

Go to Wherever with the Go To Command

Word's Go To command allows you to send the insertion pointer to a specific page or line or to the location of a number of interesting items that Word can potentially cram into your document. The Go To command is your word processing teleporter to anywhere.

To use the Go To command, follow these steps:

1. **Click the Home tab.**

2. **In the Editing group, choose the Go To command.**

The Find and Replace dialog box appears with the Go To tab forward, as shown in Figure 3-2.

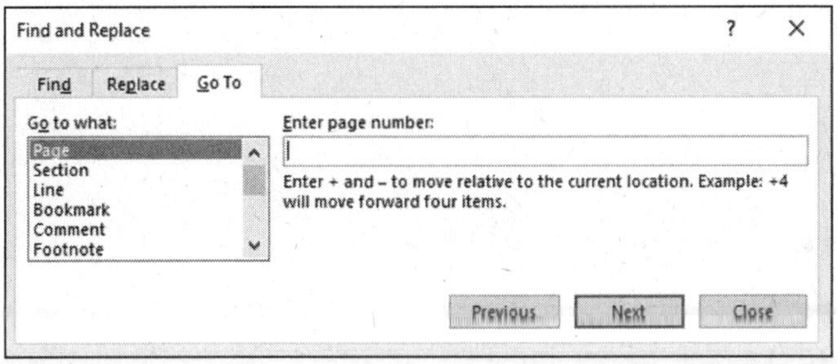

FIGURE 3-2: Telling Word to Go To you-know-where.

And now, the shortcut: Press Ctrl+G to quickly summon the Find and Replace dialog box's Go To tab.

To whisk the insertion pointer to a specific location, choose it from the Go to What list. For example, choose Page to visit a specific page. Type the page number in the Enter Page Number box, and then click the Go To button to go to that page in your document.

TIP

TECHNICAL STUFF

» The Enter Page Number box also accepts relative pages as input. For example, to go three pages forward, type +**3**. To go 12 pages backward, type –**12** in the box.

» The last item you chose from the Go to What list affects the behavior of the Ctrl+PgUp and Ctrl+PgDn keyboard shortcuts. For example, if you choose Page and click the Go To button, the Ctrl+PgUp and Ctrl+PgDn keyboard shortcuts navigate through your document a page at a time.

Chapter **4**

Text Editing

Writing is about creating text. Part of the process also includes reviewing and editing your words. My advice is to concentrate first on writing. In fact, one of the reasons budding writers get stuck is that they spend more time editing than writing.

To accommodate your text-editing desires, Word comes with a host of commands to chop, slice, stitch, and otherwise decimate your text. The commands are a necessary part of word processing, and they work best when you have oodles of text to edit. So, again, write first and edit second.

Remove Text You Don't Want

Credit the guy who put the eraser on the end of the pencil: It's a given that human beings make mistakes. The round, soft eraser counterbalances the sharp point of the pencil in more ways than one.

In Word, you use the keyboard to both create and destroy text. The majority of keys create text. Only two keys delete: Backspace and Delete. These keys gain more power when used with other keys — and even the mouse — that help them to delete great swaths of text.

>> As text is deleted, the remaining text in the line, in the paragraph, or on the page scoots up to fill the void. Deleting text doesn't leave a hole in your document.

TECHNICAL STUFF

>> Document fields cannot be deleted like regular text. When you attempt to remove a field, Word highlights the field's text as a warning. To continue and remove the field, press the Delete or Backspace key. See Chapter 23 for more information on fields.

Deleting single characters

Use the Backspace and Delete keys to delete single characters:

>> Backspace deletes the character to the left of the insertion pointer.

>> Delete deletes the character to the right of the insertion pointer.

In the following example, the insertion pointer is flashing (okay, it *would* be flashing on a computer screen) between the *v* and the *i* in *inevitably.* Pressing the Backspace key deletes the *v*; pressing the Delete key deletes the *i*:

```
It is inev|itably the duty of people who are in a
hurry to be stuck behind those who are not.
```

You can press and hold down Backspace or Delete to machine-gun-delete characters. Release the key to halt such wanton destruction, though I recommend that you use other delete commands (covered in this chapter) rather than the machine-gun approach.

Deleting a word

To gobble up an entire word, use the Ctrl key with the Backspace or Delete key:

>> Ctrl+Backspace deletes the word to the left of the insertion pointer.

>> Ctrl+Delete deletes the word to the right of the insertion pointer.

These keyboard shortcuts work best when the insertion pointer is at the start or end of a word. When the pointer is in the middle of the word, these commands delete only from that middle point to the start or end of the word.

When you use Ctrl+Backspace to delete a word to the left, the insertion pointer sits at the end of the preceding word (or paragraph). When you use Ctrl+Delete to remove a word, the cursor sits at the start of the next word. This positioning is done to facilitate the rapid deletion of several words in a row.

No mere pencil eraser can match Ctrl+Delete or Ctrl+Backspace for sheer speed and terror!

Deleting more than a word

To remove chunks of text larger than a character or a word, the keyboard must pal up with the mouse. The process involves selecting a chunk of text and then delet-ing that chunk. See Chapter 6 for more information on selecting text.

Delete a line of text

A line of text starts at one side of the page and goes to the other. It's not really a sentence or a paragraph, but the line can be removed easily:

1. **Move the mouse pointer into the left margin, next to the line of text.**

You know you've found the sweet spot when the mouse pointer changes into a northeast-pointing arrow.

2. **Click the mouse.**

The line of text is selected and appears highlighted on the screen.

3. **Press the Delete key to send that line into oblivion.**

Delete a sentence

A sentence is a grammatical thing. You know: Start with a capital letter and end with a period, a question mark, or an exclamation point. You probably mastered this concept in grammar school, which is why they call it grammar school anyway.

Making a sentence go bye–bye is cinchy:

1. **Position the mouse pointer at the offending sentence.**

2. **Press and hold down the Ctrl key and click the mouse.**

The Ctrl and mouse-click combination (Ctrl+click) selects a sentence of text.

You can release the Ctrl key.

3. **Press the Delete key.**

Delete a paragraph

A paragraph is one or more sentences, or a document heading, ending with a press of the Enter key. Here's the fastest way to delete a full paragraph:

1. **Click the mouse button thrice.**

   Thrice means "three times." The triple-click selects a complete paragraph of text.

2. **Press the Delete key.**

Another way to select a paragraph is to click the mouse twice in the left margin, next to the paragraph.

Delete a page

A page of text includes everything on a page, top to bottom. This document-chunk isn't something Word directly addresses with specific keyboard commands. To remove a page full of text requires some legerdemain. Follow these steps:

1. **Press Ctrl+G.**

   The Find and Replace dialog box appears, with the Go To tab forward.

2. **From the Go to What list, click to select Page.**

3. **Type the number of the page you want to delete.**

   For example, type **2** to delete Page 2.

4. **Click the Go To button and then click the Close button.**

   The insertion pointer is positioned at the top of the page.

5. **Press the F8 key.**

   Word enters Extended Selection mode. Now you must send the insertion pointer to the top of the next page.

6. **Press Ctrl+G to view the Find and Replace dialog box again.**

7. **Type the next page number.**

   For example, type **3** to delete page 2, which you entered in Step 3.

8. **Press the Delete key.**

All text is removed from the page.

>> If the page remains but it's blank, you might be dealing with a hard page break. See Chapter 13.

>> If you're trying to delete a blank page at the end of a document, see Chapter 9.

>> Chapter 3 offers more information on the Go To command.

>> The F8 key activates extended selection mode. See Chapter 6 for more F8 key tricks.

Delete an odd-size chunk of text

Word lets you delete any old odd-size chunk of text anywhere in your document. The key is to select that text as a *block*. After the block is marked, press the Delete key to zap it to kingdom come. Refer to Chapter 6 for more information on selecting blocks of text.

Split and Join Paragraphs

A paragraph is both an English grammatical entity and a Word formatting concept. In English, a paragraph is a collection of sentences that collectively express some thought, idea, or theme. In Word, a paragraph is a chunk of text that ends when you press the Enter key. While grammarians and software engineers duke it out over the different meanings, you can redefine a paragraph in a document by splitting or joining text.

Making two paragraphs from one

To split a single paragraph in twain, follow these steps:

1. **Click the mouse at the point where you want the new paragraph to begin.**

   Ideally, that point is at the start of a sentence.

2. **Press the Enter key.**

   Word splits the paragraph in two; the text above the insertion pointer becomes its own paragraph, and the text following it then becomes the next paragraph.

Depending on how the paragraph was torn asunder, you may need to delete an extra space lingering at the end of the first paragraph or dawdling at the start of the next.

Making one paragraph from two

To join two paragraphs and turn them into one, follow these steps:

1. **Place the insertion pointer at the start of the second paragraph.**

   Use the keyboard to position the insertion pointer, or click the mouse.

2. **Press the Backspace key.**

   The Enter character from the preceding paragraph is removed, which joins two paragraphs into one.

Depending on how neatly the paragraphs were joined, you may need to add a space between the sentences at the spot where the paragraphs were thrust together.

Soft and Hard Returns

Word defines a paragraph as a chunk of text ending with a hard return character. You press the Enter key to generate this character. The paragraph ends, and then a new paragraph starts. And so it goes throughout the document.

You can end a line of text without ending the paragraph by typing a soft return, also known as a manual line break. To do so, press Shift+Enter. The current line of text stops and the insertion pointer hops to the start of the next line. Keep typing at that point and, eventually, press Enter to end the paragraph.

TIP

The soft return is best used to split titles and headings. Using a soft return is also the secret used to type an address. That way, you can keep the address text together in a single paragraph. For example:

```
Mr. President
1600 Pennsylvania Ave.
Washington, DC 20500
```

This bit of text is a single paragraph with soft returns separating each line.

To help you see hard returns and soft returns, use the Show/Hide command: Click the Home tab and, in the Paragraph group, click the Show/Hide command button. The button is adorned with the Paragraph symbol (¶).

When the Show/Hide command is active, the soft return appears as a right-angle arrow, which looks like the symbol found on the keyboard's Enter key: ↵

The hard return appears as the paragraph mark: ¶

Figure 4-1 illustrates how these two characters appear in a document with the Show/Hide command enabled.

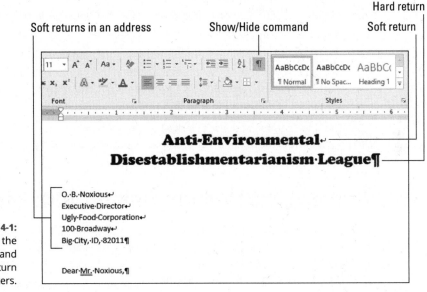

Soft returns in an address   Show/Hide command   Hard return   Soft return

Anti-Environmental·
Disestablishmentarianism·League¶

O.·B.·Noxious↵
Executive·Director↵
Ugly·Food·Corporation↵
100·Broadway↵
Big·City,·ID,·82011¶

Dear·Mr.·Noxious,¶

FIGURE 4-1: Viewing the soft- and hard-return characters.

>> See Chapter 2 for additional details on the Show/Hide command and seeing hidden characters in your text.

>> Though soft returns keep text close, the text is still affected by the paragraph's line spacing. See Chapter 11 for more information on paragraph formatting.

REMEMBER

Undo Mistakes with Undo Haste

That quaffing and drinking will undo you.
— RICHARD II, WILLIAM SHAKESPEARE

The Undo command undoes anything you do in Word, which includes formatting text, moving blocks, typing and deleting text — the whole enchilada. You have two handy ways to unleash the Undo command:

>> Press Ctrl+Z.

>> Click the Undo command button on the Quick Access toolbar.

I prefer using the Ctrl+Z key combination, but an advantage of the Undo command button is that it sports a drop-down menu that helps you review the past several things you've done, which can be undone.

> » Regrettably, you cannot pick and choose from the Undo command button's drop-down menu; you can merely undo multiple actions with a single command.

> » Word warns you should you attempt an action that cannot be undone. For example, you see a message such as "There is not enough memory to undo this operation." Proceed at your own peril.

> » The Undo command doesn't work when there's nothing to undo or something simply cannot be undone. For example, you cannot undo a document save.

Undoing the Undo command with Redo

If you undo something and — whoops! — you didn't mean to, use the Redo command to set things back to the way they were. For example, you may type some text and then use Undo to "untype" the text. You can then use the Redo command to restore the typing. You have two choices:

> » Press Ctrl+Y.

> » Click the Redo command button on the Quick Access toolbar.

The Redo command does exactly the opposite of whatever the Undo command does. So, if you type text, Undo untypes the text and Redo recovers the text. If you use Undo to recover deleted text, Redo deletes the text again.

Using the Repeat command

When the Redo command has nothing left to redo, it changes functions and becomes the Repeat command. On the Quick Access toolbar, the command button changes as shown in the margin. The Repeat command's duty is to repeat the last thing you did in Word, whether it's typing text, applying a format, or doing a variety of other things.

Lamentably, you can't use the Repeat command to ease your typing chores. That's because it repeats only the last single character you typed.

The keyboard shortcut for the Repeat command is Ctrl+Y, the same as the Redo command.

IN THIS CHAPTER

» **Finding text in your document**

» **Using special text-finding options**

» **Locating entire words**

» **Searching for text that cannot be typed at the keyboard**

» **Hunting down formatting codes**

» **Replacing found text with other text**

Chapter **5**

Search for This, Replace It with That

ittle Bo Peep has lost her sheep. Too bad she doesn't know about Word's Find and Replace commands. She could find the misplaced ruminants in a matter of nanoseconds. Not only that, she could use search-and-replace to, say, replace all the sheep with real estate. It's all cinchy after you understand and use the various Find and Replace commands. Sadly, it's only words that are replaced. True, if Word could search-and-replace real things, there'd be fewer sheep in the world.

Text Happily Found

Finding text is one of the most basic and ancient tools available in a word processor. The only issue has been whether the command is called Find or Search. The terms Relentlessly Hunt Down and Fiendishly Locate were never considered.

In Word, finding duties are split between the traditional Find dialog box and the navigation pane.

Finding a tidbit o' text

Don't bother with the Ribbon! To find text in your document, press Ctrl+F, the memorable keyboard shortcut for the Find command. You see the navigation pane, similar to what's shown in Figure 5-1.

Search text

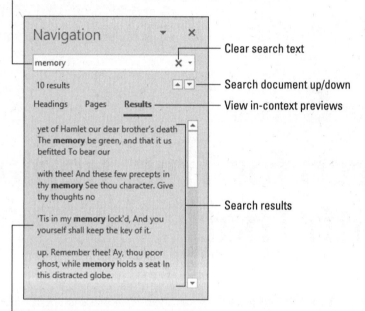

Clear search text

Search document up/down

View in-context previews

Search results

Click or tap a result to see that text in your document

FIGURE 5-1:
The navigation pane.

In the Search Document box, type the text you want to locate. As you type, instances of the text are highlighted in the document. In-context chunks of text appear in the navigation pane under the Results heading, as illustrated in Figure 5-1. To peruse found text, use the up and down arrows in the navigation pane or click a snippet to view that particular part of your document.

When text can't be found, the navigation pane explains that it can't find the text. It uses the pronoun *we*, which I find disturbing. And if too many tidbits of text are found, previews don't appear in the navigation pane, which I find disappointing.

REMEMBER

>> To clear text from the Search Document box, click the X button found at the right end of the box.

>> Do not end the text with a period unless you want to find the period, too. Word's Find command is persnickety.

>> Word finds text only in the current document (the one you see in the window). To find text in another document, switch to that document's window and try searching again. Or you can use the Find command in Windows, which isn't covered in this book.

>> Word does host the Find command on the Ribbon's Home tab. Seriously, press the Ctrl+F key. It's faster.

Scouring your document with Advanced Find

The navigation pane is a handy tool for locating text. In fact, I keep it open for all my documents. When it comes to exercising some Find command muscle, however, you must turn to a more specific tool. That's the traditional Find dialog box, called the Find and Replace dialog box, shown in Figure 5-2.

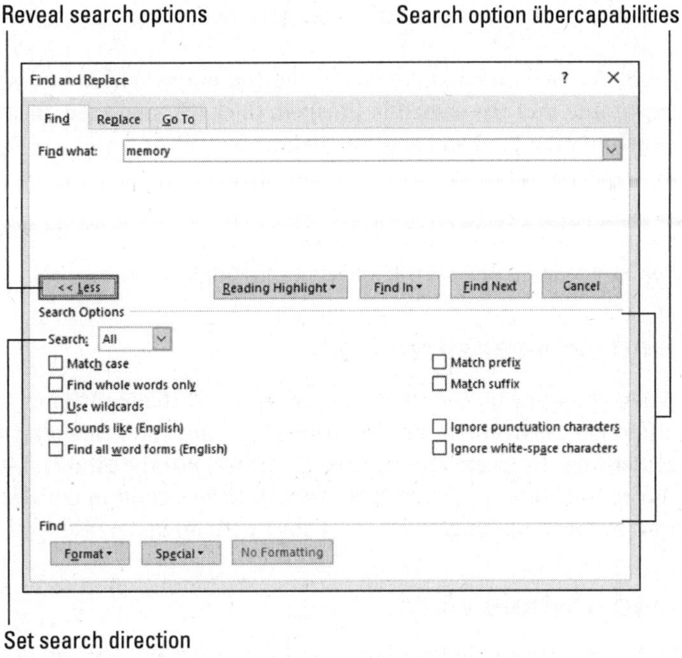

Reveal search options   Search option übercapabilities

FIGURE 5-2:
The Find and Replace dialog box.

Set search direction

Follow these steps to conjure forth the Find and Replace dialog box:

1. **Click the Home tab.**

2. **In the Editing group, choose Find ➪ Advanced Find.**

   The Find and Replace dialog box appears, with the Find tab forward. You may see only the top part of the dialog box. So:

3. **Click the More button to reveal the dialog box's powerful bits.**

   What you see now appears just like Figure 5-2.

4. **Type the search text in the Find What text box.**

5. **Use the dialog box's controls to make further adjustments.**

   Examples for using the various controls are found throughout this chapter.

6. **Click the Find Next button to locate the text.**

Once the text is found, you can do whatever to it: Edit it, change it, or click the Find Next button to continue looking for text.

After the Find command has scoured the entire document, you see an info box explaining that the search is finished. Click OK, and then click the Cancel button to dismiss the Find and Replace dialog box.

REMEMBER

Options set in the Find and Replace dialog box remain set until deactivated. When you can't seem to locate text that you *know* is in your document, review the dialog box's settings. Turn off the ones you no longer need.

Find case-sensitive text

When you want to find Pat in your document, the Find command must know the difference between *Pat* and *pat.* One is a name, and the other is to lightly touch something. To locate one and not the other, use the Find and Replace dialog box. (Refer to Figure 5-2.) Select the Match Case option under Search Options. That way, *Pat* matches only words that start with an uppercase *P.*

Find a whole word

Word's Advanced Find command can locate *Pat* and not *pat*, but it might also flag the word *Pattern* at the start of a sentence. To avoid that situation, select the Find Whole Words Only option.

Find word variations

Two options in the Find and Replace dialog box assist you with finding words that may not be exactly what you're looking for.

The Sounds Like (English) option allows you to search for *homonyms*, or words that sound the same as the search word. These words include *their* and *there*, *deer* and *dear*, and *hear* and *here*. The command doesn't, however, locate rhyming words.

The Find All Word Forms (English) option expands the search to include different forms of the same word. With this option set, you can search for the word *hop* and also find matches with *hops*, *hopped*, and *hopping*.

Search this way or that

The Find command searches from the insertion pointer's position to the end of a document and then back 'round the top again. To override its sense of direction, use the Search drop-down list, as illustrated earlier, in Figure 5-2. You see three options:

>> **Down:** The Find command searches from the insertion pointer's location to the end of your document, and then it stops.

>> **Up:** The Find command searches from the insertion pointer's location to the start of your document. Then it stops.

>> **All:** The Find command searches the entire document, from the insertion pointer's location down to the end of the document and back up to the beginning, and then stops at the point where the search began.

TIP

You can use keyboard shortcuts to search up or down. The Ctrl+PgDn key combination repeats the last search downward; the Ctrl+PgUp key combination repeats the most recent search upward.

Finding stuff you can't type

The Find command is brilliant enough to locate items in your document such as tab characters or text colored red. The puzzle is how to input that type of information in the Find and Replace dialog box. The secret is to use the Format and Special buttons lurking near the bottom of the dialog box. (Refer to Figure 5-2.)

Find special characters

To hunt down special characters in your document, such as a tab or Enter key press, click the Special button in the Advanced Find dialog box. Up pops a list of

22 items that Word can search for but that you would have a dickens of a time typing in the Find and Replace dialog box.

Despite the exhaustive list, here are the few items you may find handy:

» **Any Character, Any Digit,** and **Any Letter** are special characters that represent, well, just about anything. These items can be used as wildcards for matching lots of stuff.

» **Caret Character** allows you to search for a caret (^) symbol, which may not seem like a big deal, but it is: Word uses the ^ symbol in a special way for finding text; see the next section.

» **Paragraph Mark** (¶) is a special character that's the same as the Enter character — the one you press to end a paragraph.

» **Tab Character** moves the insertion pointer to the next tab stop.

» **White Space** is any number of blank characters: one or more spaces, tabs, empty lines, or a combination thereof.

Choose an item from the list to search for that special character. When you do, a special, funky shorthand representation for that character appears. The shorthand involves the ^ character and then another character, such as ^t to search for the tab character.

TECHNICAL STUFF

If you're a nerd, you can quickly type special characters manually. Popular options are ^p for the paragraph mark (Enter key press), ^t for a tab, ^w for white space, and ^? for any character. These symbols may not make much sense, but if you're a nerd, you won't care.

Find formatting

In its most powerful superhero mode, the Find command can scour your document for text and formatting. You can search for the formatting information itself or use it with text to locate specifically formatted text.

The secret to hunting down text formats is to use the Format button, found at the bottom of the Find and Replace dialog box, as shown earlier, in Figure 5-2. Click that button to view a menu full of formatting categories, such as Font, Paragraph, and Tabs. Choose a category to pluck out a specific format.

Suppose that you want to find the text *red herring* in your document. The text is italic and colored red. Follow these steps:

1. Click the Home tab.

2. In the Editing group, choose Find ⇨ Advanced Find.

The Find and Replace dialog box appears.

3. Type the text you're searching for.

In this example, that would be *red herring*.

4. Ensure that the dialog box details are displayed; click the More button, if necessary.

5. Click the No Formatting button to remove any previously applied formatting.

The No Formatting button is available when you've previously searched for format attributes.

6. Click the Format button and choose Font from the pop-up list.

The Find Font dialog box appears

7. Choose Italic as the font style.

8. Select Red from the Font Color menu.

Yes, many shades of red dwell on the menu. Pick the correct one.

9. Click OK.

The Find Font dialog box goes away and you return to the Find and Replace dialog box. Below the Find What text box appears the search format. It lists which attributes the Advanced Find command is looking for.

10. Click the Find Next button to locate the formatted text.

If you want to search only for a format, leave the Find What text box blank. (Refer to Step 3.) That way, you can search for formatting attributes without regard to what the text reads.

REMEMBER

» The Find command remembers your formatting options! The next time you want to search for plain text, click the No Formatting button. (Refer to Step 5.) Doing so removes the formatting attributes and allows you to search for text in any format.

» Word's Find and Replace command is powerful enough that it can find and replace text formats. Details on performing this magic are found in my book *Word 2016 For Professionals For Dummies* (Wiley).

Replace Found Text

When you want to find text and replace it with new text, summon the Find command's powerful companion, Find and Replace. This is the command Little Bo Peep used to establish her real estate empire, transforming all those useless sheep into vast land holdings.

To globally change all instances of text throughout your document, follow these steps:

1. **Click the Home tab.**

2. **In the Editing group, click the Replace command button.**

If you don't see the Replace command button directly, click the Editing button to find it.

Choosing the Replace command button summons the Find and Replace dialog box with the Replace tab forward, shown in Figure 5-3.

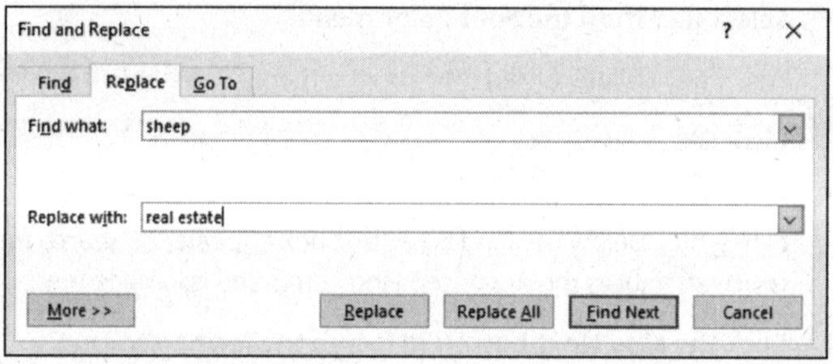

FIGURE 5-3:
The Replace tab in the Find and Replace dialog box.

3. **In the Find What box, type text you want to replace.**

For example, if you're finding *coffee* and replacing it with *tea,* type **coffee**.

4. **In the Replace With box, type the replacement text.**

To continue from the example in Step 3, you type **tea** here.

5. **Click the Find Next button.**

At this step, the Replace command works just like the Find command: Word scours your document for the text you typed in the Find What box. If the text is found, proceed with Step 6. If nothing is found, start over again with Step 3 — or just abandon your efforts and close the dialog box.

6. **Click the Replace button.**

The found word, highlighted on the screen, is replaced.

7. **Repeat Steps 5 and 6 until all the text is replaced.**

Or you can click the Replace All button to search-and-replace the text throughout your document in a single step.

Just as you can search for specific text, you can find and replace specific text. The secret is to use the More button, shown in Figure 5-3. For example, you can choose to find an entire word, which avoids finding *use* in *causes*. Refer to the section "Scouring your document with Advanced Find," earlier in this chapter. The options are set individually to either the Find What or Replace With text boxes.

WARNING

» If you don't type anything in the Replace With box, Word replaces your text with *nothing!* It's wanton destruction! Still, it may be something you need. For example, to search for extra tabs in a document and remove them: Search for two tabs and replace them with a single tab. Refer to the earlier section "Find special characters" for details on typing the tab character into the Find What and Replace With text boxes.

TIP

» Speaking of wanton destruction, the Undo command restores the document to its preceding condition if you foul up the Replace operation. See Chapter 4 for more information.

» For a large document, Word may inform you that it cannot undo a document-wide Replace All operation.

» The keyboard shortcut for the Replace command is Ctrl+H. The only way I can figure that one out is that Ctrl+F is the Find command and Ctrl+G is the Go To command. F, G, and H are found together on the computer keyboard, and Find, Replace, and Go To are found together in the Find and Replace dialog box. Go figure.

» The Find and Replace command can also locate specific text formatting and remove it or replace it with new formatting. This advanced topic is covered in my book *Word 2016 For Professionals For Dummies*.

Chapter **6**

Blocks o' Text

Writing is about blocks. From the moveable blocks used by the ancient Chinese for printing to the inevitable writer's block. In Word, *blocks* refer to selected chunks of text in a document, which I believe you'll find more useful than the other types of blocks.

Meet Mr. Block

"Hello, Mr. Block! What do you do?"

"Well! I'm a block of text. I have a beginning and an end. I can be any size, from a single character to the entire document."

To create Mr. Block in your document, you select text. You can use the keyboard. You can use the mouse. You can use both at once or employ some of Word's more esoteric text-selection commands.

A block of selected text appears highlighted in a document, similar to what's shown in Figure 6-1.

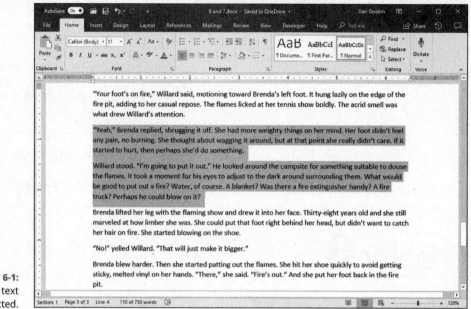

FIGURE 6-1:
A block of text
is selected.

Once a block of text is selected, you can perform certain actions that affect only the text in that block. You can also copy, move, or delete the block.

To help format a selected block of text, the mini toolbar appears, as shown in Figure 6-2.

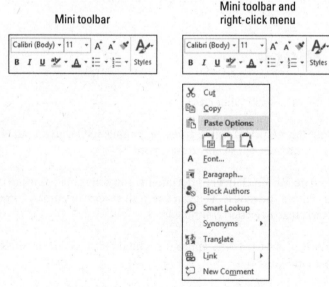

Mini toolbar

Mini toolbar and
right-click menu

FIGURE 6-2:
The mini toolbar
and the block
pop-up menu.

The mini toolbar hosts popular commands found on the Ribbon, allowing you to quickly format the block of text. You can also right-click the selected text, in which case you see both the mini toolbar and a shortcut menu, also shown in Figure 6-2.

» A block of text in Word includes text and text formatting.

» Graphics and other nontext elements can also be selected as a block. In fact, you can select graphics along with text in the same block.

» When the status bar is displaying word-count statistics, the number of words selected in the block of text is displayed next to the total number of words in the document. (Refer to Figure 6-1.)

» When the Find command locates text, the found text is selected as a block. Refer to Chapter 5 for more information on the Find command.

» The mini toolbar disappears after a few moments of neglect. Refer to Chapter 33 for information on disabling the mini toolbar.

TECHNICAL STUFF

» Selecting text also means selecting invisible characters such as the tab or the Enter character, which marks the end of a paragraph. Word shows the Enter character as an extra blank space at the end of a paragraph. When you select that blank, you select the whole paragraph as a block. To avoid selecting the Enter character, don't select the blank space at the end of a paragraph.

Mark a Block of Text

Before you can work with a block of text, you must tell Word where the block starts and where it ends. The process is known as *marking* or *selecting* a block of text.

Using the keyboard to select text

You can use the keyboard's cursor keys to select text, but only when you know the secret: Press and hold down the Shift key as you move the cursor. When the Shift key is down, Word's standard cursor-key commands not only move the insertion pointer but also select chunks of text. Table 6-1 lists common key combinations.

TABLE 6-1

Keyboard Selection Wizardry

To Select This	Press This
A character at a time to the right of the insertion pointer	Shift+→
A character at a time to the left of the insertion pointer	Shift+←
A block of text from the insertion pointer to the end of the line	Shift+End
A block of text from the insertion pointer to the beginning of the line	Shift+Home
A block of text from the insertion pointer to a line above	Shift+↑
A block of text from the insertion pointer to a line below	Shift+↓

TIP

Though you can use any keyboard cursor-movement command, including some that move the insertion pointer a great distance, I recommend using this Shift key technique for selecting only small chunks of text. Otherwise, you may end up tying your fingers into knots.

>> See Chapter 3 for the full list of Word's cursor key commands.

>> Either Shift key works, although I prefer to use the left Shift key and then work the arrow keys on the right side of the keyboard.

Marking a block with the mouse

Mickey may rule a kingdom, but your computer's mouse rules over text selection in your computer.

Drag over text to select it

Position the mouse pointer at the start of the text block, and then drag the mouse over the text you want to select. As you drag, the text becomes highlighted or selected.

TIP

>> This technique works best when you use the mouse to drag over only the text you can see on the screen. When you try to select text beyond what you see on the screen, you have to select and scroll, which can be unwieldy.

>> Using the mouse to select text in a table is funky. See Chapter 19.

>> Also see Chapter 33, which covers how to adjust Word so that you can use the mouse to select individual letters instead of entire words at a time.

Click the mouse to select text

A speedy way to select specific sizes of chunks of text is to match the power of the mouse with the dexterity of your index finger. Table 6-2 explains some clicking-and-selecting techniques worth noting.

TABLE 6-2

Mouse-Selection Arcana

To Select This Chunk of Text	Click the Mouse Thusly
A single word	Double-click the word.
A line	Move the mouse pointer into the left margin beside the line you want to select. The mouse pointer changes to an arrow pointing northeastward. Click the mouse to select a line of text. Drag the mouse up or down to select several lines.
A sentence	Position the insertion pointer over the sentence and Ctrl+click. (Press the Ctrl key and click the mouse.)
A paragraph	Point the mouse somewhere in the paragraph's midst and click thrice (triple-click).

Select text with the old poke-and-point

TIP

Here's the best way to select a chunk of text of any size, especially when that chunk of text is larger than what you can see on the screen at one time:

1. **Click the mouse to set the insertion pointer wherever you want the block to start.**

   I call this location the *anchor point.*

2. **Scroll through your document.**

   You must use the scroll bar or the mouse wheel to scroll through your document. If you use the cursor-movement keys, you reposition the insertion pointer, which isn't what you want.

3. **Hold down the Shift key and click the mouse where you want the block to end.**

   The text from the insertion pointer to wherever you clicked the mouse is selected as a block.

Using the F8 key to mark a block

A relic from the old days, the F8 key activates Word's Extend Selection command. Press this key to "drop anchor" at the insertion pointer's location. Then use either the mouse or the cursor keys to select text. In fact, you cannot do anything but select text when Extend Selection mode is active.

To exit Extend Selection mode, you can either do something with the block of text or press the Esc key to cancel.

>> To help you with the F8 key and Extend Selection mode, right-click the status bar and choose the Selection Mode item. The text *Extend Selection* appears on the status bar when this mode is active.

>> Not only can you use the cursor keys while in Extend Selection mode, any of the character keys works as well; text is selected from the anchor point to the character you type. Type an *N*, for example, and all text between the insertion pointer and the next letter *N* is selected.

>> You can also use the Find command to locate a specific bit of text in Extend Selection mode. Word marks all text between the anchor and the text that the Find command locates.

>> Press the F8 key twice to select the current word.

>> Press the F8 key thrice (three times) to select the current sentence.

>> Press the F8 key four times to select the current paragraph as a block of text.

>> Press the F8 key five times to select the entire document, from top to bottom.

>> No matter how many times you press F8, be aware that it always drops anchor. Whether you press F8 once or five times, Word is still in Extend Selection mode. Do something with the block or press Esc to cancel this mode.

Blocking the whole dang-doodle document

The biggest block you can mark is an entire document. Word has a specific command to do it. Follow these steps:

1. **Click the Home tab.**

2. **In the Editing group, choose Select ⇨ Select All.**

The entire document is marked as a single block o' text.

And now, the keyboard shortcut: Press Ctrl+A to select an entire document as a block.

Deselecting a block

When you mark a block of text and change your mind, you must unmark, or *dese-lect*, the text. Here are a few handy ways to do it:

>> **Move the insertion pointer.** It doesn't matter how you move the insertion pointer, with the keyboard or with the mouse, but doing so deselects the block. (This trick doesn't work when you use the F8, Extend Selection, key to select text.)

>> **Press the Esc key and then the ← key.** This method works to end Extend Selection mode.

>> **Press Shift+F5.** The Shift+F5 key combo (refer to Chapter 3) is the "go back" command, but it also deselects a block of text *and* returns you to the text you were editing before making the selection.

Manipulate a Block of Text

You can block punches, block hats, block and tackle, play with building blocks and engine blocks, take nerve blocks, suffer from mental blocks, jog for blocks, and, naturally, block text. But what can you do with those marked blocks of text?

Why, plenty of things! You can apply a format to all text in the block, copy a block, move a block, search for text in a block, proof a block, print a block, and even delete a block. The information in this section explains a few of those tricks.

REMEMBER

>> Blocks must be selected before you can manipulate them. See the first half of this chapter.

>> When a block of text is marked, various Word commands affect only the text in that block.

>> To replace a block, type some text. The new text (actually, the initial character) replaces the entire block.

>> To delete a block, press the Delete or Backspace key. Thwoop! The block is gone.

>> Formatting commands can be applied to any marked block of text — specifically, character and paragraph formatting. See Part 3 of this book.

>> Also see Chapter 32 for information on Word's bizarre yet potentially useful Collect and Paste feature.

Copying a block

After a block is marked, you can copy it to another part of your document. The original block remains untouched by this operation. Follow these steps to copy a block of text from one place to another:

1. **Mark the block.**

Detailed instructions about doing this task are offered in the first part of this chapter.

2. **Click the Home tab.**

3. **In the Clipboard group, click the Copy command button.**

You get no visual clue that the text has been copied; it remains selected.

4. **Click to set the insertion pointer at the position where you want to place the block's copy.**

Don't worry if there's no room! Word inserts the block into your text.

5. **Click the Paste command button.**

The block of text is inserted into your text just as though you had typed it there by yourself.

The keyboard shortcuts for copy and paste are Ctrl+C and Ctrl+V, respectively. You'll probably use these keyboard shortcuts more than the command buttons in the Home tab's Clipboard group.

TIP

» See the later section "Setting the pasted text format" to discover various ways you can paste text into your document.

» The Paste command continues to paste the copied text, over and over — that is, until new text is selected and copied (or cut). Pasting text again simply pastes down a second copy of the block, spit-spot (as Mary Poppins would say).

» You can paste the block into another document you're working on or even into another application. This is a Windows trick that works in any program that can accept text as input.

Moving a block

To move a block of text, you select the text and then *cut* and paste. This process is almost the same as copying a block, described in the preceding section, although in Step 3 you choose the Cut command button (shown in the margin) or press Ctrl+X on the keyboard. Otherwise, all steps are the same.

Don't be alarmed when the block of text vanishes! That's cutting in action; the block of text is being *moved*, not copied. You see the block of text again when you paste it.

REMEMBER

If you screw up, the Ctrl+Z Undo shortcut undoes a block move.

Setting the pasted text format

When you paste text in Word, you may see the Paste Options icon appear, as shown in the margin. This button allows you to select formatting to apply to the pasted block. For example, you can choose to retain the formatting as pasted, choose to paste in the text plain and unformatted, or choose to have the pasted text match the style of the text around it.

To work the Paste Options button, click it with the mouse or press and release the Ctrl key on the keyboard. You see a menu of options, illustrated in Figure 6-3.

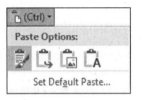

FIGURE 6-3:
Pasting options.

Table 6-3 summarizes some of the common paste options.

TABLE 6-3   **Paste Option Options**

Icon	Keyboard Shortcut	Name	Description
	K	Keep Source Formatting	The formatting is okay; don't do a thing.
	M	Merge Formatting	Reformat the pasted block so that it matches the text it's being pasted into.
	T	Keep Text Only	Just paste in the text — no formatting.

For example, to keep only text with a copied or cut block (no formatting), press the Ctrl key and then tap the T key after pasting. That's two separate keys, not Ctrl+T.

Using the Paste Options icon is utterly optional. In fact, you can continue typing or working in Word and the icon bows out, fading away like some nebbish who boldly asked a power blonde to go out with him and she utterly failed to recognize his existence. Like that.

>> Click the Set Default Paste text to direct Word to permanently deal with pasted text. It's a handy trick, especially when you find yourself repeatedly choosing the same Paste Options format.

>> You can control whether the Paste Options icon appears after pasting text: Click the File tab and choose Options to summon the Word Options dialog box. Choose Advanced. In the Cut, Copy, and Paste area, add or remove the check mark by the option Show Paste Options Button When Content Is Pasted to show or hide the icon, respectively.

Using the mouse to copy or move a block

When you need to move a block only a short distance, you can use the mouse to drag-move or drag-copy the block.

To move any selected block of text, hover the mouse pointer anywhere in the blocked text and then drag the block to its new location. As you drag the block, the mouse pointer changes, as shown in the margin. That means you're moving a block of text.

To copy a block of text, point the mouse pointer at the block — just as though you were going to move the block — but press and hold down the Ctrl key as you drag. When you drag the block, the mouse pointer changes to resemble the icon shown in the margin. That's your clue that the block is being copied and not just moved.

REMEMBER

This trick works best when you're moving or copying a block to a location you can see right on the screen. Otherwise, you're scrolling your document with the mouse while you're playing with blocks, which is like trying to grab an angry snake.

>> When you drag a block of text with the mouse, you're not copying or cutting it to the Clipboard. You cannot use the Paste (Ctrl+V) command to paste in the block again.

TECHNICAL STUFF

>> To create a *linked copy* of the block, drag the mouse and hold down *both* the Shift and Ctrl keys. When you release the mouse button, the copied block plops down into your document with a dark highlight. It's your clue that the copy is linked to the original; changes in the original are reflected in the copy and vice versa. If the linked copy doesn't update, right-click the text and choose the Update Link command.

Viewing the Clipboard

All text you copy or cut is stored in a location called the Clipboard. This is the standard cut-copy-paste holding bin for text in Windows. In Word, however, the Clipboard is more powerful than in other Windows programs. Specifically, you can use the Clipboard task pane to examine items cut or copied, and paste them again in your document in any order.

To copy a chunk of text from the task pane to your document, heed these steps:

1. **Place the insertion pointer in your document where you want the pasted text to appear.**

2. **Click the Home tab.**

3. **In the Clipboard group, click the dialog box launcher.**

   You see the Clipboard task pane, along with all text cut or copied since you've started the Word program, similar to what's shown in Figure 6-4.

4. **Position the mouse pointer at an item in the task pane.**

   A menu button appears to the right of the item.

5. **Click the menu button and choose the Paste command.**

   The text is pasted into your document.

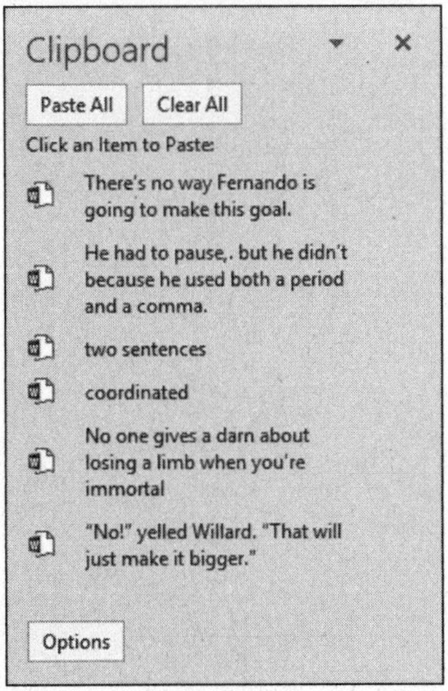

FIGURE 6-4:
The Clipboard task pane.

Unlike using the Ctrl+V keyboard shortcut, or the Paste button on the Ribbon, you can paste text from the Clipboard in any order, and even summon text you copied or cut hours ago or text you copied or cut from other Microsoft Office programs.

Also see Chapter 32 for information on using the Collect and Paste feature, which takes advantage of the Clipboard task pane.

Chapter **7**

Spell It Write

Spelling in English really wasn't a thing until Noah Webster published his dictionary. Suddenly, busybodies had another reason to criticize you: Your spelling wasn't up to Webster's standard. And though Mark Twain wrote that he pitied the man who knew only one way to spell a word, Webster has prevailed. Spelling matters. Grammar does, too. For these reasons, Word features document proofing, a feature that's automatic and irritating at the same time.

Check Your Spelling

Word's Spell Check feature works the second you start typing. Offending or unknown words are immediately underlined with the red zigzag of shame. Leave the word be, correct it, or add it to your own dictionary just to spite Mr. Webster.

» Spell checking works thanks to a digital dictionary stocked with zillions of words, all spelled correctly. Every time you type a word, it's checked against that dictionary. When the word isn't found, it's marked as suspect in your document.

TIP

» Don't let the red zigzag of a failed elementary education perturb you. My advice is to keep typing. Focus on getting your thoughts on the page. Go back later to fix the inevitable typos.

» The spell-check feature also flags repeated words by underlining them with a red zigzag. Your choice is to either delete the repeated word or just ignore ignore it.

» Word doesn't spell-check certain types of words, such as words with numbers in them or words written in all capitals.

» To disable automatic spell checking, see the later section "Document Proofing Settings."

» An alternative to on-the-fly spell checking is to perform a manual spell check. See the later section "All-at-Once Document Proofing."

Fixing a misspelled word

Don't let that red zigzag of shame vex you any longer! Follow these steps:

1. **Right-click the misspelled word.**

Up pops a shortcut menu, with the Spelling submenu displayed, as shown in Figure 7-1.

2. **From the submenu, choose the word you intended to type.**

In Figure 7-1, the word *deadlines* fits the bill. Click that word to replace the spurious word.

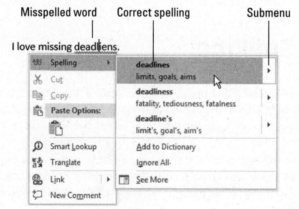

FIGURE 7-1: Deal with that typo.

YEW RIGHT GRATE

Word's document-proofing tools are as technologically advanced as the programmers at Microsoft can make them. As the title of this sidebar suggests, however, there's something to be said about context.

Just because your document appears to contain no proofing errors doesn't mean that everything is perfect. You have no better way to proof a document than to read it with human eyes.

If the word you intended to type isn't on the list, don't fret: Just take another stab at spelling the word phonetically and then correct it again. For extremely difficult spelling, type word into a Google search on the web, which may also offer a correct spelling.

Dealing with incorrectly flagged words

Occasionally, Word's spell checker bumps into a word it doesn't recognize, such as your last name or perhaps your city. Word dutifully casts doubt on the word by scribbling beneath it the notorious red zigzag. Yes, this is one of those cases where the computer is wrong.

To correct a falsely accused word, right-click it. Choose one of these options (shown earlier, in Figure 7-1):

Add to Dictionary: This command adds the word to your custom dictionary. The word is no longer flagged as misspelled in the current document or any other document.

Ignore All: This command directs Word to ignore the term and accept it as correctly spelled throughout the entire document.

If the word is intentionally misspelled and you don't want to ignore all instances or add it to the custom dictionary, just leave it be.

>> See the section "Rechecking a document," later in this chapter, for information on reversing your decision to ignore a spelling error.

>> For information on viewing or editing the custom dictionary, see the later section "Customizing the custom dictionary."

THE 25 MOST FREQUENTLY MISSPELLED WORDS

a lot	embarrass	realize
accidentally	gauge	receive
acquire	grammar	ridiculous
amateur	independent	separate
argument	kernel	supersede
atheist	liaison	their
collectible	maneuver	weird
consensus	no one	
definite	occurrence	

AutoCorrect in Action

Word quickly fixes hundreds of common typos and spelling errors on the fly, meaning you may never see the embarrassing red zigzag. The AutoCorrect feature is responsible, and you have to be quick to see it.

For example, in Word you can't type the word *mispell* (with only one *s*). That's because AutoCorrect fixes that typo the split second you press the spacebar or use punctuation to end the word.

AutoCorrect also converts common text shortcuts into their proper single characters. For example, type **(C)** and AutoCorrect properly inserts the © copyright symbol. Ditto for **(TM)** for the trademark. Typing ⇨ is translated into an arrow, and **:)** becomes a happy face. ☺

Beyond spelling, AutoCorrect fixes common punctuation. It automatically capitalizes the first letter of a sentence. AutoCorrect capitalizes *I* when you forget to, properly capitalizes the names of days, fixes the iNVERSE cAPS lOCK pROBLEM, plus other common typos.

Undoing an AutoCorrect correction

You can reverse AutoCorrect instant changes, but only when you're quick. The secret is to press Ctrl+Z (the Undo command) immediately after AutoCorrect makes its correction. The change is gone.

Even when you're not quick with the Undo command, you can peruse AutoCorrect changes. These are flagged by a weensy blue rectangle that appears under the first letter of the corrected text, as illustrated in Figure 7-2. Position the mouse pointer at that rectangle, and click to see various AutoCorrect options, also illustrated in Figure 7-2.

Point the mouse

Blue rectangle/AutoCorrect hint

Click to display menu

To restore the text to how it was typed originally, choose the option Change Back to *whatever*, where *whatever* is the original text (shown as the :) in Figure 7-2).

To prevent AutoCorrect from ever making the change again, choose the option Stop Automatically Correcting *whatever*. Keep in mind that though the text won't be automatically corrected, it may still show up as a typo or a spelling error.

See the later section "Adjusting AutoCorrect settings" for information on the final option, Control AutoCorrect Options.

Adding a new AutoCorrect entry

I'm proud to announce that, after a long absence, Microsoft has decided to return to you the capability to create your own AutoCorrect entries. The process is similar to correcting any spelling mistake, but you must remember to take a few extra steps:

1. **Right-click a misspelled word that you want to add as an AutoCorrect entry.**

   The word must be flagged as misspelled, underlined by the red zigzag of shame.

2. **Point the mouse at the correct spelling, but instead of choosing that word, click its submenu button (illustrated in Figure 7-1).**

3. **Choose Add to AutoCorrect.**

   You'll never see the word misspelled again.

Words you accidentally add as AutoCorrect entries can be removed, should you make a mistake. See the next section.

Adjusting AutoCorrect settings

To control how AutoCorrect behaves, as well as manage the words it corrects, follow these steps:

1. **Click the File tab.**

2. **Choose Options.**

   The Word Options dialog box appears.

3. **Choose the Proofing category on the left side of the window.**

4. **Click the AutoCorrect Options button.**

   The AutoCorrect dialog box appears, with the AutoCorrect tab forward.

The AutoCorrect tab lists all of AutoCorrect's superpowers, such as capitalizing the first letter of a sentence. Click the Exceptions button to manage specific words where the rules need not apply.

More specific to your AutoCorrect desires is the long list showing the words automatically replaced as you type. This list is where you'll find items such as *teh*, which is autocorrected to *the*. You'll also find words you've added to the list as described in the preceding section.

To remove an entry from the AutoCorrect list, scroll to find that item, such as :) for the happy face. Click to select the entry, and then click the Delete button.

To add an entry, use the Replace and With text boxes. For example, to replace *kludge* with *kluge*, type **kludge** in the Replace box and **kluge** in the With box.

Click the OK button when you're done adjusting, and then close the Word Options dialog box.

Also see Chapter 33 for information on disabling various AutoCorrect and Auto-Format features.

Grammar Be Good

Mark Twain once referred to English spelling as "drunken." If that's true, English grammar must be a hallucination. To help you detox, Word offers on-the-fly grammar checking. It's just like having your eighth-grade English teacher inside your computer — only it's all the time and not just during third period.

Word's grammar checker works like its spell checker. The main difference is that offenses are underlined with a frigid blue zigzag, such as the one shown in Figure 7-3 (although the zigzag looks gray in this book). That's your hint of Word's sense of grammatical justice. Even then, the offense is most likely mild and, given the illusionary nature of English grammar, can probably be ignored.

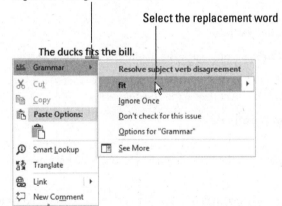

FIGURE 7-3:
A grammatical error is flagged.

To address a grammar issue, right-click the blue-underlined text, as shown in Figure 7-3. Use the pop-up menu to discover what's wrong and, optionally, choose an alternative. You can also choose to ignore the error, which I find myself doing quite often.

>> The most common source of grammatical woe in English is verb agreement, or matching the subject to the correct verb. In Figure 7-3, the subject *ducks* is plural, but the verb *fits* is third person singular.

>> The grammar checker is excellent at spotting two spaces between words when you need only one space. It's not so good at spotting fragments.

>> You may see false grammar errors when using Word's revision-tracking feature with the No Markup setting enabled. Reveal all revision marks to see what's up. Refer to Chapter 26 for details.

>> To customize or turn off grammar checking, refer to the sections "Disabling automatic proofing" and "Curtailing grammar checking," later in this chapter.

All-at-Once Document Proofing

If you prefer to ignore the red zigzag underline of shame, or perhaps you've disabled that feature, you can resort to performing a final document proof. It's an all-in-one spelling- and grammar-checking process, which is how spell check worked before it became an on-the-fly feature.

Reviewing all those errors

To perform all-at-once document proofing, top to bottom, follow these steps:

1. **Click the Review tab.**

2. **In the Proofing group, click the Spelling & Grammar button.**

The Editor pane appears. Errors are shown one at a time as they occur in your document. You must review them sequentially.

3. **Deal with the offense.**

Depending on the transgression, either the Spelling pane or the Grammar pane appears. Options presented let you deal with each abuse of the mother tongue:

- *Ignore:* Click this button to ignore the error once. You'll be reminded of the same spelling error or similar grammatical errors again.

- *Ignore All:* Use this button to direct Word to merrily skip the error throughout the entire document.

- *Delete Repeated Word:* Click this button to remove one of the twin words.

- *Don't Check for This Issue:* Choose this button to inform Word's grammar checker that you're fine with the specifically mentioned grammatical *faux pas*.

- *Add to Dictionary:* Use this button to thrust a misspelled word into the custom dictionary. It won't be flagged as incorrect ever again. Well, unless you edit the dictionary, as described elsewhere in this chapter.

- *Change:* For spelling boo-boos and grammatical flubs, click to select a correct option from the list that's presented and then click the Change button to replace the offending text.

- *Change All:* For spelling errors only, click the correct word and then click Change All to replace all instances of your spelling mistake.

You can also edit the word directly: Click in the document to make necessary textual repairs. Click the Resume button in the Editor pane when you're done, to continue scouring the text.

4. **Continue checking the next affront to the English language.**

5. **Click the OK button when the checking is done.**

You can easily enter a trancelike state while you're document proofing. You might find yourself clicking the Ignore button too quickly. My advice: Use the Undo command, Ctrl+Z, to go back and change text that you may not have paid attention to.

>> Another way to sequentially peruse spelling and grammar errors is to use the Spelling and Grammar Check button on the status bar (shown in the margin). To proof your document, click that button to hop from one spelling or grammar error to the next.

>> Word disables its on-the-fly proofing when your document grows larger than a certain size — say, 100 pages. You see a warning message when this change happens. At that point, you must perform an all-at-once document check, as described in this section.

Rechecking a document

Clicking the Ignore or Ignore All button has consequences for accidentally ignored spelling errors in your document. If you've abused these options too often, you can direct Word to recheck your document, which re-admits ignored misspelled words and grammatical blunders back into the realm of document proofing. Obey these steps:

1. **Click the File tab.**

2. **Choose Options to display the Word Options dialog box.**

3. **Choose the Proofing category.**

4. **Click the Recheck Document button.**

   It's found beneath the heading When Correcting Spelling and Grammar in Word.

5. **Click the Yes button to confirm that you want to un-ignore things you've chosen to ignore before.**

6. **Click the OK button to dismiss the Word Options dialog box.**

The document represents itself, again flagging all those words and items you've chosen to ignore before.

>> Rechecking a document doesn't undo any additions you've made to Word's custom dictionary. See the later section "Customizing the custom dictionary."

>> If spelling and grammar errors fail to appear after rechecking, consider that the option to hide them may be enabled, as described in the later section "Hiding all proofing errors in a document."

Document Proofing Settings

Whether you adore or detest Word's capability to ridicule your language abilities, you have the final say-so. Plenty of settings and options are available to control Word's document-proofing tools.

Customizing the custom dictionary

You build the custom dictionary by adding properly spelled words that are flagged as misspelled. You can also manually add words, remove words, or just browse the dictionary to see whether you're making old Noah Webster jealous. Follow these steps:

1. **Click the File tab.**

2. **Choose Options to display the Word Options dialog box.**

3. **Choose Proofing.**

4. **Click the Custom Dictionaries button.**

   The Custom Dictionaries dialog box appears.

   Word 2019 uses the RoamingCustom.dic file as the custom dictionary. You may see other files in the list, especially if you've upgraded from older versions of Microsoft Word.

5. **Select the item RoamingCustom.dic (Default).**

6. **Click the button labeled Edit Word List.**

    You see a scrolling list of words you've added to the custom dictionary.

To add a word to the custom dictionary, type it in the Word(s) text box. Click the Add button.

To remove a word from the custom dictionary, select the word from the scrolling list. Click the Delete button.

Click the OK button when you're done with the custom dictionary. Then click the various OK buttons to close the open dialog boxes and return to your document.

Disabling automatic proofing

To banish the angry red zigzag underlines and bitter blue underlines from your document, which effectively disables on-the-fly document proofing, follow these steps:

1. **Click the File tab and choose Options.**

    The Word Options dialog box appears.

2. **On the left side of the dialog box, choose Proofing.**

3. **Remove the check mark by the item Check Spelling as You Type.**

4. **While you're at it, remove the check mark by the item Mark Grammar Errors as You Type.**

5. **Click the OK button.**

See? You've just improved your spelling, though I wouldn't get cocky about it.

Also see the later section "Hiding all proofing errors in a document."

Curtailing grammar checking

I find Word's grammar checker to be insistently incorrect. After all, English is fluid. Especially if you're writing poetry or you just know the rules and prefer to bend them or toss them asunder, consider throttling back some of Word's more aggressive grammar flags.

To adjust grammar settings, follow these steps:

1. **Click the File tab.**

2. **Choose Options to display the Word Options dialog box.**

3. **Choose Proofing.**

Below the heading, When Correcting Spelling and Grammar in Word, look for the Writing Style item. Next to is the Grammar and Refinements menu. And to the right you see a Settings button.

4. **Click the Settings button.**

The Grammar Settings dialog box appears.

5. **Uncheck those items you no longer desire Word to mark as offensive.**

The categories are general, which makes deselecting a rule difficult. That's because whenever Word flags a grammar error, you see a specific rule and not the general ones listed in the Grammar Settings dialog box.

6. **Click the OK button to dismiss the Grammar Settings dialog box.**

7. **Click OK to close the Word Options dialog box.**

REMEMBER

You can train Word to ignore specific grammar incidents by clicking the option to ignore a rule when it's flagged in your document.

Hiding all proofing errors in a document

It's possible to direct Word to continue to spell-check yet hide the angry red zig-zag and chilling blue underlines. All-at-once document checking still works, and words are still flagged as misspelled, but they don't appear as such in the text. To hide the proofing marks, obey these steps:

1. **Summon the Proofing area in the Word Options dialog box.**

Refer to Steps 1–3 in the preceding section.

2. **At the bottom of the right side of the Word Options dialog box, remove the check marks by the options Hide Spelling Errors in This Document Only and Hide Grammar Errors in This Document Only.**

3. **Click OK.**

The proofing flags disappear throughout your document.

TIP

You might want to confirm the status of these options when you believe Word's document proofing to be broken. For example, you type a misspelled word on purpose and the red zigzag underline doesn't appear! In that situation, document proofing marks may be disabled. If so, follow the steps in this section but remove the check marks in Step 2.

IN THIS CHAPTER

» **Understanding terms**

» **Creating a new document**

» **Saving documents**

» **Updating (resaving) a document**

» **Opening a document**

» **Inserting one document inside another**

» **Retrieving a lost document**

Chapter **8**

Documents New, Saved, and Opened

I like the word *document.* It's elegant. It's much better than saying "a file" or "that thing I created with my word processor." A document could include everything from a quick shopping list to a vast cycle of medieval fantasy novels you keep reading despite knowing that your favorite protagonist will die a sudden, horrific death.

Regardless of size or importance, a word processing file is called a *document.* It's the end result of your efforts in Word. You create new documents, save them, open up old documents, and close documents. That's the document cycle.

Some Terms to Get Out of the Way

TECHNICAL STUFF

To best understand the document concept, you must escape the confines of Word and wander into the larger dominion of computer storage. A basic understanding of files and storage is necessary if you're to get the most from your word processing efforts.

File: A Word document is a file. A *file* on a computer is information stored for the long term, which can be recalled again and shared with others. Windows manages files and their storage, backup, copying, moving, and renaming.

Folder: Files dwell in containers called folders. A *folder* stores files and other folders, which creates a hierarchical system for data storage. This is how folders play a role in file organization.

Local storage: Files are kept for the long term, saved to your computer's hard drive or solid-state drive (SSD). Because this hardware exists on your computer, it's referred to as local storage.

Cloud storage: Files can also be kept for long-term storage on the Internet. This storage is commonly referred to as *cloud storage*. With regard to Word (and the rest of Microsoft Office), the preferred form of cloud storage is Microsoft OneDrive. Files saved to cloud storage are available to your computer as well, but the benefit is that you can access your cloud storage from any Internet-connected device.

Word also works with other cloud storage services, such as Dropbox or Google Drive. These locations are accessed through their shadow copies on local storage. For some quirky reason, only Microsoft's OneDrive cloud storage is closely integrated with Word.

Behold! A New Document

To conjure a new document when Word first starts, choose a template thumbnail on the Word Start screen; the Blank thumbnail presents a fresh, empty document. But here's a shortcut: Press Ctrl+N to summon a new document. It's quicker.

If you've disabled the Word Start screen (as revealed in Chapter 33), you can see its contents and peruse various document templates to start a new document, by obeying the following steps. You can also follow these steps anytime you're using Word, not just when it first starts:

1. **Click the File tab.**

   The File screen appears.

2. **Choose New from the left side of the window.**

   The New screen lists the same templates that appear on the Start screen. Category tabs are titled Featured and Personal for Word's templates and your own templates, respectively.

TECHNICAL STUFF

HOW LONG CAN A WORD DOCUMENT BE?

The quick answer is that no length limit is assigned to a Word document. If you like, your document can be thousands of pages long. Even so, I don't recommend putting that limit to the test.

The longer a document, the more apt Word is to screw up. You probably won't encounter any issues for typical-size documents, even those up to 100 pages or more. For larger projects, however, I recommend splitting your work into chapter-size chunks. Organize those chapter documents in their own folder.

To stitch together several documents into a larger document, use Word's Master Document feature, as described in Chapter 25. The book *Word 2016 For Professionals For Dummies* (Wiley) offers a host of hints for managing large manuscripts, including publishing novels and other weighty tomes.

3. **Click the Blank Document thumbnail to create a new, blank document (probably because you forgot the Ctrl+N keyboard shortcut), or select a template.**

A new Word window appears, ready for typing action.

You can produce as many new documents as are needed. Word lets you work with several documents at a time.

>> See Chapter 24 for details on how to best work with multiple document windows all open at once.

>> Chapter 16 contains information on templates, which can greatly boost your performance by providing common document elements, including preset text and styles, automatically for you.

Save Your Stuff!

It doesn't matter whether you're writing the next Great American Novel or jotting down notes for tonight's PTA meeting, the most important thing you can do to a document is *save it*.

Save! Save! Save!

Saving creates a permanent copy of your document, encoding the text as a file on the computer's storage system. That way, you can work on the document again, publish it electronically, or have a copy ready in case the power goes *poof*. All these tasks are possible, providing you save your stuff.

Saving a document for the first time

You don't have to finish a document before you save it. No! You should save immediately — as soon as you have a few sentences or paragraphs.

To save a document for the first time, follow these steps:

1. Press Ctrl+S.

You see the Save As screen on the File tab. In fact, you could also click the File tab and choose Save As, but Ctrl+S is a universal keyboard shortcut and using it is quicker.

If you don't see the Save As screen, the document has already been saved. See the later section "Saving or updating a document."

2. Choose a location for the document.

All documents (files) are saved in folders, so your job is to pick an appropriate one. You can choose local storage or cloud storage, or select a pinned or recently used folder from the right side of the window, as illustrated in Figure 8-1.

To browse local storage, choose This PC.

To browse cloud storage on OneDrive, choose OneDrive.

To use a recent folder, choose it on the right side of the screen.

After you choose a location, the traditional Save As dialog box appears. Or you can quickly summon that dialog box by clicking the Browse button, as illustrated in Figure 8-1.

You can use the Save As dialog box to navigate to a specific folder if it doesn't appear on the Save As screen.

TIP

3. Type a name for your document in the File Name box.

Word automatically selects the first several words of your document as a filename and places that text in the File Name box. If that's okay, continue with Step 5. Otherwise, type a better name.

Be descriptive with the filename! The more concisely you name your document, the easier it is to recognize it by that name in the future.

REMEMBER

Locations to save your document   Pinned folders

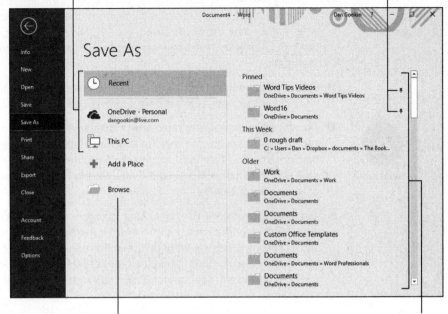

FIGURE 8-1:
The Save As
screen.

Summon the traditional Save As dialog box   Recent folders

4. **Click the Save button.**

The file is safely stored.

The document window doesn't close after you save. You don't need to quit Word. You can keep working. As you do so, continue to save. See the later section "Saving or updating a document."

>> The Save As screen on the File tab is known as the *backstage.* It's an updated way to save documents and integrate cloud storage.

>> If you prefer to use the traditional Save As dialog box directly, press the F12 key.

>> If the computer's current folder-organization scheme isn't to your liking, click the New Folder button to create a new folder in the current folder. Word proceeds to save your document in the newly created folder.

>> For a folder you use frequently, such as a current project folder, point the mouse at the folder name and click the Pushpin icon, shown in the margin. Clicking the pushpin pins the folder to the top of the folder list, as shown in Figure 8-1. That way, you can keep favorite folders handy for quick selection when saving documents.

>> Your clue that the document is saved successfully is that its filename appears on the document's title bar, at the top center of the Word window. Further, when the document is freshly saved, you see the text *Saved to . . .* followed by the folder name. This extra text vanishes as you continue to work on the document.

>> The Save As command can also be used to save a document with a new name, to a different location, or in a different format. See Chapter 24.

WARNING

>> Do not save a document to removable media, such as a thumb drive or media card. Instead, save the document to the computer's main storage device: the hard drive or SSD. Then you can copy the file to the removable media. If you save directly to a thumb drive and it's accidentally removed, you run the risk of losing your document.

>> The advantage of using OneDrive cloud storage is that your document is available to any device you use with Internet access. If you have an Office 365 subscription, you can use Word on the web to edit the document. You can also employ Word's collaboration features to share and work with others on the same document. See Chapter 26 for collaboration information.

Dealing with document-save errors

Saving a document involves coordination between Word and Windows. This complexity doubles the chances of something going wrong, so it's high time for an error message. One such error message is

The file *whatever* already exists

Here are your choices and my suggestions:

>> **Replace Existing File:** Nope.

>> **Save Changes with a Different Name:** Yep.

>> **Merge Changes into Existing File:** Nope.

Choose the middle option and click OK. Type a different filename in the Save As dialog box.

Another common problem occurs when a message that's displayed reads something like this:

The filename is not valid

TRIVIAL — BUT IMPORTANT — INFORMATION ABOUT FILENAMES

Be creative in your document, but also be creative when saving the document and christening it with a name. These names must abide by the Windows rules and regulations for all filenames:

- Short, descriptive filenames are best.

- A filename can be longer than 200 ridiculous-something characters, but don't tempt the gods.

- A filename can include letters, numbers, and spaces, and can start with a letter or a number.

- A filename can contain periods, commas, hyphens, and even underlines.

- A filename cannot contain any of these characters: \ / : * ? " < > |.

Word automatically appends a *filename extension* to all documents you save — like a last name. You may or may not see the filename extension, depending on how you've configured Windows. Either way, don't type the extension. Only concern yourself with giving the document a proper and descriptive filename.

That's Word's less-than-cheerful way of telling you that the filename contains a forbidden character. To be safe, use letters, numbers, and spaces when naming a file. Check the nearby sidebar, "Trivial — but important — information about filenames."

Saving or updating a document

As you continue to work on your document, you should save as you work: Ctrl+S. The frequent re-save captures any changes you've made since the last time you saved, keeping it fresh. It never hurts to save a document multiple times.

>> I save my document whenever I pause to think, rise to pour another cup of coffee, or answer the phone.

>> You can also perform a quick save by clicking the Save button on the Quick Access toolbar.

>> If you haven't yet saved a document, using the Save command, Ctrl+S, or the Save button on the Quick Access toolbar, brings up the Save As screen. Refer to the earlier section "Saving a document for the first time."

Saving automatically on OneDrive

If you've saved a document to OneDrive and the AutoSave feature is active, you never really need to save again. Word automatically updates your documents for you.

AutoSave On

To ensure that AutoSave is active, look for the AutoSave item on the Quick Access toolbar, similar to what's shown in the margin. If the switch is off, click it. AutoSave is active when you see the word *On* (as shown nearby).

>> When the AutoSave item is disabled, the document has been saved to local storage or a location other than OneDrive. This feature might also be disabled for some versions of Word.

>> If you don't see the AutoSave item, click the menu button on the far right of the Quick Access toolbar. Choose Automatically Save from the menu.

Forgetting to save before you quit

When you're done writing in Word, you close the document, close the window, or quit Word outright. No matter how you call it quits, when your document hasn't yet been saved, or was changed since the last save, you're asked to save one last time before leaving.

The warning dialog box that appears when you attempt to leave before saving features three options:

Save: Click this button to save the document and close. If you've been naughty and haven't yet saved the document, the Save As screen appears.

Don't Save: When you click this button, the document is closed without saving. It might still be available for later recovery. See the later section "Recover a Draft."

Cancel: Click this button to forget about saving and return to the document for more editing and stuff.

I recommend that you choose the Save option.

Open a Document

Saving a document means nothing unless you have a way to retrieve that document later. As you might suspect, Word offers multiple ways to *open* a document on either local storage or cloud storage.

TECHNICAL STUFF

The original "open" command in Word was File, Transfer, Load. I think "open" sounds better.

Using the Open command

Open is the standard computer command used to fetch an existing document. Once you find and open the document, it appears in Word's window as though it's always been there.

To open a document in Word, follow these steps:

1. **Click the File tab.**

2. **Choose the Open command.**

The Open screen materializes, similar to what's shown in Figure 8-2.

Choose a recent document

Places to look for a document

Pinned documents appear here

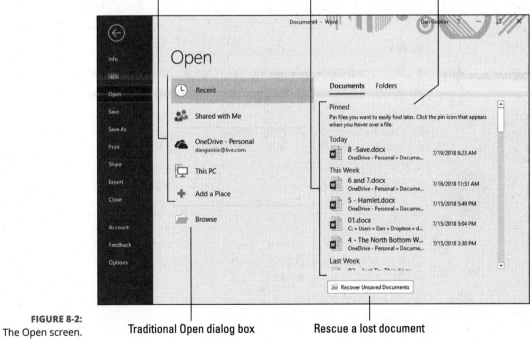

FIGURE 8-2:
The Open screen.

Traditional Open dialog box

Rescue a lost document

3. **Choose a location where the document may lurk.**

   Your choices are Recent Documents, which is shown in Figure 8-2, cloud storage such as OneDrive, or local storage titled This PC.

   If you spy the desired document lurking on the Recent list, click it. The document opens on the screen. Congratulations — you're done.

4. **Choose a recent folder from the list.**

5. **Click a document when you find it.**

   The document opens, ready for editing.

6. **If you can't find the document, or you just yearn to use the traditional Open dialog box, click the Browse button.**

   The traditional Open dialog box appears, which you can use to locate the file you want to open: Click to select the file, and then click the Open button.

The file you open appears in the Word window. Word may highlight the last location where you were writing or editing, along with a *Welcome back* message.

After the document is open, you can edit it, look at it, print it, or do whatever you want.

>> The shortcut key to access the Open screen is Ctrl+O. Also, an Open command button appears on the Quick Access toolbar.

>> The keyboard shortcut to directly access the traditional Open dialog box is Ctrl+F12. Good luck remembering that one.

>> You can open a document by locating its icon in a folder window, which happens in Windows, not in Word. Double-click the icon to open the document. Refer to Chapter 1 for information.

>> To access recently opened documents, right-click the Word icon on the taskbar. Choose a document from the pop-up list (called the *jump list*) to open it.

>> Opening a document doesn't erase it from storage. In fact, the file stays on the storage system until you use the Save command to save and update the document with any changes.

>> When you position the mouse pointer at a recently opened document on the Open screen, you see a Pushpin icon, similar to what's shown in the margin. Click that icon to make the document "stick" to the Open screen. That way, the document is always available for quick access later.

>> To remove a document from the Recent list, right-click the document's entry. Choose the command Remove from List.

>> Avoid opening a file on any removable media, such as a thumb drive or media card. Though it's possible, doing so can lead to headaches later, should you remove the media before Word is done with the document. Because of that, I recommend that you use Windows to copy the document from the removable media to the computer's main storage device. Then open it in Word.

Opening one document inside another

Inserting the contents of one document into another is possible in Word, and no surgery or screaming is involved. For example, at the end of a paper you can insert another document that may have a short bio – including your picture. To do so, follow these steps:

1. **Position the insertion pointer where you want the other document's contents to appear.**

The text is inserted at that spot.

2. **Click the Insert tab.**

3. **From the Text group, click the menu (down-pointing triangle) by the Object button.**

The Object button is shown in the margin.

4. **Choose the menu item Text from File**

The Insert File dialog box appears. It's similar to the Open dialog box.

5. **Locate and select the document you want to insert.**

Browse the various folders to find the document icon. Click to select its icon.

6. **Click the Insert button.**

The document's text is inserted into the current document, just as though you had typed and formatted it yourself.

The resulting combined document retains the name of the first document. The document you inserted remains unchanged.

>> You can insert any number of documents into another document.

>> Inserting text from one document into another is often called *boilerplating*. For example, you can save a commonly used piece of text in a document and then insert it into other documents as necessary. This process is also the way that sleazy romance novels are written.

>> If you find yourself inserting common bits of text into documents consider instead creating a document template. See Chapter 16.

>> Biography. Résumé. Curriculum vitae. The more important you think you are, the more alien the language used to describe what you've done.

Recover a Draft

When you forget to save a document or the computer crashed or the power went out, you can recover some — but perhaps not all — of an unsaved document Valiantly make this attempt:

1. **Press Ctrl+O to summon the Open screen.**

2. **Ensure that Recent is chosen as the file location.**

3. **Click the Recover Unsaved Documents button, found at the bottom of the list of recent files. (Refer to Figure 8-2.)**

   The Open dialog box appears, listing the contents of a special folder, UnsavedFiles. It's Word's graveyard. Actually, it's more like a morgue in a county with a lousy EMS.

4. **Select a document to recover.**

   The document may have an unusual name, especially when it's never been saved.

5. **Click the Open button to open and recover the document.**

The document you recover might not be the one you wanted it to be. If so, try again and choose another document.

You might also find that the recovered document doesn't contain all the text you typed or thought would be there. You can't do anything about it, other than *remember to save everything* in the first place!

TECHNICAL STUFF

The recovery of drafts is possible because of Word's AutoRecover feature. Refer to Chapter 31 for more information on AutoRecover.

IN THIS CHAPTER

» Previewing a document before printing

» Printing a specific part of a document

» Printing multiple copies of a document

» Canceling a print job

» Making a document compatible for sharing

» Sending a document as an attachment

» Exporting a document as a PDF

Chapter **9**

Publish Your Document

After writing, editing, formatting, and proofing, the final step in document preparation is publishing. Don't get all excited: Publishing in Word has nothing to do with seeing your book on the *New York Times* bestseller list (although it could happen). Publishing is a general topic that includes printing a document to paper as well as generating an electronic document you can share online. Times have changed.

Your Document on Paper

The word processor is the best writing tool ever invented. It's also the first writing tool that avoids paper until your document is complete. Even then, you choose whether to generate a dead-tree version of the document, also called a *printout* or *hard copy.*

» Configuring the printer is done in Windows, not Word. Use the Control Panel or Settings app to set up and configure a printer, though it's pretty much an automatic operation.

» I assume that your computer has a printer attached or available on a network and that everything is set up just peachy. That setup includes stocking the printer with ink or toner and plenty of paper.

Previewing before printing

TIP

Before you print, preview the look of the final document. Yeah, even though your document is supposed to look the same on the screen as it does on paper, you may still see surprises: missing page numbers, blank pages, screwy headers, and other jaw-dropping blunders, for example.

Fortunately, a print preview of your document appears as part of the Print screen, as shown in Figure 9-1.

Back button/Return to document

Print document

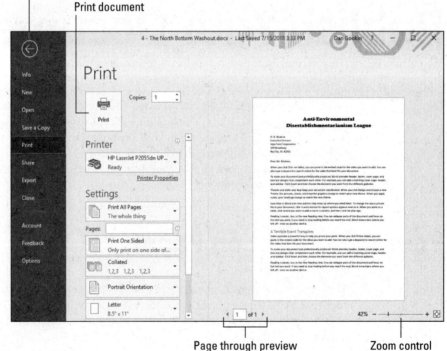

FIGURE 9-1:
The Print screen.

Page through preview

Zoom control

To preview your document, follow these steps:

1. **Save your document.**

   Yep — always save. Saving before printing is a good idea.

2. **Press Ctrl+P.**

   The Ctrl+P keyboard shortcut is the common Windows printing command. You can also click the File tab and choose chose the Print item from the left side of the File screen. Ctrl+P is quicker.

   The Print screen appears, similar to what's shown in Figure 9-1.

3. **Use the buttons at the bottom of the Print screen to peruse your document.**

   You can use the Zoom control (refer to Figure 9-1) to enlarge or reduce the image. Look at the margins. If you're using footnotes, headers, or footers, look at how they lay out. The idea is to spot anything that's dreadfully wrong *before* you print.

When you're ready, print the document. Details are offered in the next section, but basically you click the big Print button, labeled in Figure 9-1. Or when things need to be repaired, click the Back button or press the Esc key to return to your document.

Printing the entire document

It's time for your scribbling to hit paper. Heed these directions:

1. **Make sure that the printer is on and ready to print.**

   Printing works fastest when the printer is on.

2. **Save your document.**

   Click the little Save button on the Quick Access toolbar for a quickie save.

3. **Press Ctrl+P, or if you're being paid by the hour: Click the File tab and choose the Print item.**

   The Print screen appears. (Refer to Figure 9-1.)

4. **Click the big Print button.**

   The Print screen closes, and the document spews forth from the printer.

DELETE THAT EXTRA BLANK PAGE AT THE END OF A DOCUMENT

Occasionally, you may be surprised when your document prints one extra page — a blank page. And you're not only bothered because you forgot to preview before printing (which I recommend in this chapter) but also vexed because you cannot get rid of it! Until now.

To remove the ugly, blank page that follows your document like a phantom caboose, press Ctrl+End. With the insertion pointer at the end of your document, press the Backspace key repeatedly until the extra page is gone. How can you tell? Keep an eye on the total page-count tally on the status bar. When the page count decreases by one, you know that the extra page is gone.

Printing speed depends on the complexity of the document and how dumb the printer is. Fortunately, you can continue working while the document prints.

» Obligatory Ctrl+P joke goes here.

» If nothing prints, don't use the Print command again! Most likely, nothing is awry; the computer is still thinking or sending information to the printer. If you don't see an error message, everything will probably print, eventually.

» The computer prints one copy of your document for every Print command you incant. If the printer is just being slow and you impatiently click the Print button ten times, you end up printing ten copies of your document. (See the section "Canceling a print job," later in this chapter.)

» When the document format specifies a unique paper size, the printer prompts you to load that paper size. Stand by to produce and load the proper paper when the printer prompts you.

Printing a specific page

Because the printer chewed up page 16 in your document, you must print that page again. Rather than reprint the entire document and throw away everything but page 16, print only that page. Follow these steps:

1. **Move the insertion pointer so that it's sitting somewhere on the page you want to print.**

   Double-check the page number on the status bar to ensure that you're on the correct page.

   TIP

2. **Press Ctrl+P.**

3. **Click the Print Range button below the Settings heading.**

   Refer to Figure 9-2 for the button's location. It typically says Print All Pages.

4. **Choose Print Current Page from the menu.**

   The page number can also be confirmed by viewing the Page Range box at the bottom of the Print screen. (Refer to Figure 9-1.)

5. **Click the Print button.**

Print the document

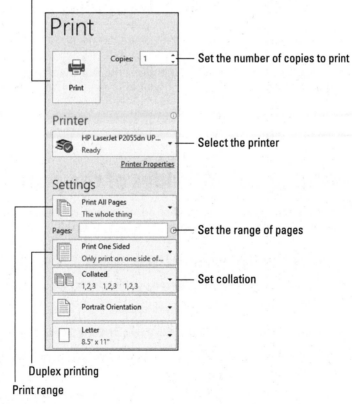

Set the number of copies to print

Select the printer

Set the range of pages

Set collation

FIGURE 9-2:
Specific buttons
on the Print
screen.

Duplex printing

Print range

The single page prints with all the formatting you applied, including footnotes and page numbers and everything else, just as though you plucked that page from a complete printing of the entire document.

Printing a range of pages

Word enables you to print a range of pages, odd pages, even pages, or a hodge-podge combination of given pages from within your document. To print a range or group of pages, summon the Print screen: Press Ctrl+P.

On the Print screen, look for the Pages text box, illustrated in Figure 9-2. Here are some suggestions for what to type in that text box:

> To print pages 3 through 5, type **3-5**.
>
> To print pages 1 through 7, type **1-7**.
>
> To print pages 2 and 6, type **2,6**.
>
> To print page 3, pages 5 through 9, pages 15 through 17, and page 19 (boy, that coffee went everywhere, didn't it?), type **3, 5-9, 15-17, 19**.

Typing any value into the box changes the selection from Print All Pages to Custom Print.

Click the big Print button when you're ready to print. Only the pages you specify churn from the printer.

Printing on both sides of the page

If the printer is capable of duplex printing, you can direct Word to print your document on both sides of a sheet of paper. Follow these steps:

1. **Press Ctrl+P right after saving the document.**

2. **Click the Duplex Printing button on the Print screen.**

   Refer to Figure 9-2 for the button's location.

3. **Choose Print on Both Sides, Flip Pages on Long Sides.**

   Don't bother with the Short Sides option unless you plan to bind your document that way.

   If you don't see the Print on Both Sides options, you must manually print on both sides of the paper. See the next section.

4. **Make other settings as necessary on the Print screen.**

5. **Click the big Print button to print your document.**

I've discovered that Word (Windows, actually) isn't that smart when it comes to knowing which printers are duplex and which aren't. Alas, when Windows doesn't recognize your duplex printer as such, there's little you can do.

Printing odd and even pages

Say you have a printer that doesn't print on both sides of the page. If so, you can print all the odd pages in your document. Flip the paper and reinsert it in the printer. Then print all the even pages. The result is text printed on both sides of the page.

To print all odd pages or all even pages, follow these steps:

1. **Press Ctrl+P to summon the Print screen.**

2. **Click the Print Range button below the Settings heading.**

   Refer to Figure 9-2 for the button's location.

3. **Choose Only Print Odd Pages from the menu.**

4. **Click the Print button to print odd pages in your document.**

To print even pages, repeat these steps, but in Step 3 choose Only Print Even Pages.

TIP

I recommend printing only one odd-and-even page first, to ensure that when you reinsert the paper it's set in the proper orientation.

REMOVE THE DOCUMENT PROPERTIES SHEET

A printing problem that can potentially annoy you is finding the Document Properties sheet printing with your document. This extra sheet of paper prints first, listing document trivia. The Document Properties sheet isn't printed unless its option is set, and for some reason the option gets set on some folks' computers.

To prevent the Document Properties sheet from printing, click the File tab and choose the Options command. In the Word Options dialog box, choose Display from the left side of the window. In the Printing Options area on the Display screen, remove the check mark by the Print Document Properties item. Click OK.

Printing a block

After you mark a block of text in your document, you can beg the Print command to print only that block. Here's how:

1. **Mark the block of text you want to print.**

    See Chapter 6 for all the block-marking instructions in the world.

2. **Press Ctrl+P to summon the Print screen.**

3. **Click the Print Range button below the Settings heading.**

4. **From the menu, choose the Print Selection item.**

    The Print Selection item is available only when a block is selected in the document.

5. **Click the Print button.**

The block you selected prints at the same position with the same formatting (including headers and footers) as though you had printed the entire document.

Printing more than one copy of something

When it comes time to provide a copy of your report to all five members of the cult and the photocopier is broken, just print multiple copies. Here's how:

1. **Press Ctrl+P on the keyboard to summon the Print screen.**

2. **Enter the number of copies in the Copies text box.**

    To print five copies, for example, click the box and type **5**.

3. **Click the big Print button to print your copies.**

Under normal circumstances, Word prints each copy of the document one after the other. This process is known as *collating*. However, if you're printing five copies of a document and you want Word to print five copies of page 1 and then five copies of page 2 (and so on), choose the Uncollated option from the Collated menu button, illustrated in Figure 9-2.

Choosing another printer

Your computer may have access to several printers, such as one connected directly plus perhaps a selection of network or wireless printers. To choose a specific printer, such as that fancy color printer that's available on the network even though Ed has hidden it in his office, follow these steps:

1. **Press Ctrl+P to summon the Print screen.**

2. **Click the Select Printer button below the Printer heading.**

   The button shows the name of the currently selected printer, the one set by Windows as the default.

3. **Choose another printer from the list.**

   Unfortunately, not every printer features a clear and descriptive name. Also, not every printer listed is a physical printer. Some are document printers, such as Microsoft Print to PDF, which is covered later in this chapter.

4. **Click the Print button to print your document on the selected printer.**

TECHNICAL STUFF

Adding and managing printers falls under the domain of Windows, not Word. To add printers, rename them, or set the default printer, use Windows.

Canceling a print job

The fastest, easiest way to cancel a print job is to rush up to the printer and set it on fire. Lamentably, this method is frequently met with frowns by local fire officials.

A majority of modern computer printers feature a Cancel button. Press this button to stop a print job run amok. The Cancel button typically features an X, often colored red. Touch that button, and the printer stops — maybe not at once, but the button cancels the rest of the document from printing.

For slow printers, or those without a Cancel button, you can attempt to use Windows to halt a print job run amok. Obey these steps:

1. **Double-click the little Printer icon on the right end of the taskbar.**

   If you don't see the li'l printer icon, it's too late to cancel the print job. Otherwise, you see the printer's control window, which lists any queued printing jobs.

2. **Select your document in the job list.**

3. **Choose either the Document ⇨ Cancel command or the Document ⇨ Cancel Printing command.**

4. **Click Yes or OK to terminate the job.**

5. **Close the printer's control window.**

This method frequently meets with failure simply because the printer is fast and working these steps takes time. Still, it's worth a try, especially when the printer lacks a Cancel button.

>> It may take awhile for the printer to stop printing. That's because printers have their own memory, and a few pages of the document may be stored *and* continue to print even after you tell the printer to stop.

>> Stopping a print job is a Windows task, not one that Word has control over.

Electronically Publishing Your Document

Not every document needs to hit paper. For example, I never print my books. They're sent electronically to the publisher and edited right on the screen. eBooks don't need to be printed. And sometimes documents can be more effectively distributed by email than by paper. It's all part of electronically publishing your document.

Preparing a document for publishing

Lots of interesting things can find their way into your Word document, information that you may not want published. These items include comments, revision marks, hidden text, and other tidbits useful to you or your collaborators, which would mess up a document you share with others. The solution is to use Word's Check for Issues tool, like this:

1. **Ensure that your document is finished, finalized, and saved.**

2. **Click the File tab.**

   On the File screen, the Info area should be selected. If not, click the word *Info*.

3. **Click the Check for Issues button.**

4. **Choose Inspect Document.**

   The Document Inspector window appears. All items relevant to your document are selected.

5. **Click the Inspect button.**

   After a few moments, the Document Inspector window shows up again, listing any potential problems. The issues shown are explained, which allows you to cancel the Document Inspector to address individual items.

6. **Optionally, click the Remove All button next to any issues you want to clear up.**

   Now that you know what the issues are, you can always click the Close button and return to your document to manually inspect them.

7. **Click the Close button, or click Reinspect to give your document another once-over.**

After completing inspection, you can go forward with publishing your document or continue working.

Making a PDF

Word document files are considered a standard. Therefore, it's perfectly acceptable to send one of your document files as an email attachment or make it available for sharing with others, such as on cloud storage.

It's also possible to save, or publish, your document in the Adobe Acrobat document format, also known as a PDF file. This type of electronic publishing is secretly a form of printing your document. Obey these steps:

1. **Finish your document.**

   Yes, that includes saving it one last time.

2. **Press Ctrl+P to summon the Print screen.**

3. **Click the Printer button.**

   A list of available printers appears.

4. **Choose Microsoft Print to PDF.**

5. **Click the Print button.**

   Nothing is printed on paper, but the document is "printed" to a new PDF file. That requires the use of the special Save Print Output As dialog box.

6. **Choose a location for the PDF file.**

   Use the dialog box's controls to locate the proper folder.

7. **Type a filename.**

8. **Click the Save button.**

The PDF file is created. The original document remains in the Word window, unchanged by the print-to-PDF operation.

>> You can also open and edit PDF files in Word. In the traditional Open dialog box, choose the item PDF Files (*.pdf) from the File Type menu. Only PDF documents appear in the folder window. Choose one. Click OK to confirm that the process may take awhile. Once complete, the PDF file is open for editing as a Word document.

>> You need a copy of the Adobe Reader program to view PDF files. Don't worry: It's free. Go to get.adobe.com/reader.

Exporting your document

Beyond the Word document format and PDF, you can export your document into other, common file formats. These formats allow for easy document sharing, though they're not as common as they once were.

To export your document into another file format, follow these steps:

1. **Click the File tab.**

2. **Choose Export from the items on the left side of the screen.**

3. **Choose Change File Type.**

A list of available file types appears on the right side of the screen. These types include Word formats and other file types such as Plain Text, Rich Text Format (RTF), and Web Page (HTML).

4. **Select a file type.**

5. **Click the Save As button.**

You may have to scroll down the list to find the Save As icon.

The Save As dialog box appears. It's the same Save As dialog box as covered in Chapter 8, though the Save As Type menu lists the file type you selected in Step 3.

6. **Work the dialog box to set a folder or another location for the file, or to change its name.**

7. **Click the Save button to export the document into the alien file type.**

It may look like the document hasn't changed, but it has! The title bar now specifies that you're working on the exported document, not the original Word document.

WARNING

8. **Close the document.**

Press Ctrl+W or otherwise dismiss the document.

By closing the document, you ensure that any changes you make aren't made to the exported copy. To continue working on the original document, open it again in Word.

3

Fun with Formatting

Learn how to format your characters by choosing a font, text size, and color.

Apply paragraph formats, including line spacing, space before and after, and indenting.

Get to know the ruler and all the ways you can use tabs to align your text.

Find out how to change page size, orientation, and margins.

Get familiar with adding headers, footers, and cover pages.

Learn all you need to know about creating and applying styles and using templates.

Chapter **10**

Character Formatting

A t the atomic level, the most basic element you can format in a document is text — letters, numbers, and characters. You can format text to be bold, underlined, italicized, small or large, in different fonts or colors, and all sorts of pretty and distracting attributes. Word gives you a magnificent amount of control over the appearance of your text.

TIP

For an in-depth examination of fonts, typefaces, and character formatting in Word, refer to *Word 2016 For Professionals For Dummies* (Wiley).

Text-Formatting Techniques

You can format text in a document in two ways:

» Use text-formatting commands as you type, turning them on or off.

» Type the text first. Go back and select the text to format. Apply the format.

Either method works, though I recommend you concentrate on your writing first and return to formatting later.

Suppose that you want to write and format the following sentence:

```
His toe was severely swollen.
```

The first way to format is to type the sentence until you reach the word *severely*. Press Ctrl+I to apply the italic format. Type the word. Press Ctrl+I again to turn off the format. Continue typing.

The way I formatted the sentence was to type the entire thing first. Then I double-clicked the word *severely* to select it. Finally, I pressed Ctrl+I to apply the italic format.

Refer to Chapter 6 for more information on marking blocks of text.

Basic Text Formats

Word stores the most common text-formatting commands on the Home tab, in the Font group, as illustrated in Figure 10-1.

The Font group's gizmos not only control the text format but also describe the format for currently selected text: In Figure 10-1, the text format uses the Calibri font, and the text size is 11 points.

In addition to the Home tab's Font group, text-formatting commands are available on the mini toolbar. It appears whenever text is selected, as described in Chapter 6.

Selecting a font

The base attribute of text is its *typeface,* or *font.* The font sets the way the text looks and its overall style. Choosing the best font can be agonizing (and, indeed, many graphic artists are paid well to choose just the right font), but the process isn't too difficult. It generally goes like this:

1. **Click the Home tab.**

2. **In the Font group, click the down arrow by the Font item.**

   A list of fonts appears, shown on the right in Figure 10-1.

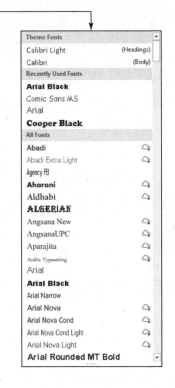

Dialog Box Launcher

FIGURE 10-1:
Text-formatting
commands in the
Font group.

3. Choose a font.

As you point the mouse pointer at a font, text in the document changes to preview the font. Click to choose the font and change the text format.

The Font menu is organized to help you locate the font you need. The top part of the menu lists fonts associated with the document theme. The next section contains fonts you've chosen recently, which is handy for reusing fonts. The rest of the list, which can be quite long, shows all fonts available to Word. The fonts appear in alphabetical order and are displayed as they would appear in the document.

TIP

>> To quickly scroll to a specific part of the Font menu, type the first letter of the font you need. For example, type **T** to find Times New Roman.

>> When a font name doesn't appear in the Font group (the text box is blank), it means that more than one font is selected in the document.

>> Refer to Chapter 16 for more information on document themes.

>> Fonts are the responsibility of Windows, not Word. Thousands of fonts are available for Windows, and they work in all Windows applications.

>> Graphic designers prefer to use two fonts in a document: one for the text and one for titles. Word is configured this way as well. The Body font is set for text. The Heading font is set for titles. These two fonts are set as part of the document theme.

Applying character formats

On the lower left side of the Font group, you find some of the most common character formats. These formats enhance the selected font or typeface.

B To make text bold, press Ctrl+B or click the Bold command button.

Use **bold** to make text stand out on a page — for titles and captions or when you're uncontrollably angry.

I To make text italic, press Ctrl+I or click the Italic command button.

Italic has replaced underlining as the preferred text-emphasis format. Italicized text is light, wispy, poetic, and often lacking undergarments.

<u>U</u> Underline text by pressing Ctrl+U or clicking the Underline command button. You can click the down arrow next to the Underline command button to choose from a variety of underline styles or set an underline color.

The double-underline format is available from the Underline command button's menu, but it does have a keyboard shortcut: Ctrl+Shift+D.

Also available is word-underlining format. <u>Word</u> <u>underlining</u> <u>looks</u> <u>like</u> <u>this</u>. The keyboard shortcut is Ctrl+Shift+W.

 Strike through text by clicking the Strikethrough command button. (A keyboard shortcut is unavailable.)

I don't know who the Strikethrough command bribed to make it into the Font group. If I were king of Microsoft, I would have put small caps up there instead. But who am I? Strikethrough is commonly used in legal documents, when you mean to say something but then ~~change your mind~~ think of something better to say.

Click the Subscript command button to make text subscript. The keyboard shortcut is Ctrl+= (equal sign).

Subscript text appears below the baseline, such as the 2 in H_2O.

To make text superscript, click the Superscript command button. The keyboard shortcut is Ctrl+Shift+= (equal sign), which is the shifted version of the subscript keyboard shortcut.

Superscript text appears above the line, such as the 10 in 2^{10}.

Another popular format, but apparently not popular enough to sport a command button in the Fonts group, is small caps. The small caps keyboard shortcut is Ctrl+Shift+K.

Small caps formatting is ideal for headings. I use it for character names when I write a script or play:

> BILL. That's a clever way to smuggle a live grenade into prison.

The All Caps text format sets the text to uppercase letters only. As with small caps, this format doesn't feature a command button, though it has a shortcut key: Ctrl+Shift+A.

To find all these text formats and more, open the Font dialog box. Refer to the section "Behold the Font Dialog Box," later in this chapter.

TIP

TECHNICAL STUFF

>> More than one character format can be applied at a time to any text. For example, use Ctrl+B and then Ctrl+I to apply bold and italic formats.

>> The best way to use superscript or subscript is to write text first and then apply the superscript or subscript format to selected text. So 42 becomes 4^2 and CnH2n+1OH becomes $C_nH_{2n+1}OH$. If you apply superscript or subscript as you type, the text can become difficult to edit.

>> When will the Underline text attribute die? I'm baffled. Honestly, I think we're waiting for the last typewriter-clutching librarian from the 1950s to pass on before underlining officially disappears as a text attribute. And please don't fall prey to the old rule about underlining book titles. It's *Crime and Punishment,* not <u>Crime and Punishment.</u>

Text Transcending Teensy to Titanic

Text size is set in a document based on the ancient typesetter measurement known as *points*. One point is equal to $\frac{1}{72}$ of an inch. Although that value is mysterious and fun, don't bother committing it to memory. Instead, here are some point pointers:

» The bigger the point size, the larger the text.

» Most printed text is either 10 or 12 points tall.

» Headings are typically 14 to 24 points tall.

» In Word, fonts can be sized from 1 point to 1,638 points. Point sizes smaller than 6 are generally too small for a human to read.

» A 1-inch-high letter is roughly 72 points.

TECHNICAL STUFF

» The point size of text is a measure from the bottom of the descender to the typeface's cap height, which is often above the ascender — for example, from the bottom of the lowercase *p* to the top of the capital *E*. Because of this measurement, the typical letter in a font is smaller than its given point size. In fact, depending on the font design, text formatted at the same size but with different fonts *(typefaces)* doesn't appear to be the same size. It's just one of those typesetting oddities that causes regular computer users to start binge-drinking.

Setting the text size

To set the size of text you're about to type, or text in a selected block, heed these steps:

1. **Click the Home tab.**

2. **In the Font group, click the down arrow next to the Font Size box.**

   A menu of font sizes appears, as shown in the center in Figure 10-1.

3. **Choose a font size.**

   As you point the mouse pointer at various values, text in the document (an individual word or a selected block) changes to reflect the size. Click to set the size.

The Size menu lists only common text sizes. To set the text size to a specific value, type the value in the box. For example, to set the font size to 11.5, click in the Size box and type **11.5**.

Nudging text size

Rare is the student who hasn't fudged the length of a term paper by inching up the font size a notch or two. To accommodate those students, or anyone else trying to set text size visually, Word offers two command buttons in the Home tab's Font group.

 To increase the font size, click the Increase Font Size command button. The keyboard shortcut is Ctrl+Shift+>.

The Increase Font Size command nudges the font size up to the next value as listed on the Size menu. (Refer to Figure 10-1.) So, if the text is 12 points, the command increases its size to 14 points.

To decrease the font size, click the Decrease Font Size command button. Its keyboard shortcut is Ctrl+Shift+<.

The Decrease Font Size command works in the opposite direction of the Increase Font Size command: It reduces text size to the next-lower value displayed on the Size menu. (Refer to Figure 10-1.)

 To remember the text-size keyboard shortcuts, think of the less-than and greater-than symbols. To make the text size greater than the current size, use the Ctrl+Shift+> shortcut. To make the text size less than its current size, use Ctrl+Shift+<.

TIP

To increase or decrease the font size by smaller increments, use these shortcut keys:

Ctrl+]	Makes text one point size larger
Ctrl+[	Makes text one point size smaller

More Colorful Text

Adding color to your text doesn't make your writing more colorful. All it does is make you wish that you had more color ink when it's time to print the document. Regardless, you can splash color on your text, without the need to place a drop cloth below the computer.

Coloring the text

To change the color of text in a document, follow these steps:

1. **Click the Home tab.**

2. **In the Font group, click the Font Color command button.**

   The current word, any selected text, or any new text you type is assigned the button's color.

The Font Color button shows which color it assigns to text. To change the color, click the menu triangle to the button's right and choose a color from the palette that's displayed.

>> To restore the font color, choose Automatic from the Font Color menu. The Automatic color is set according to the text style. See Chapter 15 for details on styles.

>> Theme colors are associated with the document theme. Refer to Chapter 16.

>> To craft your own, custom colors, select the More Colors item from the Font Color menu to display the Colors dialog box.

REMEMBER

>> The printer companies would love it if you'd use more colored text in your documents. Colored text works only on a color printer, so buy more ink!

>> Avoid using faint colors for a font, which can make text extremely difficult to read.

WARNING

>> Don't confuse the Font Color command button with the Text Highlight Color command button, to its left. Text highlighting is used for document markup, as described in Chapter 26.

Shading the background

To set the text background color, use the Shading command. Follow these steps:

1. **Click the Home tab.**

2. **In the Paragraph group, click the Shading command button.**

   The color shown on the button shades the current word or selected block, or sets the background color for new text typed.

To switch colors, click the menu button to the right of the Shading command button. Select a color from the list, or choose More Colors to create a custom color.

>> If you want to remove the background color, choose No Color from the Shading command's menu.

>> The Shading command is used also to shade other objects on the page, such as cells in a table. That's why it dwells in the Paragraph group and not in the Font group.

>> To create white-on-black text, first select the text. Change the text color to white, and then change the background (shading) to black.

>> If you need to apply a background color to an entire page, use the Page Color command. See Chapter 13.

Change Text Case

When you forget to type text the proper way in the first place, or when the AutoCorrect and AutoFormat features forget their jobs, a Change Case command is available. Follow these steps:

Aa ▼

1. **Click the Home tab.**

2. **In the Font group, click the Change Case command button.**

3. **Choose the proper case from the menu.**

The list of menu items reflects how the case is changed, as shown in Figure 10-2.

Aa ▼
Sentence case.
lowercase
UPPERCASE
Capitalize Each Word
tOGGLE cASE

FIGURE 10-2:
Options for changing the text case.

The Change Case command isn't really a formatting command; its effect doesn't stick with the text you type.

>> The keyboard shortcut for the Change Case command is Shift+F3. Press this key combination to cycle between three case options: ALL CAPS, lowercase, and Capitalize Each Word.

>> Back in the days of mechanical type, a font came in a case, like a briefcase. The upper part of the case held the capital letters. The lower part held the miniscule letters. This is where the terms *uppercase* and *lowercase* originated.

Clear Character Formatting

So many Word formatting commands are available that it's possible for your text to look more like a pile of runes than modern text. Word understands this problem, so it offers the Clear Formatting command. Use this command to peel away all formats from your text, just like you peel the skin from a banana.

To remove text formatting, follow these steps:

1. **Click the Home tab.**

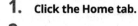

2. **In the Font group, click the Clear Formatting command button.**

    Text formats are removed from selected text or from all new text typed.

The formatting isn't removed as much as it's restored: After you issue the Clear Formatting command, text reflects the currently applied style. This style includes font, size, and other attributes.

>> The keyboard shortcut for the Clear Formatting command is Ctrl+Space (the spacebar).

>> The Clear Formatting command removes the ALL CAPS text format, but doesn't otherwise change the text case.

>> You cannot use the Clear Formatting command to remove text highlighting. See Chapter 26.

>> Using the Clear Formatting command to change the text color doesn't reset the background color. See the section "Shading the background," earlier in this chapter.

Behold the Font Dialog Box

Word features a single location where all your font-formatting dreams can come true. It's the Font dialog box, shown in Figure 10-3.

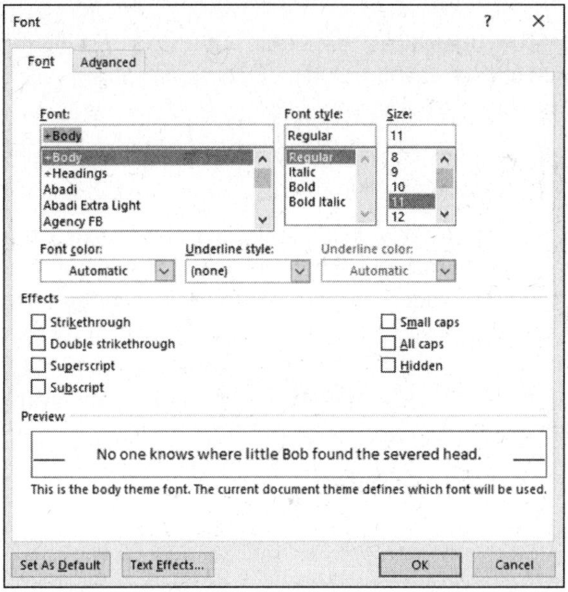

FIGURE 10-3:
The neatly organized Font dialog box.

To summon the Font dialog box, obey these steps:

1. **Click the Home tab.**

2. **In the Fonts group, click the Dialog Box Launcher button thing.**

The button is found in the lower-right corner of the Font group. (Refer to Figure 10-1.)

The Font dialog box hosts *all* the commands for formatting text, including quite a few that didn't find their way into the Font group on the Ribbon. As with all text formatting, the commands you choose in the Font dialog box affect any new text you type or any selected text in your document.

When you've finished setting up your font stuff, click the OK button. Or click Cancel if you're just visiting.

>> Use the Ctrl+D keyboard shortcut to quickly summon the Font dialog box.

>> The best benefit of the Font dialog box is its Preview window, at the bottom. This window shows you exactly how your choices affect text in your document.

>> The Font names *+Body* and *+Heading* refer to the fonts selected by the current document theme. This is done so that you can use Word's theme commands to quickly change body and heading fonts for an entire document all at one time.

>> Click the Font dialog box's Text Effects button to access interesting text attributes such as Shadow, Outline, Emboss, and Engrave. See Chapter 17 for information on this button.

>> The Font dialog box's Advanced tab hosts options for changing the size and position of text on a line.

TIP

>> The Set As Default button in the Font dialog box changes the font that Word uses for new documents. If you prefer to use a specific font for all your documents, choose the font (plus other text attributes) in the Font dialog box, and then click the Set as Default button. In the dialog box that appears, choose the option All Documents Based on the Normal Template. Click the OK button. Afterward, all documents start with the font options you selected.

Chapter **11**

Paragraph Formatting

I f you're after formatting fun, a standard paragraph of text presents you with the most opportunities. Word's paragraph-formatting commands are vast, mostly because so many aspects of a typical paragraph can be adjusted and customized to present text just the way you like.

TIP

For specific and grueling details on paragraph formatting, see the tome *Word 2016 For Professionals For Dummies* (Wiley). It goes into scintillating detail on paragraph formatting, covering topics not mentioned here, including fancy indentation, spacing, hyphenation, and more.

Paragraph-Formatting Rules and Regulations

Word's paragraph-level formatting commands affect paragraphs in a document. This notion is obvious, so what's a paragraph?

Writing conventions aside, to Word a *paragraph* is any chunk of text that ends when you press the Enter key. A single character, a word, a sentence, or a document full of sentences is a paragraph, so long as you terminate the chunk-o-text by pressing the Enter key.

The Paragraph symbol (¶) appears in a document to mark the end of a paragraph. Normally this character is hidden, but you can order Word to display it for you. Follow these steps:

1. **Click the File tab.**

2. **Choose the Options command.**

The Word Options dialog box appears.

3. **Click Display.**

4. **Place a check mark by Paragraph Marks.**

5. **Click OK.**

Now, every time you press the Enter key, the ¶ symbol (called a *pilcrow*) appears, marking the end of a paragraph.

Also see Chapter 2 for information on the Show/Hide command, which also displays paragraph symbols in a document as well as other hidden text.

Formatting a paragraph

You can format a paragraph in several ways:

Change an existing paragraph. With the insertion pointer in a paragraph, use a paragraph-formatting command. Only the current paragraph format is changed.

Change a block of paragraphs. Select one or more paragraphs and then use the formatting command to affect the lot.

Just start typing. Choose a paragraph-formatting command, and then type a paragraph. The chosen format is applied to the new text.

» To format all paragraphs in a document, press Ctrl+A to select all text in the document and then apply the format.

» If your desire is to apply the same format to multiple paragraphs in your document, consider creating a style. See Chapter 15.

Locating the paragraph-formatting commands

In a vain effort to confuse you, Word uses not one but *two* locations on the Ribbon to house paragraph-formatting commands. The first Paragraph group is found on the Home tab. The second is located on the Layout tab. Both groups are illustrated in Figure 11-1.

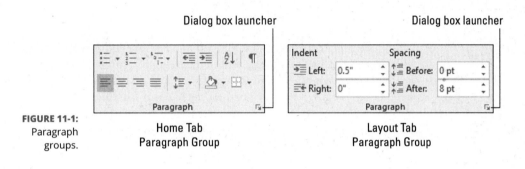

FIGURE 11-1:
Paragraph groups.

Home Tab
Paragraph Group

Layout Tab
Paragraph Group

But wait! There's more.

To conjure the Paragraph dialog box, shown in Figure 11-2, click the Dialog Box Launcher button in either of the Paragraph groups. (Refer to Figure 11-1.) In it, you find controls and settings not offered by the command buttons on the Ribbon.

FIGURE 11-2:
The Paragraph dialog box.

The obnoxious keyboard shortcut to summon the Paragraph dialog box is Alt+H, P, G. Don't mock me! Memorizing this keyboard shortcut saves you time.

REMEMBER

A smattering of paragraph-formatting commands are also found on the mini toolbar, which appears after you select text.

Justification and Alignment

Paragraph alignment has nothing to do with politics, and justification has little to do with the reasons behind putting text in a paragraph. Instead, both terms refer to how the left and right edges of the paragraph look on a page. The four options are Left, Center, Right, and Fully Justified, each covered in this section.

>> All alignment-formatting command buttons are found on the Home tab, in the Paragraph group.

>> The left and right indents of a paragraph are measured from the page margin. See Chapter 13 for information on page margins.

Line up on the left!

Left alignment is considered standard, probably thanks to the mechanical type-writer and, before that, generations of grammar school teachers who preferred text lined up on the left side of a page. The right side of the page? Who cares!

To left-align a paragraph, press Ctrl+L or click the Align Left command button, found in the Home tab's Paragraph group.

TIP

>> This type of alignment is also known as *ragged right.*

>> Left-aligning a paragraph is how you undo the other types of paragraph alignment.

Everyone center!

Centering a paragraph places each line in that paragraph in the middle of the page, with an equal amount of space to the line's right and left.

To center a paragraph, press Ctrl+E or use the Center command button, found on the Home tab's Paragraph group.

>> Centering is ideal for titles and single lines of text. It's ugly for longer paragraphs and makes reading the text more difficult.

>> Use a center tab stop to center a single word in the middle of a line. See Chapter 12.

Line up on the right!

The mirror image of left alignment, right alignment keeps the right edge of a paragraph even. The left margin, however, is jagged. When do you use this type of formatting? I have no idea, but it sure feels funky typing a right-aligned paragraph.

To flush text along the right side of the page, press Ctrl+R or click the Align Right command button.

>> This type of alignment is also known as *ragged left* or *flush right.*

>> To right-justify text on a single line, use a right tab stop. See Chapter 12 for more info.

Line up on both sides!

Lining up both sides of a paragraph is *full justification:* Both the left and right sides of a paragraph are neat and tidy, flush with the margins.

To give your paragraph full justification, press Ctrl+J or click the Justify command button located, as you might guess, on the Home tab's Paragraph group.

>> Fully justified paragraph formatting is often used in newspapers and magazines, which makes the narrow columns of text easier to read.

>> Word makes each side of the paragraph line up by inserting tiny slivers of extra space between words in a paragraph. The extra space is recycled from government computers designed to look impressive, but which merely create extra space.

Make Room Before, After, or Inside Paragraphs

Sentences in a paragraph can stack as tightly as a palette of plywood. Alternatively, you can choose to keep paragraphs all light and airy, like a soft, fluffy cake. Space can cushion above or below the paragraph. These paragraph air settings are illustrated in Figure 11-3.

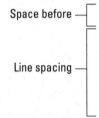

Space before —

Line spacing —

Jackie wanted feet like an elephant. She was insistent. "Elephant toenails are magnificent," she pointed out. "Human toenails are molecular by comparison. Imagine how lovely my elephant toenails could be if painted well!" Further, she gushed, "I would be most excellent at making pancakes with my flat, round elephant feet." Indeed, it was her dream.

Space after —

FIGURE 11-3: Spacing in and around a paragraph.

Commands to control paragraph spacing include the traditional line-spacing commands as well as the Space Before and Space After commands. These commands are found in the Paragraph groups on both the Home and Layout tabs.

Setting the line spacing

To set the space between all lines in a paragraph, follow these steps:

1. **Click the Home tab.**

2. **In the Paragraph group, click the Line Spacing command button.**

   A menu appears.

3. **Choose a new line spacing value.**

The line spacing is set for the current paragraph or all selected paragraphs. Word adds the extra space below each line of text.

TIP

Three keyboard shortcuts are available for the most common line-spacing values:

» To single-space, press Ctrl+1. Use this command to remove other line-spacing styles.

» To double-space, press Ctrl+2. This setting formats the paragraph with one blank line below each line of text.

PERSNICKETY LINE-SPACING OPTIONS

For seriously precise line spacing, turn to the Paragraph dialog box: Click the Home tab, and in the lower right corner of the Paragraph group, click the Dialog Box Launcher icon.

In the Paragraph dialog box, the Line Spacing drop-down list features some specific items: At Least, Exactly, and Multiple. These items are used with the At box to indicate line spacing as follows:

At least: The line spacing is set to a minimum value. Word can disobey that value and add more space whenever necessary to make room for larger type, different fonts, or graphics on the same line of text.

Exactly: Word uses the specified line spacing and doesn't adjust the spacing to accommodate larger text or graphics.

Multiple: Use this option to enter line-spacing values other than those specified in the Line Spacing drop-down list. For example, to set the line spacing to 4, choose Multiple from the Line Spacing drop-down list and type **4** in the At box.

Click the OK button to confirm these settings and close the Paragraph dialog box.

>> To use 1½-space lines, press Ctrl+5. Yes, this keyboard shortcut is for 1.5 lines, not 5 lines. Use the 5 key in the typewriter area of the computer keyboard. Pressing Ctrl+5 using the 5 key on the numeric keypad activates the Select All command.

The Ctrl+0 (zero) keyboard shortcut applies Word's default line spacing, which is 1.15. According to experts in white lab coats, that extra 0.15-size chunk of space below each line adds to readability.

TIP

When you want text to stack up one line atop another line, such as when typing a return address, use the *soft return* at the end of a line: Press Shift+Enter. See the section in Chapter 4 about soft and hard returns.

Making space between paragraphs

To help separate one paragraph from another, you add space either before or after the paragraph. What you don't do is to press Enter twice to end a paragraph. That's extremely unprofessional, and doing so causes rooms full of educated people to frown at you.

To add space before or after a paragraph, follow these steps:

1. **Click the Layout tab.**

2. **In the Paragraph group, use the Before gizmo to add space before a paragraph of text or use the After gizmo to add space after the paragraph.**

   Measurements are made in points, the same measurement used for font size.

To create the effect of pressing the Enter key twice to end a paragraph, set the After value to a point size about two-thirds the size of the current font. As an example, for a 12-point font, an After value of 8 looks good.

TIP

>> Most of the time, space is added after a paragraph. You can add space before a paragraph, for example, to further separate text from a document heading or subhead.

>> The space you add before or after a paragraph becomes part of the paragraph format. Like other formats, it sticks with subsequent paragraphs you type or can be applied to a block of paragraphs.

TECHNICAL STUFF

>> Graphics designers prefer to insert more space between paragraphs when the first line of a paragraph isn't indented, as in this book. When you indent the first line, it's okay to have less spacing between paragraphs. See the next section.

Paragraph Indentation Madness

Paragraphs fill the page's margin from side to side, as dictated by the justification, or alignment. Exceptions to this rule can be made. A paragraph's first line can be indented, the rest of the lines can be indented, and the left and right sides can be indented. It's paragraph indentation madness!

>> Adjusting a paragraph's indentation doesn't affect the paragraph's alignment.

>> Paragraphs are indented relative to the page's margins. Refer to Chapter 13 for information on page margins.

Indenting the first line of a paragraph

Back in the old days, it was common to start each paragraph with a tab. The tab would indent the first line, helping the reader identify the new paragraph. Word can save you tab-typing energy by automatically formatting each paragraph with an indent on the first line. Here's how:

1. **Click the Home tab.**

2. **In the Paragraph group, click the dialog box launcher.**

   The Paragraph dialog box appears.

3. **Click the Special drop-down list and choose First Line.**

4. **Confirm that the By box lists the value 0.5".**

   The By box shows half an inch, which is the standard tab stop and a goodly distance to indent the first line of text.

5. **Click OK.**

   The first line of the current paragraph, or all paragraphs in a selected block, are indented per the amount specified in the By box.

To remove the first-line indent from a paragraph, repeat these steps but select (none) from the drop-down list in Step 3.

Word's AutoCorrect feature can automatically indent the first line of a paragraph, which is handy but also annoying. What AutoCorrect does is convert the tab character into the First Line Indent paragraph format, which may not be what you want. If so, click the AutoCorrect icon (shown in the margin), and choose the command Convert Back to Tab. I recommend using the steps in this section and not AutoCorrect to format first-line indents.

If you choose to indent the first line of a paragraph, you don't really need to add space after it. See the earlier section "Making space between paragraphs."

REMEMBER

Making a hanging indent (an outdent)

A *hanging indent* isn't in imminent peril. No, it's a paragraph in which the first line breaks the left margin or, from another perspective, in which all lines but the first are indented. Here's an example:

```
Dr. Cornelius: Never mind! The effects are only temporary.
    Eventually your sense of balance will be restored, the nausea
    will diminish, and your desire to continue spending on your
    credit card will be fully restored.
```

The simple way to create such a beast is to press Ctrl+T, the Hanging Indent keyboard shortcut. The command affects the current paragraph or all selected paragraphs.

The not-so-simple way to hang an indent is to use the Paragraph dialog box: In the Indentation area, click the Special menu and choose Hanging. Use the By text box to set the indent depth.

TIP

>> Every time you press Ctrl+T, the paragraph is indented by another half-inch.

>> To undo a hanging indent, press Ctrl+Shift+T. That's the Unhang keyboard shortcut, the chiropractor that puts the paragraph's neck back in shape.

Indenting a whole paragraph

To draw attention to a paragraph, its left side can be sucked in a notch. This presentation is often used for quoted material in a longer expanse of text.

To indent a paragraph, heed these steps:

1. **Click the Home tab.**

2. **In the Paragraph group, click the Increase Indent command button.**

The paragraph's left edge hops over one tab stop (half an inch).

To unindent an indented paragraph, click the Decrease Indent command button in Step 2.

When you want to get specific with indents, as well as indent the paragraph's right side, click the Layout tab and use the Indent Left and Indent Right controls to set specific indentation values. Set both controls to the same value to set off a block quote or a nested paragraph.

>> The keyboard shortcut to indent a paragraph is Ctrl+M. The shortcut to un-indent a paragraph is Shift+Ctrl+M.

>> To undo any paragraph indenting, click the Layout tab and in the Paragraph group set both Left and Right indent values to 0.

>> Indent only one paragraph or a small group of paragraphs. This format isn't intended for long stretches of text.

WARNING

>> Do not try to mix left and right indenting with a first-line indent or a hanging indent while drowsy or while operating heavy equipment.

Using the ruler to adjust indents

The most visual way to adjust a paragraph's indents is to use the ruler. This tip is helpful only when the ruler is visible, which it normally isn't in Word. To unhide the ruler, follow these steps:

1. **Click the View tab.**

2. **In the Show area, ensure that the Ruler option is active.**

Click to place a check mark by the Ruler option if it isn't active.

The ruler appears above the document text. In Print Layout view, a vertical ruler also appears on the left side of the document.

On the ruler, you see the page margins left and right, and to the far left is something I call the tab gizmo (covered in Chapter 12). Figure 11-4 illustrates the important parts of the ruler with regard to paragraph formatting.

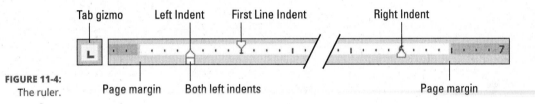

FIGURE 11-4:
The ruler.

Four doojobbies on the ruler reflect the current paragraph indents. Use these controls to adjust the paragraph indents in a visual manner.

Drag the Left Indent control left or right to adjust a paragraph's left margin. Moving this gizmo does not affect the first-line indent.

Drag the First Line Indent control left or right to set the first-line indent independently of the left margin.

Drag the Both control to adjust both the left indent and first-line indent together.

Drag the Right Indent control right or left to adjust the paragraph's right margin.

As you drag controls on the ruler, a vertical guide drops down into the document. Use that guide to help adjust indents for the current paragraph or any selected paragraphs.

TIP

>> The ruler doesn't appear in Read mode or Outline view.

>> The ruler measures from the page's left *margin,* not from the left edge of the page. The page's left margin is set when you format a page of text. See Chapter 13.

>> For more precise setting of indents, use the Paragraph dialog box instead of the gizmos on the ruler.

PARAGRAPH-FORMATTING SURVIVAL GUIDE

TECHNICAL STUFF

This table contains all the paragraph-formatting commands you can summon by holding down the Ctrl key and pressing a letter or number. By no means should you memorize this list.

Format	Key Combination	Command Button
Center	Ctrl+E	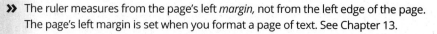
Fully justify	Ctrl+J	
Left-align (flush left)	Ctrl+L	
Right-align (flush right)	Ctrl+R	
Indent	Ctrl+M	
Unindent	Ctrl+Shift+M	
Hanging indent	Ctrl+T	n/a
Unhanging indent	Ctrl+Shift+T	n/a
Line spacing	Alt+H, K	n/a
Single-space lines	Ctrl+1	n/a
1.15 line spacing	Ctrl+0	n/a
Double-space lines	Ctrl+2	n/a
1.5-space lines	Ctrl+5	n/a

Chapter **12**

Tab Formatting

On my ancient Underwood typewriter, the Tab key is located on the right side of the keyboard. It's named Tabular Key. On other old typewriters, I've seen it named Tabulator. The root for these words is the same as the root for *table*, which is the Latin word *tabula*, meaning "list."

In Word, tabs are used to make lists or indent text. That sounds simple, but for some reason tabs remain one of the most complex formatting topics.

Once Upon a Tab

Like other keys on the keyboard, pressing the Tab key inserts a tab *character* into your document. The tab character works like the space character, with the exception that the character that's inserted has a variable width. The width is set at a predefined location marked across a page. That location is called the *tab stop*.

It's the tab stop that makes the tab character work: Press the Tab key, and the insertion pointer hops over to the next tab stop. That way, you can precisely line up text on multiple lines. Using a tab is definitely neater than whacking the space-bar multiple times to line up columns of text.

REMEMBER

>> Word presets tab stops at every half-inch position across the page. And, of course, you can create your own tab stops.

>> Anytime you press the spacebar more than once, you *need* a tab. Believe me, your documents will look prettier and you'll be happier after you understand and use tabs instead of spaces to line up your text.

>> What happens to text after you type the tab character is determined by the type of tab stop. In Word, multiple tab stop types help you format a line of text in many ways.

>> As with any other characters, you use the Backspace or Delete keys to remove a tab character.

>> Tabs work best for a single line of text or for only the first line of a paragraph. For more complex lists, use Word's Table command. See Chapter 19.

TECHNICAL STUFF

>> The diet beverage Tab was named for people who like to keep a tab on how much they consume.

Seeing tab characters

Tab characters are normally hidden in your document. They look like blank spaces, which is probably why too many Word users use spaces instead of tabs.

It's not necessary to see tab characters to use them, although if you're having trouble setting tab stops and using tabs, viewing the tab characters is helpful.

Use the Show/Hide command to quickly view tabs in a document: Click the Home tab and in the Paragraph group, click the Show/Hide command button, which looks like the Paragraph symbol (¶).

When Show/Hide is active, tab characters appear in the text as left-pointing arrows, similar to what's shown in the margin.

To direct Word to show tab characters at all times, regardless of the Show/Hide command setting, follow these steps:

1. Click the File tab.

2. Choose Options.

The Word Options window appears.

3. **Click the Display item on the left side of the window.**

4. **Put a check mark by the Tab Characters option.**

5. **Click OK.**

With the Tab Characters option set, tabs always appear in a document. They don't print that way, but viewing them in the text may help you solve some formatting puzzles.

Seeing tab stops

Tab stops are invisible; you can't see them in your document, but they exist, and they affect the text that's typed after you press the Tab key. The best way to view the tab stop locations and types, as well as to set new ones, is to summon the ruler. Follow these steps:

1. **Click the View tab.**

2. **In the Show area, ensure that the check box by the Ruler item has a check mark in it.**

   If not, click to set the check mark.

The ruler appears just above the document. Figure 12-1 illustrates how the ruler might look when various tab stops are set. It also shows the location of the tab gizmo, which is a handy tool you can use to access different tab stop types.

Tab gizmo

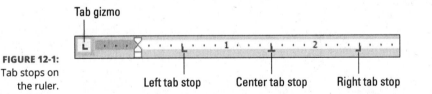

FIGURE 12-1:
Tab stops on the ruler.

Left tab stop   Center tab stop   Right tab stop

If tab stops are not visible on the ruler, Word is using its default setting of one tab stop every half-inch. The default tab stops don't appear on the ruler.

>> When several paragraphs are selected, you may spot a light gray, or *phantom*, tab stop on the ruler. The ghostly appearance indicates that a tab stop is set in one paragraph but not in all. To apply the tab stop to all selected paragraphs, click the phantom tab stop once.

>> See the later section "Tab Stop, Be Gone!" for information on using the ruler to remove, or unset, a tab stop.

Using the ruler to set tab stops

The visual and quick way to set a tab stop is to use the ruler. Assuming that the ruler is visible (see the preceding section), the process involves two steps:

1. **Click the tab gizmo until the desired tab stop type appears.**

   Later sections in this chapter discuss what each of the five types of tab stops does.

   The tab gizmo also shows paragraph-indent controls, which are covered in Chapter 11. They don't relate to setting tabs.

2. **Click the ruler at the exact spot where you want the tab stop set.**

   For example, click the number 2 to set a tab stop 2 inches in from the page's left margin.

The Tab Stop icon appears on the ruler, marking the paragraph's tab stop position. You can further adjust the tab by dragging left or right with the mouse. If a tab character already sits in the current paragraph, its format updates as you drag the top stop hither and thither.

REMEMBER

The tab stop is a paragraph-level format. The tab stop you set applies to the current paragraph or any selected paragraphs. Refer to Chapter 6 for details on selected text.

Using the Tabs dialog box to set tabs

For precisely setting tabs, summon the Tabs dialog box. It's also the only way to get at certain types of tabs, such as dot leader tabs, which are covered elsewhere in this chapter.

Keep in mind that the Tabs dialog box doesn't work like a typical Word dialog box: You must set the tab position and type first and then click the Set button. Click the OK button only when you're done setting tabs. Generally speaking, the process works like this:

1. **Click the Home tab.**

2. **In the lower right corner of the Paragraph group, click the dialog box launcher.**

   The Paragraph dialog box appears. The tab is, after all, a paragraph-level format.

3. Click the Tabs button.

The Tabs dialog box appears, as shown in Figure 12-2.

4. Enter the tab stop position in the Tab Stop Position box.

You can be precise, if you like, such as 3.11 inches.

5. Choose the type of tab stop from the Alignment area.

Word's five tab stop types are covered elsewhere in this chapter.

6. Click the Set button.

The tab stop is added to the Tab Stop Position list.

7. Continue setting tab stops.

Repeat Steps 2–6 for as many tab stops as you need to set.

8. Click OK.

REMEMBER

You must click the Set button to set a tab stop! I don't know how many times I click OK instead, thinking that the tab stop is set when it isn't.

The tab stops you set affect the current paragraph or a selected group of paragraphs.

TIP

If the ruler is visible, you can quickly summon the Tabs dialog box: Double-click any existing tab stop.

RESET WORD'S DEFAULT TAB STOPS

Word presets default tab stops, marching them across the page at half-inch intervals. That way, though you haven't set any tab stops yourself, when you press the Tab key, a (left) tab stop is available for text-positioning.

The default tab stops are removed when you set your own tab stop. For example, setting a tab stop at the 3-inch position erases all default tab stops to the left of that location.

You can't eliminate the default tab stops, but you can change their spacing. In the Tabs dialog box, type a new interval value in the Default Tab Stops box. (Refer to Figure 12-2.) For example, to set default tab stops to 1-inch intervals, type **1** in the box and then click the OK button.

The Standard Left Tab Stop

The left tab stop is the traditional type of tab stop. When you press the Tab key, the insertion pointer advances to the left tab stop position, where you continue to type text. This type of tab stop works best for typing lists, organizing information in single-line paragraphs, and indenting the first line of a multiline paragraph.

Creating a basic tabbed list

A common use for the left tab stop is to create a simple 2-column list, as shown in Figure 12-3.

Tab gizmo   Left tab stop   Left tab stop

Film	Android
Metropolis	Maria
The Day the Earth Stood Still	Gort
Forbidden Planet	Robbie the Robot
King Kong Escapes	Mechani-Kong
THX-1138	The fuzz
Logan's Run	Box
Alien	Ash
Aliens	Bishop

FIGURE 12-3:
Two-column list.

Follow these steps to create this type of list:

1. **On a new line, press Tab.**

2. **Type the item for the first column.**

   This item should be short — two or three words, max.

3. **Press Tab again.**

4. **Type the item for the second column.**

   Again, make it short.

5. **Press Enter to end that line and start a new line.**

   Yes, your list looks horrible! Don't worry. Type first, then format.

6. **Repeat Steps 2–5 for each line in the list.**

   After the list is finished, you next use the ruler to visually set the tab stops. If you don't see the rule in your document, refer to the earlier section "Using the ruler to set tab stops."

7. **Select all lines of text that you want to organize in a 2-column tabbed list.**

8. **Choose a left tab stop from the tab gizmo on the ruler.**

   If necessary, click the tab gizmo until the Left Tab Stop icon shows up, as shown in the margin.

9. **Click the ruler to set the first tab stop.**

   If the text doesn't line up right, drag the tab stop left or right.

10. **Click to set the second tab stop.**

    Drag the tab stop left or right, if necessary, to help line up text.

You could add a third column to the list, but then the text starts to get crowded. In fact, anytime you need this type of complex list, consider instead cobbling together a table. See Chapter 19.

You need only one tab between items in a column list. That's because the tab *stop*, not the tab character, lines up your text.

REMEMBER

Creating a 2-tab paragraph thing

By using the power of tabs coupled with a paragraph's hanging-indent format, you can create a tab-tab-paragraph list, similar to what's shown in Figure 12-4. It looks fancy but isn't horrendous to configure, providing you follow these steps:

1. **On a new line, type the first item.**

   The shorter, the better. This item sits at the left margin, so don't type a tab to start the line.

2. **Press Tab.**

3. **Type the second item and press Tab.**

   This step is optional; you can create a simpler tab-paragraph list, which looks just like the one shown in Figure 12-4, but without the Dish column (and spaced accordingly).

4. **Type the paragraph text.**

   Unlike with the first two items, you're free to type more text here. That's because this final paragraph column wraps, as shown in Figure 12-4.

5. **Press Enter to end the line.**

   Don't let the text's ugly appearance deceive you. You're not finished.

6. **Repeat Steps 1–5 for each item in the tab-tab-paragraph list thing.**

   Now that the list is done, you set the tab stops and make the entire thing look beautiful.

7. **Select all the lines of text you want to organize into a tab-tab-paragraph list.**

8. **Ensure that the left tab stop is chosen on the tab gizmo.**

   The margin shows the Left Tab Stop symbol. If you don't see the tab gizmo or the ruler, refer to the earlier section "Using the ruler to set tab stops."

9. **Set a left tab stop to mark the second item in the list.**

   The first item is set at the start of the line. After you set the left tab stop for the second item in the list, the second column snaps into place.

10. **Slide the paragraph's left indent to the start of the text item.**

   The Left Indent triangle is shown in the margin. It sets the left margin for all text in a paragraph, except for the first line. (See Chapter 11 for details.) Slide the triangle rightward until its location passes items in the second column, as shown in Figure 12-4.

11. **Adjust the tab stop and left margin as necessary.**

   Make the adjustments while text is selected, which provides visual feedback for the paragraphs.

As with formatting any complex list, it's perfectly okay to give up. See Chapter 19 for information on adding a table to your document. You might find that using a table works better than all this paragraph-formatting nonsense.

The Center Tab Stop

The *center tab* is a unique critter with a special purpose: Unlike when you center a paragraph, text typed at the center tab stop is centered. This feature is ideal for centering text in a header or footer, which is about the only time you need a center tab stop.

Figure 12-5 shows an example of a center tab. The text on the left is at the start of the paragraph, which is left-justified. But the text typed after the tab is centered on the line, thanks to the center tab stop. Follow these steps to create such a beast in your document:

1. **Start a new paragraph, one containing text that you want to center.**

   Center tabs inhabit 1-line paragraphs.

2. **Click the tab gizmo on the ruler until the center tab stop shows up.**

   The Center Tab Stop icon is shown in the margin.

Center tab stop

FIGURE 12-5:
Center tab stop
in action.

A Trip To Uranus   Chapter 9: Exploring the curious crevasse

Centered text

3. **Click the ruler to set the center tab stop's position.**

   Generally speaking, the center tab stop dwells in the middle of the page. That location could be the 3 inch mark or thereabouts.

4. **Optionally, type text to start the line.**

   In Figure 12-5, the text *A Trip to Uranus* appears at the start of the line.

5. **Press the Tab key.**

   The insertion pointer hops over to the center tab stop.

6. **Type the text you want to center.**

   As you type, the text is centered on the line. Don't type too much; the center tab is a single-line thing.

7. **Press Enter to end the line of text.**

TIP

When you need only centered text on a line, use the center paragraph format instead of a center tab stop. See Chapter 11.

See Chapter 14 for information on headers and footers.

The Right Tab Stop

The right tab stop's effect is to right-align text typed after you press the Tab key. As with the center tab stop, the right tab stop is frequently used in headers and footers or when a paragraph contains only a single line of text. Otherwise, to right-align text, use the Right justification paragraph-formatting command, as described in Chapter 11.

Making a right-stop, left-stop list

A clever way to format a 2-column list is to employ both a right tab stop and a left tab stop. The list lines up on a centerline, as shown in Figure 12-6.

Right tab stop   Left tab stop

```
. . . I . . 2 . . . I . . . 3 L . . I . . . 4 . .
```

Dorothy	Taylor Swift
Scarecrow	Michael Cera
Tin Man	Jude Law
Cowardly Lion	Seth Rogan
Wizard	Lewis Black
Wicked Witch of the West	Lady Gaga

To build such a list, follow these steps:

1. **Start out on a blank line, the line you want to format.**

2. **Click the tab gizmo until the right tab stop shows up.**

The Right Tab Stop icon appears in the margin.

3. **Click near the center of the ruler to place the right tab stop.**

4. **Click the tab gizmo until the left tab stop appears.**

Click, click, click until you see the Left Tab Stop icon, as shown in the margin.

5. **Click to place the left tab stop just to the right side of the right tab stop on the ruler.**

Use Figure 12-6 as your guide.

Now it's time to type the text. Don't worry about getting the tab stops correct at this point in the process; you can adjust them later.

6. **Press the Tab key.**

The insertion pointer hops over to the right tab stop's position.

7. **Type text for the first, right-justified column.**

8. **Press the Tab key.**

9. **Type some text for the second, left-justified column.**

10. **Press Enter to end the line of text.**

11. **Repeat Steps 6–10 to complete the list.**

If further adjustments are necessary after you're finished, select all lines and use the mouse to adjust the tab stops' positions on the ruler as necessary.

Building a 2-column right-stop list

The right tab stop can be used on the second column of a 2-column list. The presentation appears commonly in programs, similar to what's shown in Figure 12-7.

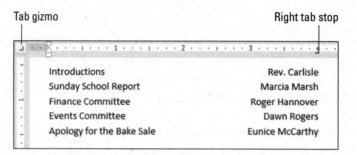

Tab gizmo

Right tab stop

Introductions	Rev. Carlisle
Sunday School Report	Marcia Marsh
Finance Committee	Roger Hannover
Events Committee	Dawn Rogers
Apology for the Bake Sale	Eunice McCarthy

FIGURE 12-7:
Right tab stops right-align the second column of this list.

Here's how to concoct such a thing:

1. **Start on a blank line of text.**

2. **Click the tab gizmo until the right tab stop appears.**

   The Right Tab Stop icon is shown in the margin.

3. **Place the right tab stop on the far right side of the ruler.**

   The position is just a guess at this point. Later, you can adjust the right tab stop position to something more visually appealing.

4. **Type the first column text.**

   The text is left-justified, as it is normally.

5. **Press the Tab key.**

   The insertion pointer hops to the right tab stop.

6. **Type the second-column text.**

   The text you type is right-justified, pushing to the left as you type.

7. **Press Enter to end the line of text.**

8. **Repeat Steps 4–7 for each line in the list.**

Afterward, you can adjust the list's appearance: Select all text as a block, and then drag the right tab stop back and forth on the ruler.

The Decimal Tab

Use the decimal tab to line up columns of numbers. You can use a right tab for this job, but the decimal tab is a better choice. Rather than right-align text, as the right tab does (see the preceding section), the decimal tab aligns numbers by their decimal — the period in the number, as shown in Figure 12-8.

Tab gizmo   Decimal tab stop

Luggage Check	$25.00
Window / Aisle Seat	$15.00
Realistic leg room	$15.00
Early boarding	$25.00
Reserved overhead bin space	$20.00
Unlimited lavatory use	Free!

FIGURE 12-8: Using the decimal tab to line up numbers.

Here's how to work with such a beast:

1. **Start a blank line of text.**

2. **On the ruler, click the tab gizmo until the decimal tab stop appears.**

   The Decimal Tab Stop icon is shown in the margin.

3. **Click the ruler to set the decimal tab stop.**

   You can adjust the position later.

4. **Type the first-column text.**

   This step is optional, though in Figure 12-8 you see the first column as a list of items.

5. **Press the Tab key.**

6. **Type the number.**

   The number is right-justified until you press the Period key. After that, the rest of the number is left-justified.

7. **Press Enter to end the line of text.**

8. **Repeat Steps 4–7 for each line in the list.**

You can make adjustments after the list is complete: Select all lines in the list, and then drag the decimal tab stop left or right.

When a line doesn't feature a period, text typed at a decimal tab stop is right-justified, as shown by the word *Free* in Figure 12-8. You can always reformat such a line to set a left tab stop, which may look better on the page.

The Bar Tab

Aside from being a most excellent pun, the bar tab isn't a true tab stop in Word; it has no effect on the tab character. Instead, the bar tab is considered a text decoration.

Setting a bar tab inserts a vertical bar in a line of text, as shown in Figure 12-9. Using a bar tab is much better than using the pipe (|) character on the keyboard to create a vertical line in a multicolumn list. That's because you can adjust all the bar tab characters just as you can adjust any tab stop.

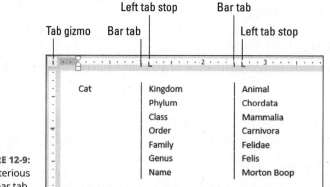

FIGURE 12-9:
The mysterious bar tab.

To set a bar tab stop, follow these steps:

1. **Click the tab gizmo until the bar tab stop appears.**

   The Bar Tab Stop icon is shown in the margin.

2. **Click the ruler to place the bar tab stop.**

   At each position, a vertical bar appears in the text. The bar appears whether or not the current line contains any tab characters.

To best use the bar tab stop, mix in a few other tab stops. For example, in Figure 12-9, left tab stops are set to the side of each bar tab stop. The effect is that text is organized into columns, but the bar tab serves only to decorate the text. It has no effect otherwise.

Fearless Leader Tabs

Press the Tab key, and the insertion pointer hops over to the next tab stop. The space occupied by the tab character is empty, but it doesn't have to be. Word lets you apply different styles to the empty tab space, which helps to create something called a leader tab.

A *leader tab* shows a series of dots or other characters where the tab character appears on the page. Three styles are available: dot, dash, and underline, as illustrated in Figure 12-10.

Left tab stop

```
· · · I · · · 1 · · · I · · · 2 · · · I · · · 3 · · I ·

Fearless dot-leader tabs ................................ 146
Zipper-line leader tabs ---------------------------- 147
U-boat underline leader tabs _____ 148
```

FIGURE 12-10:
Leader tab styles.

You can apply a leader to any tab stop in Word other than the bar tab. To do so, follow these steps:

1. **Create the tab-formatted list.**

   Refer to sections elsewhere in this chapter for information on creating a list of items.

2. **Select the text as a block.**

3. **Bring forth the Tabs dialog box.**

   The quick shortcut is to double-click a tab on the ruler. Also see the earlier section "Using the Tabs dialog box to set tabs."

4. **Select the tab stop from the Tab Stop Position list.**

5. **In the Leader area, choose the leader style.**

6. **Click the Set button.**

   Don't click OK before you set the tab stop to add the leader. This step is the one you forget most often.

REMEMBER

7. **Click OK.**

   The leader is applied.

TIP

Use the underline leader tab to create fill-in-the-blank forms. In the Tabs dialog box, set a left tab stop at the far right margin (usually, 6.0 inches). Choose the underline leader style (number 4). Click Set and then click OK. Back in your document, type a tab to create a fill-in-the-blank line, such as:

Your name: _____

This format is far better than typing a zillion underlines.

Tab Stop, Be Gone!

To unset or clear a tab stop, follow these steps:

1. Select the paragraph(s) with the offending tab stop.

2. Drag the tab stop from the ruler.

Drag downward. The tab stop is removed from the paragraph(s).

After removing the tab stop, the tab character may still lurk in the paragraph. Refer to the earlier section "Seeing tab characters," for help in hunting down rogue tabs.

REMEMBER

Word places automatic tab stops on every line of text. These cannot be removed.

For complex tab stop removal, such as when tab stops are close to each other or to the paragraph indent controls on the ruler, use the Tabs dialog box: Click to select the tab in the Tab Stop Position list, and then click the Clear button. Click OK to exit the Tabs dialog box.

» Clicking the Clear All button in the Tabs dialog box removes all tab stops from the current paragraph or selected paragraphs in one drastic sweep.

» To delete a tab character, use the Backspace key.

Chapter **13**

Page Formatting

Word is only mildly interested in the concept of a page. Unlike in the real world, where a page is a physical sheet of paper, Word conjures new pages when needed, pulling them in from the electronic ether. That makes the concept of a page ethereal. To root things in reality, Word lets you define the page format, which includes the page size, orientation, margins, as well as other page formats and attributes.

Describe That Page

Word begins its page-formatting adventure by defining exactly what a page looks like. That includes the page's physical dimensions and which portion of the page contains text.

Setting page size

You probably assume that each new document starts with a page size reflecting a typical sheet of paper.

Such foolishness.

Word's Normal template, the one used to start a new document, specifies a page size equivalent to a standard sheet of paper. In the US, that's 8½-by-11 inches. In Europe, the A4 size is used. You're not stuck with either size. That's because the page size is part of the page format, and you can change it. Follow these steps:

1. **Click the Layout tab on the Ribbon.**

2. **In the Page Setup group, click the Size button.**

   The Size icon is shown in the margin.

3. **Choose a page size from the list.**

   For example, if you want to print on that tall, legal-size paper, choose Legal from the list.

The entire document is updated to reflect the new page size, first page to last.

> ⟫ To select a size not shown on the menu (refer to Step 3), choose the More Paper Sizes menu item. The Page Setup dialog box appears. Use the controls on the Paper tab to manually specify the paper size.

> ⟫ Page size can be changed at any time, whether the document is empty or full of text. Obviously, page size affects layout, so such a major change is probably something you don't want to do at the last minute.

> ⟫ Your document can sport multiple page sizes. To do so, split the document into sections and apply the page size to one section at a time. See Chapter 14 for information on sections. Applying page formats one section at a time is done in the Page Setup dialog box, as described later in this chapter.

REMEMBER

> ⟫ Page size definitely plays a role when a document is printed. Despite your zeal to choose an oddball page size, unless the printer can handle that size paper, the document can't be printed. It can, however, be published electronically. That process is covered in Chapter 9.

Changing orientation (landscape or portrait)

An aspect of page size is whether the page is oriented vertically or horizontally. (I'm assuming it's no longer the fashion to print on square paper.) Page orientation could be set by adjusting the page size, but it's much easier to change the page orientation. Follow these steps:

1. **Click the Layout tab.**

2. **Click the Orientation button.**

The Orientation button is illustrated in the margin. It has two items on its menu: Portrait and Landscape.

3. **Choose Portrait to set the page vertically or Landscape to set the page horizontally.**

Word shifts the orientation for every page in your document. This doesn't mean that the text is sideways, but rather that the text prints wide on a page (though I suppose you could look at it as printing sideways).

TIP

>> Make the decision to have your document in landscape orientation before you do any extensive formatting. This orientation affects paragraph formatting, which may require you to adjust the document's margins; see the next section.

>> Page-orientation changes affect the entire document unless you split the document into sections. In this case, the change applies to only the current section. Read Chapter 14 for details on sections, including directions on how to stick a single landscape page into a document that's otherwise portrait oriented.

>> Scientists who study such things have determined that human reading speed slows drastically when people must scan a long line of text, which happens when you use landscape orientation. Reserve landscape orientation for printing lists, graphics, and tables for which portrait page orientation is too narrow.

>> Landscape printing is ideal for using multiple columns of text. See Chapter 20.

>> If you just want sideways text without turning the page, use a text box. See Chapter 23 for information on text boxes.

Setting the page margins

Margins create the text area on a page left, right, top, and bottom. They provide room between the text and the page's edge, which keeps the text from leaking out of a document and all over the computer.

Word automatically sets page margins at 1 inch from every page edge. Most English teachers and book editors want margins of this size because these people love to scribble in margins. (They even write that way on blank paper.)

To adjust page margins in Word, obey these steps:

1. **Click the Layout tab.**

2. **Click the Margins button.**

   It's found in the Page Setup group and shown in the margin.

   Clicking the Margins button displays a menu full of common margin options.

3. **Pluck a proper margin setting from the menu.**

The new margins affect all pages in the document — unless you split the document into sections, in which case the changes apply to only the current section. See Chapter 14 for information on sections.

The choices available on the Margins menu list settings for the top, left, bottom, and right margins. Yes, all four margins are set at once. When you want to set specific margins, choose the Custom Margins item from the bottom of the menu, and then use the Margins tab in the Page Setup dialog box to set each margin. Refer to the next section for more information.

>> The Layout tab's Margins button sets page margins. To set paragraph indents, refer to Chapter 11.

>> The orange stars appearing on the Margins menu's icons represent popular or recent margin choices you've made.

>> Many printers cannot print on the outside half-inch of a piece of paper, usually on one side — top, bottom, left, or right. This space is an *absolute* margin. You can direct Word to set a margin of 0 inches, though text may not print there. Instead, choose a minimum of 0.5 inches for all margins.

TECHNICAL STUFF

Using the Page Setup dialog box

When you want more control over page formatting, you must beckon forth the Page Setup dialog box, as shown in Figure 13-1. Specifically, you use the Margins tab in that dialog box, which is shown in the figure.

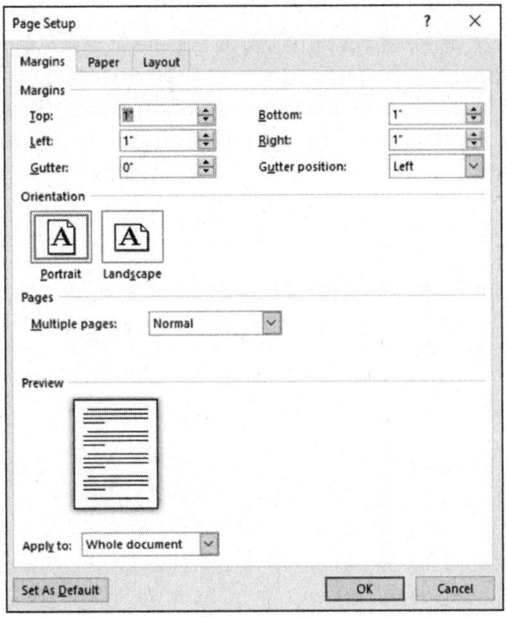

FIGURE 13-1:
The Margins
tab in the Page
Setup dialog box.

To use the Page Setup dialog box to specifically set page margins, obey these steps:

1 **Click the Layout tab.**

2. **Click the dialog box launcher in the lower right corner of the Page Setup group.**

The Page Setup dialog box appears, Margins tab forward.

3. **Type the margin offsets in the Top, Bottom, Left, and Right boxes.**

Or you can use the spinner gizmo to set the values.

Use the preview to check the margins as they relate to page size.

4. **Ensure that Whole Document is chosen from the Apply To menu button.**

You can reset margins for only a section or selected text if you instead choose those options from the menu. See Chapter 14 for information on sections.

5. **Click the OK button to confirm your new settings and close the Page Setup dialog box.**

The Gutter settings help set margins when you need extra space on one edge of the page for binding. For example, if you plan to use a 3-hole punch on the left side of a page, choose Left from the Gutter Position menu. Then increase the Gutter margin to accommodate for the three holes in the page without affecting the left margin setting.

>> The keyboard shortcut to summon the Page Setup dialog box is Alt+P, S, P.

>> The Page Setup dialog box sports three tabs: Margins, for setting margins, Paper, for selecting the page size, and Layout, for dealing with other page-formatting issues.

TECHNICAL STUFF

NUTTY MULTIPLE-PAGE OPTIONS

In the Page Setup dialog box, nestled on the Margins tab, is the Pages area. (Refer to Figure 13-1.) The Multiple Pages drop-down list tells Word how to use a single sheet of paper for printing complex documents. This is something you can avoid at all costs, yet I'm compelled by the Computer Book Writers Union to describe the various settings:

Normal means one page per sheet of paper. You can't get more normal than that.

Mirror Margins is used when the printer is smart enough to print on both sides of a sheet of paper. That way, every other page is flip-flopped so that their margins always line up. For example, the gutter may be on the left side of one page but on the right for the page's back side.

2 Pages per Sheet splits the paper right down the center and forces Word to print two "pages" per sheet of paper. Note that this option works best when the pages are in landscape orientation.

Book Fold is Word's attempt to create a multiple-page booklet by printing the proper pages on both sides of a sheet of paper. The Sheets per Booklet option that appears tells Word how long the booklet is.

Despite having these options, Word is a poor bookbinding program. If you're into document publishing, consider getting a desktop publishing program, such as Adobe InDesign or Microsoft Publisher, which are far better equipped to deal with publishing manuscripts.

Page Numbering

I remain puzzled by people who manually number their pages in Word. Such a thing is silly beyond belief. That's because

Your word processor numbers your pages for you!

Memorize it. Live it. Be it.

Adding an automatic page number

Word automatically numbers your pages. But wait! There's more: Word also lets you place the page number just about anywhere on the page and in a variety of fun and useful formats. Heed these directions:

1. **Click the Insert tab.**

2. **In the Header & Footer area, click the Page Number command button.**

A menu drops down, showing various page-numbering options. The first three are locations: Top of Page, Bottom of Page, and Page Margins (the sides of the page).

3. **Choose from the submenu where to place the page numbers.**

I want my page numbers on the bottom of the page, so I regularly choose the Bottom of Page submenu.

4. **Pluck a page-numbering style from the list.**

You see oodles of samples, so don't cut yourself short by not scrolling through the menu. You can even choose those famous *page X of Y* formats.

Dutifully, Word numbers each page in your document, starting with 1 on the first page, up to however many pages long the thing grows.

Here's the good part: If you delete a page, Word renumbers everything for you. Insert a page? Word renumbers everything for you again, automatically. As long as you insert the page number as described in this section, Word handles everything.

>> To change the page-number format, choose a new one from the Page Number menu.

>> To reference the current page number in your document's text, choose the Current Position item in Step 3. Word inserts the current page number at the insertion pointer's location. Also see Chapter 23.

>> The page numbers inserted atop or at the bottom of your document are placed in the document's header or footer. See Chapter 14 for information on headers and footers.

>> Page numbers can be removed just as easily: See the section "Removing page numbers," later in this chapter.

>> The page number is inserted as a field, not plain text. In Word, fields can be updated and changed based on changing information.

>> If the page number that's inserted looks something like this: **{ PAGE * MERGE-FORMAT }**, right-click that ugly thing and choose the Toggle Field Codes command. You can also click the mouse inside the field codes and press Shift+F9.

TECHNICAL STUFF

Starting with a different page number

You and I know that the first page of a document is page 1, but Word doesn't care. It lets you start numbering your document at whichever value you want. If you want to start numbering your document at page 42, you can do so. Follow these instructions:

1. **Click the Insert tab.**

2. **In the Header & Footer area, choose Page Number ⇨ Format Page Numbers.**

   The Page Number Format dialog box materializes, as shown in Figure 13-2.

3. **Click the Start At radio button.**

4. **Type the starting page number in the box.**

5. **Click OK.**

Page Number Format	?	✕

Number format: `1, 2, 3, ...`

☐ Include chapter number

Chapter starts with style: `Heading 1`

Use separator: `- (hyphen)`

Examples: 1-1, 1-A

Page numbering

◉ Continue from previous section

◯ Start at: `[     ]`

[OK] [Cancel]

FIGURE 13-2: Gain more control over page numbers.

Word starts numbering your document at the specified page number. So, if you enter 42 in Step 4, the first page of the document is now page 42, the next page is 43, and so on.

Of course, this trick works best when page numbers are already set for your document, as described in the preceding section.

TIP

>> For more page-number control, split the document into sections. Different page-numbering styles or sequences can be set for individual sections. You can even suppress page numbers for a section, such as not numbering the first (cover) page of a document. See Chapter 14 for more information on sections.

>> If you're working on a novel, don't worry about setting page numbers for each chapter. That's insane. Instead, use Word's Master Document feature to set page numbering when you're finished. See Chapter 25.

Numbering with Roman numerals

When the urge hits you to regress a few centuries and use Roman numerals to tally a document's pages, Word is happy to oblige. *Sic facite*:

I. **Set the location for page numbers in your document.**

Refer to the section "Adding an automatic page number." After page numbers are established, you can set a different format.

II. **Click the Insert tab.**

III. **Click the Page Number command button and choose Format Page Numbers.**

The Page Number Format dialog box appears.

IV. **Choose a style from the Number Format menu.**

Two Roman numeral styles are available: lowercase and uppercase.

V. **Click OK.**

Hail Caesar!

Removing page numbers

To banish automatic page numbers from above, below, or anywhere else around your text, follow these steps:

1. **Click the Insert tab.**

2. **Click the Page Number command button.**

3. **Choose Remove Page Numbers.**

    And they're gone.

These steps remove only the page numbers set by using the Page Number command button, as described earlier in this chapter. Page numbers you've inserted in the text are unaffected, as are any page numbers you've manually added to a document's header or footer.

To remove a manually inserted page number, use the Backspace key twice because these page numbers are actually document fields. See Chapter 23 for information on fields.

New Pages from Nowhere

With Word, you'll never have the excuse "I need more pages" when writing text. That's because Word adds new, blank pages as needed. These pages are appended to the end of the document, so even if you're typing in the midst of a chapter, the extra pages keep appearing so that no text is lost and nothing falls off the edge. That's refreshing, but it's not the end of Word's capability to thrust new pages into your document.

Starting text on a new page

You have two choices when it comes to starting text at the top of a page in the middle of a document.

The first choice is to keep whacking the Enter key until that new page shows up. This approach is horribly wrong. It works, but it leads to trouble later as you continue to create your document.

The second, and preferred, choice is to insert a hard page break:

1. **Position the insertion pointer where you want one page to end and the next page to start.**

   I recommend splitting the page at the start of a new paragraph.

2. **Click the Insert tab.**

3. **In the Pages group, click the Page Break command button.**

   Text before the insertion pointer flows to the previous page, and text after the insertion pointer rests on the next page.

The hard page break stays with your text. No matter how you edit or add text, the split between pages remains.

>> The keyboard shortcut to split pages is Ctrl+Enter.

>> To remove a hard page break, position the insertion pointer at the top of the page just after the break. Press the Backspace key. If you goof up, use Ctrl+Z to undo.

>> Use the Show/Hide command to view the hard-page-break character. See Chapter 2 for information on the Show/Hide command

>> The hard page break is easier to see in Draft view.

TIP

Inserting a blank page

Suddenly, you need a blank page in the middle of a document. Follow these steps:

1. **Click the Insert tab.**

2. **In the Pages group, click the Blank Page command button.**

   A new, blank page appears at the insertion pointer's position.

Any text before the insertion pointer appears before the blank page. Any text after the insertion pointer appears after the new page.

>> The Blank Page command inserts *two* hard page breaks in the document.

>> Be mindful of the material you place on the new, blank page. Because two hard page breaks produce the page, it's best suited for single-page items, such as graphics or a table. Anything longer than a page makes the rest of the document formatting look funky.

WARNING

>> You don't need to use this command to add a new page at the end of your document. Just keep typing.

Page Background Froufrou

A page is also a canvas, a background upon which your document rests. That background sports a few formatting options of its own, items that dwell outside a document but remain part of the page formatting.

Coloring pages

The simple way to print colored pages is to choose color paper. When the price of printer ink isn't an option, you can direct Word to format each page in a document with a different background color. Follow these steps:

1. **Click the Design tab.**

2. **In the Page Background group, click the Page Color button.**

   You see a menu full of colors.

3. **Choose a color from the palette.**

   Or choose the More Colors menu item to mix your own favorite page-background color.

The color chosen in Step 3 is applied to the document's pages.

To remove the color, choose the item No Color in Step 3.

>> The colors displayed on the Page Color menu are based on the document theme. See Chapter 16 for information on document themes.

>> Page color is independent of text foreground and background colors. See Chapter 10.

>> Unlike page size, orientation, and numbering, page background color is unaffected by document sections. The color is applied to every page in every section. See Chapter 14 for more information on document sections.

>> Choose the Fill Effects menu item in Step 3 to view the Fill Effects dialog box. Click the Gradient tab to set *gradients,* or multiple colors, as the page background. Use the Picture tab to apply an image to each page's background.

Printing colored pages

Viewing a colored page on the screen is one thing. Seeing it printed is another. In Word, you must direct the printer to print the page background color by following these steps:

1. **Click the File tab and choose Options.**

   The Word Options dialog box appears.

2. **Choose Display from the left side of the Word Options dialog box.**

3. **In the Printing Options area, put a check mark by the item labeled Print Background Colors and Images.**

4. **Click OK.**

   The page background color now appears when the document is printed — well, assuming that you have a color printer.

 TECHNICAL STUFF Because the color isn't part of the paper, it doesn't cover the entire printed page. That's because your printer cannot mechanically access the outside edge of a page, so a white border (or whatever other color the paper is) appears around the colored page. At this point, ask yourself whether it's easier to use colored paper rather than all that expensive printer ink or toner.

Adding a watermark

When fine paper is held up to the light, it shows a *watermark* — an image embedded into the paper. The image is impressive but faint. Word lets you fake a watermark by inserting faint text or graphics behind every page in your document. Here's how:

1. **Click the Design tab.**

2. **In the Page Background group, click the Watermark button.**

   A menu plops down with a host of predefined watermarks that you can safely tuck behind the text on your document's pages.

3. **Choose a watermark from the menu.**

   The watermark is applied to every page in the document.

To rid the document's pages of the watermark, choose the Remove Watermark command in Step 3.

>> To customize the watermark, choose the Custom Watermark command from the Watermark menu. Use the Printed Watermark dialog box to create your own watermark text, or import an image, such as your company logo.

>> The watermark appears on all pages in a document. It's unaffected by section breaks. See Chapter 14 for information on section breaks.

>> If the watermark doesn't show up in the printed document, you may need to enable the Print Background Colors and Images setting. Refer to the preceding section.

Chapter **14**

More Page Formatting

ord's page-formatting commands are few when compared with character- and paragraph-formatting commands, but they're not lacking in complexity. Consider the document section, which helps you craft great-looking documents, yet navigating its implementation is akin to wandering cursed archeological digs in the Jungle of Doom. Add in headers and footers as the plucky-yet-disobedient sidekick, and you have yet another action-packed chapter on page formatting.

Slice Your Document into Sections

Word page formats — such as paper size, margins, orientation, and columns — apply to an entire document, from "once upon a time" to "happily ever after." That is, unless the document is sliced into page format containers called sections.

Understanding sections

A *section* is a page-formatting container. All documents feature one section, which is why the various page-formatting commands affect the entire document; they're applied to that single section. A document, however, can sport multiple sections. Each section can sport its own page format, independent of the other sections.

Figure 14-1 illustrates three examples of how a document can be sliced up into sections.

Example 1: Change page number style

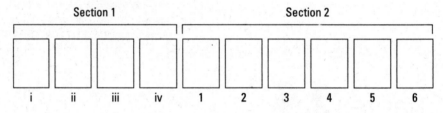

Example 2: No page number on the first page

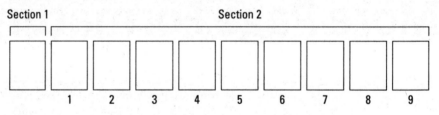

Example 3: Change page orientation

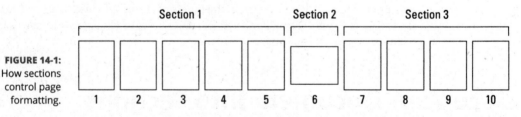

FIGURE 14-1:
How sections control page formatting.

In Example 1, a single document contains two sections. The first section uses Roman numeral page numbers. The second section uses human numerals. Each section restarts page numbering.

The document in Example 2 contains a single-page section for its cover page. The second section — all remaining pages — uses page numbering.

In Example 3, the document has three sections. The first and third sections sport the same page formatting; the second section was created so that page 6 could be presented in landscape orientation.

In all three examples, the document's text and paragraph formats remain unaffected by sections. Only page-level formatting is affected. Even then, you can choose whether to apply a page-level format to the current section or to the entire document.

Creating a section

A section is similar in concept to a page break, though it's page formatting that's "broken," not a physical page in the document. To create a new section in a document — to insert a section break — heed these steps:

1. **Position the toothpick cursor where you want the new section to start.**

Click the mouse where you need to begin a new section, similar to creating a new page break. For most new sections, position the insertion pointer at the start of a paragraph.

2. **Click the Layout tab on the Ribbon.**

3. **In the Page Setup area, click the Breaks button.**

A menu appears, listing several items. The last four items are various section breaks.

4. **Choose Next Page from the Breaks button menu.**

A new section has started, which also serves as a page break.

Pages before the section break are in one document section, pages after are in the next. Page formatting commands can be applied independently to either section.

Here is a summary of the different types of section breaks:

Next Page: Start a new section and break the page, like a hard page break. (See Chapter 13.)

Continuous: Start a new section on a flexible boundary, depending on which page-formatting command is used. A continuous section break may start a new page, or it may not.

Even Page: This one is similar to the Next Page break, but the page starting the new section will be an even-numbered page. For binding purposes, the even page is on the left side.

Odd Page: It's the same as an Even Page section break, though the page following the break will be odd, or on the right side of a bound manuscript.

TIP

When working with sections, I recommend placing the Section item on the status bar: Right-click the status bar and choose Section from the pop-up menu. The Section item shows the current section by number as you work through the document.

Using sections

You have two options to apply a page-formatting command to a specific section within your document. In both instances, the insertion pointer must roost in the section you want to format.

To apply a page format to the current section, select that format from the Ribbon, as described in Chapter 13. For example, set a new page orientation, and that format affects only the current document section.

In the Page Setup dialog box, use the Apply To drop-down menu to apply page-formatting changes to the current document section, as illustrated in Figure 14-2.

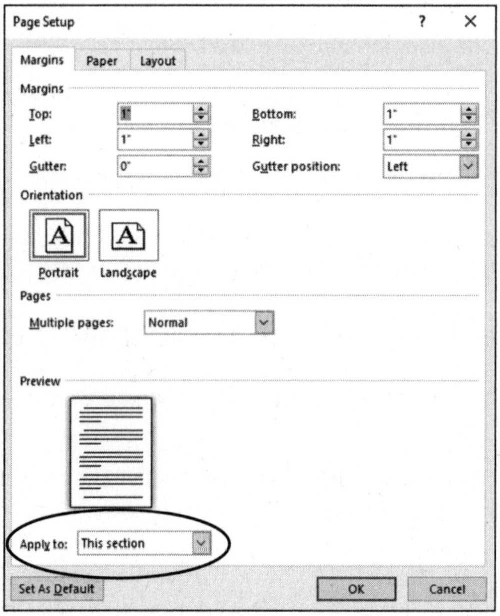

FIGURE 14-2:
Applying page formatting to one section only.

Each tab in the Page Setup dialog box features the Apply To drop-down menu. Use it to apply page-formatting changes to the entire document or to only the current section.

Removing a section break

Section breaks are invisible in Print Layout view, though you can see them in Draft view. To remove the section break, you delete it. Follow these steps, though you can start at Step 3 when using Draft view:

1. **Click the Home tab.**

2. **In the Paragraph group, click the Show/Hide command button.**

   Hidden codes and characters are revealed in the document.

3. **Position the insertion pointer to the start (left end) of the double-dashed lines that say *Section Break*.**

4. **Press the Delete key.**

   The section break is gone.

5. **Click the Show/Hide command button again to hide the codes.**

After the section break vanishes, the page formatting changes, adopting the format from the previous section. That's to be expected, but it may alter things you can't see, such as page numbering and headers and footers.

REMEMBER

If you regret your decision to remove the page number, press Ctrl+Z to undo.

That First Page

Even when you're blessed with a superior knowledge of paragraph formatting and you fully understand the magic of the section break, formatting that first page can be a bother. The kids at Microsoft are aware of your frustration, so they concocted some special first-page formatting features for Word.

Adding a cover page

The sneakiest way to slap down a cover page on your document is to use Word's Cover Page command. Here's how it works:

1. **Click the Insert tab.**

2. **In the Pages group, click the Cover Page button.**

   If you don't see the Pages group or Cover Page button, click the Pages button and then click the Cover Page icon.

   The Cover Page button displays a fat, fun menu full of various cover-page layouts.

3. **Choose a cover-page layout that titillates you.**

   The cover page is immediately inserted as the first page in the document.

Many preset cover pages feature replaceable text, such as [COMPANY NAME]. Click that text and type something appropriate, such as your actual company name, unless you actually work for the Company Name Corp. Do so for all bracketed text on the inserted cover page.

>> You can change a cover page at any time by choosing a new one from the Cover Page menu. The new cover page retains any replacement text you typed.

>> To remove a cover page, summon the Cover Page menu and choose the Remove Current Cover Page item.

>> The cover page you add is followed by a hard page break. It is not a section break. Even so, it's treated differently from certain page-formatting commands applied to the rest of the document. That means if you add page numbers or a header or footer to your document, the formatting applies to only the second page and later pages, not to the cover page.

Inserting a cover page manually

When you're dissatisfied with Word's Cover Page designs, you can craft your own cover page. All the formatting tools and document tricks presented in this book are at your disposal. You just need to insert the page at the start of the document.

Here are the general steps to take:

1. **Before writing the cover page, position the toothpick cursor at the tippy-top of the document.**

2. **Click the Layout tab.**

3. **Choose Breaks ⇨ Next Page.**

   A section break effectively inserts a new, first page into the document as its own section.

4. **Create the cover page.**

   Add a title, additional text, graphics, and various document froufrou.

Because the first (cover) page is now its own section, the page formatting it sports can be separated from the rest of the document. For example, you can apply page numbering to the second section, which keeps the cover page unnumbered. Refer to Figure 14-1, example 2.

Headers and Footers

It's easy to confuse the concept of headers and footers with headings and footnotes. To help you understand the difference, consider these definitions:

>> A *header* is text that appears at the top of every page in a document.

>> A *heading* is a text style used to break up a long document, to introduce new concepts, and to help organize the text. See Chapter 15.

>> A *footer* is text that appears at the bottom of every page in a document.

>> A *footnote* is a tiny bit of text that appears at the bottom of a page, usually a reference to some text on that page. See Chapter 21.

In Word, headers and footers dwell in special, exclusive areas outside the realm of regular text. These areas are found top and bottom on all pages in a document. Unless you place some text or other items inside these areas, they remain invisible.

Text that typically finds its way into a header or footer (or both) includes page numbers, your name, the document name, the date, and other information that's handy to have on every page.

Using a preset header or footer

Most documents use standard, noncreative headers and footers, placing common information into one or both areas. To accommodate your hurried desires, you can quickly shove one of these preset headers or footers into your document. Heed these steps:

1. **Click the Insert tab.**

2. **From the Header & Footer group, choose the Header button.**

   The Header menu shows a list of preformatted headers.

3. **Choose a header design.**

   The design's contents are added to the document, saved as part of the page format. Also, the Header & Footers Tools Design tab appears on the Ribbon.

4. **Change any [Type here] text in the header.**

   Click the bracketed text and type to personalize your header.

5. **Use the commands on the Insert group of the Header & Footer Tools Design tab to add specific items in the header.**

   Examples are offered in the sections that follow.

6. **When you're done working on the header, click the Close Header and Footer button.**

   Or you can double-click in the main text body.

To add a footer, choose the Footer button in Step 2 and think of the word *footer* whenever you see the word *header* in the preceding steps.

After you exit from the header or footer, you can see its text at the top or bottom of the document in Print Layout view. It appears ghostly, to let you know that it's there but not part of the document. To edit the header or footer, double-click that ghostly text.

Creating a custom header or footer

When one of the preset header/footer designs doesn't cut it, consider creating your own. The secret is to double-click the space at the top or bottom of the page in Print Layout view. This location is the header or footer area, respectively. When it becomes active, you can manually craft a header or footer to match your innermost desires.

A header or footer can contain text, a graphical goober, a field, or any other item you can slap down into the main part of the document. Common and useful commands appear on the Header & Footer Tools Design tab, but you can use other tabs on the Ribbon to create and customize a header or footer.

TIP

To switch between the header and footer while editing, click the Go to Footer or Go to Header button. These buttons are found on the Header & Footer Tools Design tab in the Navigation group.

Type text

Any text you type in a header or footer becomes part of the header or footer. It doesn't have to be fancy text, — just whatever text you want appearing at the top or bottom of every page in the document.

The standard format for lines in a header or footer includes two tab stops: a center tab stop in the middle of the page and a right tab stop aligned with the right margin. Use these tab stops, as illustrated in Figure 14-3, to create useful header text.

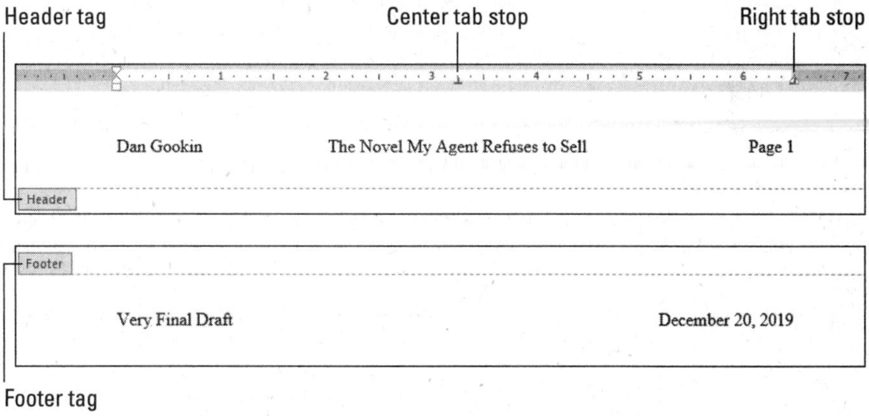

Header tag   Center tab stop   Right tab stop

Dan Gookin   The Novel My Agent Refuses to Sell   Page 1

Header

Footer

Very Final Draft   December 20, 2019

FIGURE 14-3:
Text in a header and a footer.

Footer tag

Add a page number

It's tempting, and it seems like the obvious choice, but don't use the Page Number command on the Header & Footer Tools Design toolbar. If you need a page number in a header or footer, add a document page-number field. Follow these steps:

1. Position the insertion pointer where you want the page number to appear.

2. Click the Header & Footer Tools Design tab.

3. **In the Insert group, click the Document Info button and choose Field.**

The Field dialog box appears. It's a busy place, covered in full detail in Chapter 23.

4. **From the Categories menu, choose Numbering.**

5. **In the Field Names list, click to select Page.**

6. **Choose a Format.**

For example, choose the item 1, 2, 3, to use that numbering style.

7. **Click the OK button.**

The Page field is inserted in the header. It reflects the current page number for every page printed in the document.

REMEMBER

TIP

>> You don't have to go to page 1 to insert a page number in a header. Word is smart enough to place the proper number on the proper page, no matter where you're editing the header in the document.

>> If you want one of those *Page 3 of 45* indicators in a header or footer, you need two fields: the Page field, as described in this section, and the NumPages field. To add that field, repeat the steps in this section, but in Step 4 choose Document Information and in Step 5 choose NumPages.

Add the date and time

To place the current date or time or an updating time field in a header or footer, follow these steps:

1. **Position the insertion pointer where you want the date or time to appear.**

2. **Click the Header & Footer Tools Design tab.**

3. **In the Insert group, click the Date & Time command button.**

The Date and Time dialog box appears.

4. **Choose a format for the date or the time, or both.**

5. **To keep the date and time information current, place a check mark by the Update Automatically option.**

6. **Click OK.**

Also see Chapter 23 for information on the PrintDate field.

Working with multiple headers and footers

Headers and footers come in a variety of types, allowing you to change them depending on whether the page is odd or even, or to alter the header or footer for a given document section. You can even suspend the header and footer for a page or two. Such agility requires knowing a few tricks, which I'm happy to share.

Odd and even headers and footers

See how this book has different headers on its odd- and even-numbered pages? The even-numbered pages show the page number and part title; the odd-numbered pages show the chapter title and page number. To configure such odd/even headers (and footers) for your document, obey these steps:

1. **Create or edit a header or footer, as described elsewhere in this chapter.**

2. **Click the Header & Footer Tools Design tab.**

3. **Click the Different Odd & Even Pages check box.**

   With this feature active, Word sets up headers and footers for odd- and even-numbered pages. The Header and Footer tags in the document reflect the change as well, saying Odd Page Footer or Even Page Footer. The tag tells you which header or footer you're editing.

4. **Create the header and footer for the odd-numbered pages.**

   Follow the suggestions listed in this chapter.

5. **On the Ribbon's Header & Footer Tools Design tab, in the Navigation group, click the Next button.**

   Word displays the even page header or footer, allowing you to create or edit its contents. The Header or Footer tag changes to reflect which header you're editing.

   If clicking the Next button does nothing, your document has only one page! Add a page to enable the even-page headers and footers.

   To return to the odd-page header or footer, click the Previous button.

6. **Close the header or footer when you're done.**

To return to using only one header and footer for a document, repeat these steps but in Step 3 remove the check mark. Any even-page header or footer you've set is removed, leaving only the odd-page header and footer.

REMEMBER

The even-numbered page is always on the left.

No header or footer on the first page

Most people don't want the header or footer on their document's first page, which is usually the title page or the cover page. Suppressing the header for that page is easy, if you follow these steps:

1. **Edit the document's header or footer.**

2. **Click the Header & Footer Tools Design tab.**

3. **In the Options group, place a check mark by Different First Page.**

    That's it.

The Header or Footer tag on the first page changes to read First Page Header or First Page Footer. It's your visual clue that the first page of the document sports a different header from the ones in the rest of the document. If you don't want anything to appear there, leave it blank.

Headers, footers, and sections

One way to apply different headers and footers to your document is to use sections. That way, you can change the header and footer between sections, but only when you unlink the headers and footers. Unless you know this trick, working with headers and footers in different sections can be frustrating.

To break the link between the current section's header and footer and the previous section's header and footer, follow these steps:

1. **Edit the document's header or footer in the section that you want to be different from the previous section's head and footer.**

2. **Click the Header & Footer Tools Design tab.**

3. **In the Navigation Group, click the Next button to locate the start of the next section's header or footer.**

    The Header tag or Footer tag is updated to reflect the current section, as shown in Figure 14-4. You also see the tag Same as Previous, which is your clue that the header is identical to the one in the previous section. For example, if you change something in the first section's header, the change is reflected in all linked headers.

4. **In the Navigation group, click the Link to Previous button.**

    The link is broken. The Same as Previous tag disappears. The header or footer doesn't change — yet.

5. **Edit the section's header or footer.**

    Changes made apply to only the current section.

Section 2 header   Headers are linked

FIGURE 14-4:
Header in
Section 2, linked
to Section 1.

| Dan Gookin | The Novel My Agent Refuses to Sell | Page 2 |

Header -Section 2-   Same as Previous

The link is what confuses a lot of people. They know about sections, but when they change the header or footer in one section, the text isn't updated. That's because the link hasn't been broken, as described in these steps.

To restore the link, return to the given section's header or footer and repeat the steps in this section. Clicking the Link to Previous button a second time reestablishes the link.

>> This trick may not work if your document uses different headers and footers on odd- and even-numbered pages, as described earlier in this chapter.

>> The Different First Page option, described earlier in this chapter, doesn't link the header or footer between the first page and the rest of the document.

**TECHNICAL
STUFF**

Removing a header or a footer

You can't destroy the header or footer area in a document, but you can remove all text and other stuff: Edit the header or footer, press Ctrl+A to select everything, and press the Delete key. Poof!

The more official way to remove a header or footer is to follow these steps:

1. **Edit the document's header or footer.**

2. **Click the Header & Footer Tools Design tab.**

3. **In the Header & Footer group, click the Header button.**

4. **Choose Remove Header.**

   The header is gone.

5. **Click the Footer button and choose Remove Footer.**

   The footer is gone.

Chapter **15**

Style Formatting

I f all of Word's formatting commands are ingredients, a style is a recipe. A style is a single command that applies a virtual stew of formatting commands, everything at once. Even better, when you update or change a style, all text formatting with that style applied changes as well. Styles help you save time and make your documents look fabulous.

The Big Style Overview

A *style* is a collection of text and paragraph formats given a single name and applied to text, just like any other format. When you apply a style, you apply all the formats stored in that style. For heavy-duty formatting, creating and using styles saves time.

Styles are available in all documents. The default style is called Normal, and it's applied to text in a new document unless you apply another style. The Normal style is available for use along with a bunch of other default styles, though using them is up to you.

For Word 2019, the Normal style is defined as the Calibri font, 11 points tall, left-justified paragraphs, multiple line spacing at 1.08 lines, no indenting, zero margins, and 8 points of space after every paragraph.

Other default styles include the Heading styles and Caption. You use the Heading styles, such as Heading 1 for a document's top-level heading, and the Caption style for figure and table captions. The names reflect how to use the style.

Styles are also categorized by which part of the document they affect. Five style types are available:

Paragraph: The paragraph style contains both paragraph- and text-formatting attributes: indent, tab, font, text size — you name it. It's the most common type of style.

Character: The character style applies only to characters. This type of style uses the character-formatting commands, which are mentioned in Chapter 10.

Linked: The linked style can be applied to both paragraphs and individual characters. The difference depends on which text is selected when the style is applied.

Table: The table style is applied to tables, to add lines and shading to the table cells' contents. Refer to Chapter 19 for more information on tables in Word.

List: The list style is customized for presenting lists of information. The styles can include bullets, numbers, indentation, and other formats typical for the parts of a document that present lists of information. See Chapter 21 for info on lists.

These types come into play when you create your own styles as well as when you're perusing styles to apply to text.

Finding the styles

Styles dwell on the Home tab, in the aptly named Styles group, illustrated in Figure 15-1. What you see on the Ribbon is the Style Gallery, which can be expanded into a full menu of style choices, as shown in the figure.

Click the dialog box launcher in the lower right corner of the Styles group to view the Styles pane, also shown in Figure 15-1. To dismiss the Styles pane, click the X (Close) button in its upper right corner.

>> The Styles pane lists more styles than the Style Gallery, including styles you've created.

>> To preview the styles in the Styles pane, put a check mark in the box by the Show Preview option, found at the bottom of the Styles pane.

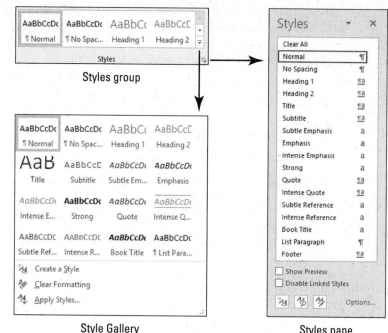

Styles group

Style Gallery

Styles pane

FIGURE 15-1:
Where Word
styles lurk.

>> You can see more information about a style by simply hovering the mouse pointer over the style's name in the Styles pane.

>> To view all available styles in the Styles pane, click the Options link (in the lower right corner). In the Styles Pane Options dialog box, choose All Styles from the Select Styles to Show menu. Click OK.

>> Word's predefined styles are specified in the Style Gallery, though you can customize the list to replace Word's styles with your own. See the section "Customizing the Style Gallery," later in this chapter.

Using a style

Styles are applied to text, just like any other formatting: Select a block of text and then apply the style: Select the style from the Style Gallery or Styles pane. (Refer to the preceding section.) You can also choose a style and start typing. In both cases, the formats held in the style are applied to the text.

>> As you hover the mouse pointer over a style in the Style Gallery, text in the document is updated with a style preview.

>> Some styles are assigned a keyboard shortcut. For example, the shortcut for the Normal style is Ctrl+Shift+N. Use the keyboard shortcut to apply the style.

» Heading styles play a special role in Word. They're used for document navigation and outlining as well as for creating a table of contents. See the later section "Creating heading styles" for details.

» As with any other formatting, applying a style replaces the previously applied style in the text.

» Also see the later section "Removing style formatting."

Discovering the current style

To determine which style is currently in use, refer to the Style Gallery. The style of text where the insertion pointer is blinking, or of any selected text, is highlighted. The current style is also highlighted if the Styles pane is visible.

To specifically examine the style for any text, use the Style Inspector. Follow these steps:

1. **Place the insertion pointer in a specific chunk of text.**

2. **Click the Home tab.**

3. **Click the Launcher icon in the lower right corner of the Styles group.**

   The Styles pane appears.

4. **Click the Style Inspector button.**

   The Style Inspector icon is shown in the margin.

Upon success, you see the Style Inspector window, similar to what's shown in Figure 15-2. The Style Inspector discloses the formatting of the text based on the style plus any additional formatting applied to the style.

To see even more details, such as the specific formats used, click the Reveal Formatting button, as illustrated in Figure 15-2. Use the Reveal Formatting pane to examine all details for the style.

» The shortcut key to summon the Reveal Formatting pane is Shift+F1.

» The Reveal Formatting pane shows the exact formatting applied to your document's text. Click any jot or tittle to see a specific formatting command or dialog box, where you can remove or alter the formatting.

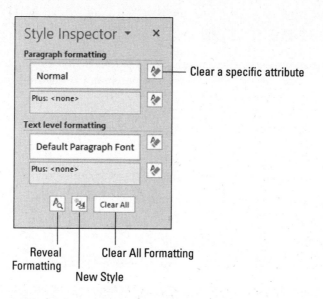

Clear a specific attribute

Reveal
Formatting

New Style

Clear All Formatting

FIGURE 15-2:
Style Inspector.

Removing style formatting

You don't remove style formatting from text as much as you reapply another style. In Word, to effectively remove a style, you replace it with the default style, Normal.

Because many Word users don't understand styles, Word comes with Clear Formatting commands. You can see such commands referenced in Figure 15-2, which illustrates the Style Inspector. Clicking those buttons replaces the given style with the Normal style.

>> See the section "Changing the Normal style," for more details on setting default formatting.

>> Also see Chapter 10 for information on using the Clear Formatting command, which applies to font formats.

Make Your Own Styles

To convince you that styles are important, consider this: You create a custom format for your document's headings. You pick the right font, size, and color and add just enough space after the heading. Then you decide to change the font. If you'd created a style, you'd make only one change and all the document's headers would be updated. Otherwise, you must change each individual heading. And that sucks.

Creating a style

The easiest way to make up a new style is to format a single paragraph just the way you like. After the character and paragraph formatting has been applied, follow these steps to create the new style:

1. **Select the text you've formatted.**

2. **Click the Home tab.**

3. **In the Styles group, display the full Quick Styles Gallery.**

    Click the down-pointing arrow in the lower right corner of the gallery. Refer to Figure 15-1.

4. **Choose the Create a Style command.**

    The Create New Style from Formatting dialog box appears.

5. **In the Name box, type a short and descriptive name for your style.**

    For example, you might type *proposal body* for the main text of a proposal or *dialog* for a character's lines in a play.

6. **Click the OK button to create the style.**

    The style is created and applied to the selected text.

The style you create appears on the Ribbon in the Style Gallery as well as in the Styles pane (if visible).

>> Styles you create are saved with the document, along with the text and other document info.

>> To make the style available to other documents, build a template, as described in Chapter 16. Styles in a template are available to all documents created by using that template.

>> To fine-tune a style after it's created, see the later section "Modifying a style."

Using the Create New Style from Formatting dialog box

A more detailed way to build a style is to summon the Create New Style from Formatting dialog box, which has the same name as its tiny cousin, described in the preceding section, but offers far more controls and details.

The Create New Style from Formatting dialog box lists all of Word's formatting settings and options in one place. If you're familiar with using Word's formatting commands, this dialog box serves as a useful tool to create new styles. Follow these steps:

1. **Summon the Styles pane.**

   The keyboard shortcut is Ctrl+Shift+Alt+S. If you don't want to tie your fingers in a knot, see the earlier section "Finding the styles" for the long way to bring up the Styles pane.

   Because I use a lot of styles, I prefer to keep the Styles pane opened in my documents. If you drag the pane over the document window's right edge, it docks permanently.

2. **Click the New Style button.**

   The button is shown in the margin. Click it to see the Create New Style from Formatting dialog box, as shown in Figure 15-3.

3. **Type a short, descriptive name for the new style.**

4. **Ensure that Paragraph is chosen as the style type.**

   Or, if the format is a character style, choose Character. An example of a character style is blue, bold, Courier, 12-point — the one that I use in my documents for filenames.

5. **Choose an existing style as a base from the Style Based On drop-down list.**

   Following this step saves time. If the style you're creating features similar formatting as an existing style, choose that style from the list. The formats from that style are copied over, letting you build upon them or reuse them in a different way.

6. **Use the controls in the dialog box to set the style's format.**

   The Create New Style from Formatting dialog box is brimming with style command buttons.

   Use the Format button in the dialog box's lower left corner to apply specific formatting commands. Choose a category from the button's menu to see a dialog box specific to one of Word's formatting categories.

7. **Click the OK button when you're done.**

   The new style is created.

Modifying a style

Styles change. Who knows? Maybe blow-dried hair and wide lapels will creep back into vogue someday.

TIP

THE FOLLOW-ME STYLE

A great way to quickly apply styles in a document is to take advantage of the Style for Following Paragraph menu, found at the top of the Create New Style from Formatting dialog box. When you choose a style from this item's menu, Word switches automatically to that style after using the current style. It's what I call the "follow-me style."

Suppose that your Document Title style is followed by the First Paragraph style. After you type the Document Title text and press Enter, Word switches to the First Paragraph style for you. That type of formatting control saves you time formatting a document where you know that one style always follows another.

When you change your mind about a style and want to update a specific element, heed these steps:

1. Summon the Styles pane.

Keyboard shortcut: Ctrl+Shift+Alt+S.

2. Position the mouse pointer over the style you want to change.

Don't click, which selects the style. Instead, hover the pointer in the style's entry; a menu button appears on the right.

3. Click the menu button.

The style's menu appears.

4. Choose Modify.

The Modify Style dialog box appears, though it's the same Create New Style from Formatting dialog box (refer to Figure 15-3), just with a shorter name.

5. Change the style's formatting.

Use the Format button to alter specific styles: font, paragraph, tab, and so on. You can even add new formatting options or assign a shortcut key (covered in the next section).

6. Click OK when you're done.

Modifying the style instantly updates text with that style applied. For example, if you change the font for your Figure Caption style, all figure–caption text changes at once. That's the power of using styles.

Assigning a shortcut key to a style

When you find yourself applying the same styles over and over, assign them a special shortcut key. Follow these steps:

1. Press the keyboard shortcut Ctrl+Shift+Alt+S to summon the Styles pane.

Okay, so you can't use Ctrl+Shift+Alt+S for the style, because it's already assigned to the Styles pane.

2. In the Styles pane, click a style's menu button.

Position the mouse pointer over the style you want to change; the menu button appears.

3. Choose Modify.

The Modify Style dialog box appears.

4. **Click the Format button and choose Shortcut Key from the menu.**

The Customize Keyboard dialog box appears. The two items you must pay attention to are the Press New Shortcut Key box and the area just below the Current Keys list.

5. **Press the shortcut-key combination.**

TIP

Use at least two of the shift keys — Shift, Alt, or Ctrl — when pressing the shortcut-key combination. Most of the Ctrl+Alt key combinations are unassigned in Word.

The keys you press are named in the Press New Shortcut Key box.

If you make a mistake, press the Backspace key and then choose another key combination.

6. **Confirm that the key combination you chose isn't already in use.**

Look below the Current Keys list. The text there explains which Word command uses the key combination you've pressed. When you see [unassigned], it means that your key combination is available for use.

7. **Click the Assign button.**

8. **Click the Close button.**

The Customize Keyboard dialog box skulks away.

9. **Click the OK button to dismiss the Modify Style dialog box.**

Try out your shortcut: Position the insertion pointer in a block of text and press the key combination. The style is applied instantly.

TECHNICAL
STUFF

I'll be honest: All the good shortcut keys are taken. Word uses most of them for its important commands. That leaves you with some Shift+Alt and Ctrl+Alt key combinations. They're better than nothing.

Deleting a style

To peel away any style you've created, follow these steps:

1. **Display the Styles pane.**

The keyboard shortcut is Ctrl+Shift+Alt+S.

2. **Right-click the style you want to obliterate.**

3. **Choose the Delete item.**

The Delete item is followed by the style's name.

4. **Click the Yes button to confirm.**

   The style is removed from the document.

The Normal style is applied to the old style's text.

You cannot delete any of Word's default styles, including Normal and the various heading styles.

Style Tips and Tricks

Awash in a sea of styles, it's easy to overlook some of the more subtle aspects of Word's styles. For example, the Normal style need not be stuck as the default for all new documents. And those heading styles offer more power than you may suspect.

Changing the Normal style

All documents sport the Normal style, which is the standard text-and-paragraph style and probably the style upon which all your personal styles are based. Like just about anything in Word, the Normal style can be modified — but I urge caution if you do so.

To modify the Normal style's font or paragraph formats, summon the Font or Paragraph dialog boxes. Refer to specific steps in Chapters 10 and 11, respectively, for details. In both dialog boxes, you find a Set As Default button. Click that button to update the Normal style.

For example, to reset the Normal style's font to Times New Roman, follow these steps:

1. **Apply the Normal style to the current paragraph.**

2. **Press Ctrl+D to summon the Font dialog box.**

3. **Choose Times New Roman as the font.**

4. **Click the Set As Default button.**

   A dialog box appears.

5. **Choose the All Documents option to update the Normal template and change the Normal style for all documents.**

   If you choose the This Document Only option, the style is updated only for the current document.

6. **Click OK.**

I don't recommend making this choice unless you're determined to alter the Normal style. Mostly, people get into trouble when they accidentally change the Normal style and then want to change it back. If so, follow the steps in this section to restore the Normal style. A description of Word 2019's Normal style can be found in the earlier section "The Big Style Overview."

Creating heading styles

Word's heading styles are numbered Heading 1, Heading 2, on down to Heading 9. You use them to identify different parts of a document, but they also take advantage of other Word features.

For example, text formatted with a heading style appears whenever you use the vertical scroll bar to skim a document. Headings can be expanded or collapsed, as part of Word's Outline feature, as described in Chapter 25. Headings appear in the navigation pane when you search for text. They can be used when creating a table of contents.

TIP

You're not stuck with using Word's preset heading styles; you can create your own heading- or document-level styles. The key is to set the paragraph's outline level: In the Paragraph dialog box, use the Outline Level menu to set the heading level: Set Level 1 for top-level headings. For the next heading level (subheading), choose Level 2, and so on. These paragraph formats are used by Word's document organization tools, such as the navigation pane and Table of Contents command.

Follow the steps in the earlier section "Using the Create New Style from Formatting dialog box" to update your heading styles to reflect the proper outline-level paragraph format.

>> Heading text is typically only one line long. Larger font sizes are usually selected. The Space After paragraph format is frequently applied.

>> Word's predefined Title style isn't a heading style.

Customizing the Style Gallery

To ensure that the styles you use the most appear in the Style Gallery, follow these steps:

1. **Summon the Styles pane.**

   Press the ungainly Ctrl+Shift+Alt+S key combination.

2. **Right-click the style you want to add to the Style Gallery.**

3. **Choose the command Add to Style Gallery.**

To remove a style from the Style Gallery, right-click the style in the gallery and choose the command Remove from Style Gallery.

REMEMBER

This trick can be useful, but the Style Gallery shows only a pittance of the styles available to a document. When you find yourself using a lot of styles, use the Styles pane instead.

IN THIS CHAPTER

» **Understanding templates**

» **Using templates**

» **Attaching a template to a document**

» **Creating a document template**

» **Changing a template**

» **Understanding themes**

» **Formatting a document with a theme**

» **Creating your own themes**

Chapter **16**

Template and Themes Formatting

Computers are supposed to save you time, so why exert great effort on the formatting task, specifically with regard to selecting fonts and colors? Instead, you can save time by using a template or a theme, or both. These tools format your prose easily and rapidly. You can choose from a preset template or theme, or you can craft your own to preserve previous formatting choices.

Instant Documents with Templates

A template is a timesaver. It lets you create documents that use the same styles, formatting, and common text elements without the need to re-create all the work and effort. A template saves time.

REMEMBER

TECHNICAL STUFF

» Choosing a specific template for a document is optional.

» When you don't choose a template, you use Word's default new-document template called Normal.

» All documents in Word are based on a template. The template is attached to the document.

» Word offers templates in two categories: Featured and Personal. The Featured templates are those supplied by Microsoft and made available over the Internet. The Personal templates are those you create.

» Using a template doesn't mean you can neglect saving your work. The template merely helps you get started by providing common document elements.

» Word uses three filename extensions for its document templates: .dot, .dotx, and .dotm. Older Word templates use the .dot extension. Word 2007 and later uses the .dotx extension, with macro-enabled templates using the .dotm extension. Filename extensions are not normally visible in Windows, though these extensions are referenced when choosing a file type in the Open dialog box.

Using a template to start a new document

When you press Ctrl+N to create a new, blank document in Word, you see a new document based on the Normal template. To use another template, either one supplied by Microsoft or one you've created, follow these steps:

1. **Click the File tab.**

The File screen appears.

2. **Choose New from the left side of the File screen.**

You see a list of template thumbnails. The list is divided into two categories or tabs, Featured and Personal, as illustrated in Figure 16-1.

3. **To peruse your own templates, click the Personal tab; otherwise, browse the available templates in the Featured list.**

When you choose Personal, the screen shows only the templates you crafted yourself.

4. **Click a template.**

5. **If prompted, click the Create button.**

The button appears when you use one of Word's predefined templates.

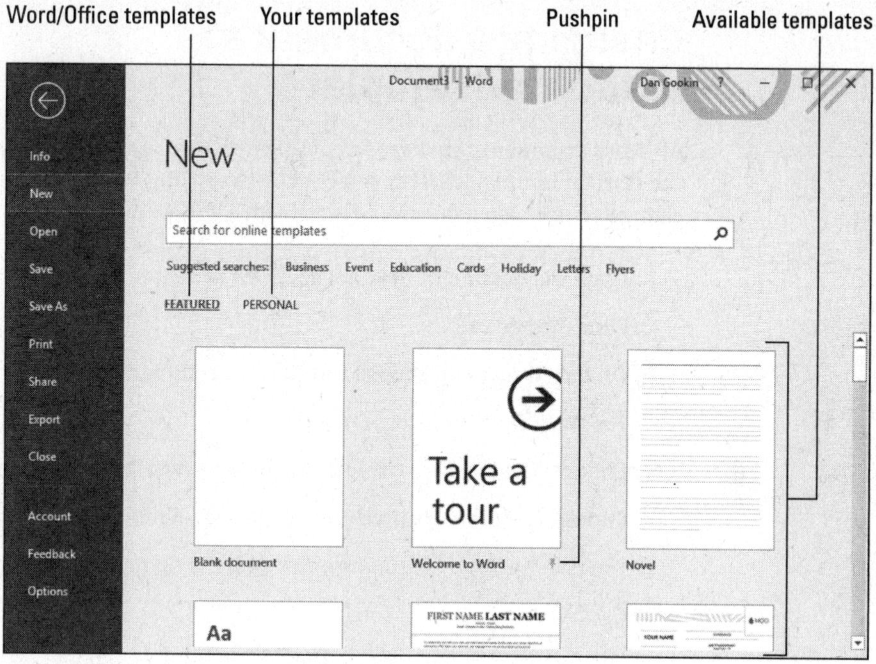

FIGURE 16-1:
Choosing a template from the New screen.

6. **Start working on the new document.**

   Text, graphics, headers, and footers appear in the document — if these items were supplied with the template. You also have access to all styles saved in the template.

REMEMBER

Save your work! You use a template to start the document, but if you check the window's title bar, you see that it isn't saved: Use the Save command, and give your document a proper name as soon as possible.

>> Using a template to create a new document doesn't change the template. To modify a template, see the section "Modifying a template," later in this chapter.

>> Refer to the later section "Templates of Your Own" for information on making your own templates.

TIP

>> It's possible to pin your personal templates to the Featured screen: Click the Pushpin icon, as illustrated earlier, in Figure 16-1. That way, you can skip Step 3 (in the preceding list) and choose one of your own templates to quickly start a new document.

Changing a document's associated template

All Word documents are based on a specific template. Even a blank document uses the Normal template. When you choose the wrong template or suddenly desire to change or reassign a document's template, follow these steps:

1. **Open the document that needs a new template attached.**

2. **Click the File tab.**

3. **On the File screen, choose the Options command.**

   The Word Options dialog box appears.

4. **Choose Add-Ins from the left side of the Word Options dialog box.**

5. **Choose Templates from the Manage drop-down list.**

   You find the Manage drop-down list near the bottom of the dialog box.

6. **Click the Go button.**

   The Templates and Add-Ins dialog box appears. You should see which template is attached to the document, such as Normal.

7. **Click the Attach button.**

   Word displays the Attach Template dialog box, which looks and works like the Open dialog box.

8. **Select the template you want to attach.**

   The templates listed are stored on your computer, so you don't see the full range of templates that you would find on the New screen.

9. **Click the Open button.**

   The template is attached to your document.

10. **Ensure that the option Automatically Update Document Styles is selected.**

    Updating styles means that your document's current styles are changed to reflect those of the new template, which is probably what you want.

11. **Click OK.**

    The styles stored in that template are available to your document, and the document is now attached to the template.

If the template has any preset text or graphics, reassigning that template doesn't import those items into your document. Only the styles, custom toolbars, and macros are merged into your document.

You can also follow these steps to unattach a template. Do that by selecting Normal (normal.dotm) as the template to attach.

Templates of Your Own

If you enjoy the thrill and excitement of templates, you'll just burst at the thought of creating your own. Over time, you build up a collection. Your own, custom templates greatly help expedite your document production duties.

Creating a template based on a document you already have

The easiest way to create a new template (the way I do it about 90 percent of the time) is to base the template on an existing document — for example, a document you've already written and formatted to perfection. The template retains the document's formatting and styles so that you can instantly create a new document with those same settings.

To make a template based on a document you've already created, follow these steps:

1. **Open or create the document, one that has styles or formats or text that you plan to use repeatedly.**

2. **Strip out any text that doesn't need to be in every document.**

   For example, my play-writing template has all my play-writing styles in it, but the text includes only placeholders — just to get me started.

3. **Click the File tab.**

4. **On the File screen, choose the Save As command.**

5. **Click the Browse button.**

   The Save As dialog box appears. It's the same Save As dialog box that Word uses for saving everything. Refer to Chapter 8 for a refresher.

6. **Type a name for the template.**

   Type the name in the File Name box. Be descriptive. You don't need to use the word *template* when naming the file.

7. **From the Save As Type drop-down list, choose Word Template.**

   Ah-ha! This is the secret. The document must be saved in a document template format. That's what makes a template different from a typical, boring Word document.

   Don't worry about choosing the document's location. All Word templates are saved in a predefined folder, which Word automatically chooses for you after you set the file type as a Word template.

8. **Click the Save button.**

   Your efforts are saved as a document template, nestled in the proper storage location, where Word keeps all its document templates.

9. **Close the template.**

   The reason for closing it is that any changes you make from now on are saved to the template. If you want to use the template to start a new document, you choose that template from the New window, as described earlier in this chapter.

Refer to the later section "Modifying a template" for information on updating or changing a template.

Making a new template from scratch

If you want a simple template, you can create it from scratch, especially when you're well-versed in using Word's style commands and you know exactly which elements the template needs.

To start, create any common text. Next, create the styles and any text formatting you plan on using in the template.

When everything is set, use the Save As dialog box to save the document as a template, as described in the preceding section.

Modifying a template

You have two options for changing a template. The first is to start a new document by using the template. Make the changes you want. Then save the document as a template file, overwriting the original file.

The second way is to open the template file directly. This way is more difficult because Word keeps the template files in a special folder that may not be easy for you to find. The good news is that in Word 2019, the folder is named Custom Office Templates and is found in the My Documents folder. Use the Open dialog box to open a template file held in that location.

>> If you use Word's Open command to open a template but no templates appear to be in the folder, don't panic! Instead, click the File Type menu button and choose Word Template. You should see the lot.

WARNING

>> Changing a template has a widespread effect. When you update or modify a template, you change all documents using the template. Although such a change can be beneficial, and one of the best reasons for using a template, be mindful of your changes!

TECHNICAL STUFF

>> That template folder pathname is

```
%USERPROFILE%\Documents\Custom Office Templates
```

The Theme of Things

Themes apply decorative styles, such as fonts and colors, to your document, giving your written efforts a professionally formatted feel while keeping hordes of graphics designers unemployed.

A theme consists of three elements:

Colors: A set of colors is chosen to format the text foreground and background, any graphics or design elements in the theme, plus hyperlinks.

Fonts: Two fonts are chosen as part of the theme — one for the heading styles and a second for the body text.

Graphical effects: These effects are applied to any graphics or design elements in your document. The effects can include 3D, shading, gradation, drop shadows, and other design doodads.

Each of these elements is organized into a theme, given a name, and placed on the Design tab's Themes menu for easy application in your document.

>> A professionally licensed, certified mentally stable graphics designer creates a theme's fonts, colors, and design effects so that they look good and work well together.

>> A theme doesn't overrule styles chosen for a document. Instead, it accents those styles. The theme may add color information, choose different fonts, or present various graphical elements. Beyond that, it doesn't change any styles applied to the text.

>> The graphical effects of a theme are only applied to any graphics in the document; the theme doesn't insert graphics into your text. See Chapter 22 for information on graphics in Word.

REMEMBER

>> Choosing a theme affects the entire document all at once. To affect individual paragraphs or bits of text, apply a style or format manually. Refer to Chapter 15.

Applying a document theme

To apply a theme to your document, follow these directions:

1. **Click the Design tab.**

2. **Click the Themes button.**

Built-in themes are listed along with any custom themes you've created. Figure 16-2 illustrates the Themes menu.

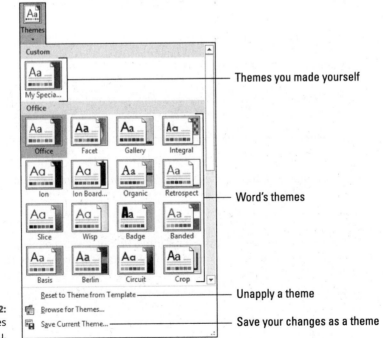

FIGURE 16-2:
The Themes menu.

Each built-in theme controls all three major theme elements (colors, fonts, graphical effects), changing your document's contents accordingly. Hover the mouse pointer over a theme to visually preview its effect. Click a theme to choose it.

TIP

>> Because a document uses only one theme at a time, choosing a new theme replaces the current theme.

>> To unapply a theme from your document, choose the Office theme or the menu command Reset to Theme from Template. (Refer to Figure 16-2.)

>> If you would rather change only one part of a theme, such as a document's fonts, use the Colors, Fonts, or Effects command button on the Design tab.

Modifying or creating a theme

You can't create your own themes from scratch, but you can modify existing themes to make your own, custom theme. You start by modifying existing theme colors and fonts. Choose one of these options while viewing the Design tab:

To create a custom color theme, choose Colors ⇨ Customize Colors. Use the Create New Theme Colors dialog box to pick and choose which colors to apply to text or various graphical elements in your document.

To create a custom font theme, choose Fonts ⇨ Customize Fonts. Use the Create New Theme Fonts dialog box to select fonts — one for the headings and another for the body text.

For each option, give the new theme a name and save it. You can then choose that theme from the Custom area of either the Colors menu or the Fonts menu.

After customizing various elements, on the Design tab, click the Themes menu button and choose Save Current Theme. Use the Save Current Theme dialog box to give your theme a proper descriptive name and save it. The theme you create then appears in the Custom area of the Themes menu, as illustrated earlier, in Figure 16-2.

To remove a custom theme, right-click it on the Themes menu and choose the Delete command. Click the Yes button to confirm and remove the theme.

Chapter **17**

Random Drawer Formatting

E veryone has one, even neatniks who proudly profess to be organized. It's the random-stuff drawer. Maybe it's in the kitchen or a desk drawer in your home office. Perhaps you have several such random stuff drawers. These are necessary because everyone needs a location for stuff that just doesn't fit anywhere else.

Welcome to the random-drawer formatting chapter. Here you find formatting commands various and sundry. They just don't fit in well with the other formatting chapters found in this part of the book.

Weird and Fun Text Effects

On the Home tab, in the Font group, is a button adorned with a fuzzy *A*, as shown in the margin. It's the Text Effects and Typography button. Click that button to view the Text Effects menu, as shown on the far left in Figure 17-1. This menu lists special text decorations, well beyond the standard text attributes shown in Chapter 10. Choose an effect from the menu to apply it to your text.

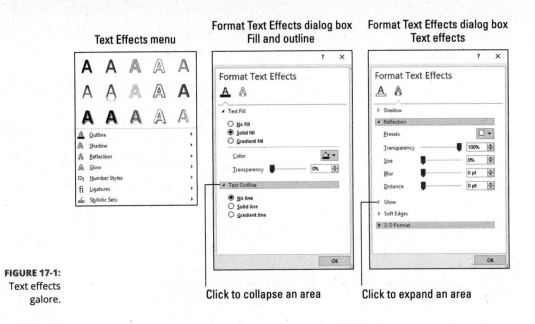

Text Effects menu

Format Text Effects dialog box
Fill and outline

Format Text Effects dialog box
Text effects

Click to collapse an area   Click to expand an area

If the effects on the Text Effects menu aren't exactly what you want, you can create your own: You can choose custom effects from the submenus on the Text Effects and Typography menu, or you can use the Format Text Effects dialog box, shown in the center and on the right in Figure 17-1. To access this dialog box, follow these steps:

1. **Press Ctrl+D.**

   The Font dialog box appears.

2. **Click the Text Effects button.**

   The Format Text Effects dialog box appears. It features two categories: Text Fill & Outline and Text Effects, shown in the center and on the right in Figure 17-1, respectively.

3. **Manipulate the controls in the dialog box to customize text effects.**

   Choose a category, and then click a triangle to expand items in a subcategory. Controls appear, as illustrated in Figure 17-1, which let you customize the effect. Sadly, the dialog box lacks a preview window, so you have to make your best guess about the results.

4. **Click the OK button to dismiss the Format Text Effects dialog box.**

5. **Click the OK button to close the Font dialog box.**

The options that you select affect any selected text in the document or any text you type from that point onward.

>> Font effects are best used for document headings and other decorative text.

>> The Text Effects button is unavailable (dimmed) if you attempt to use this command on an older Word document. See Chapter 24 for information on converting older Word documents. If the document is based on an older template, you need to update the template and then reattach the document to that template. See Chapter 16.

Steal This Format!

It's not a whisk broom, and it's definitely not a shaving brush. No, it's a paintbrush. Not only that, but it's also a *special* paintbrush — one that steals text and paragraph formatting, lifting it from one place in your document and splashing it down in another. It's the Format Painter, and here's how it's used:

1. **Place the insertion pointer in the midst of the text that has the formatting you want to copy.**

   Think of this step as dipping a brush into a bucket of paint.

2. **Click the Home tab.**

3. **In the Clipboard group, click the Format Painter command button.**

   The mouse pointer changes to a paintbrush/I-beam, as depicted in the margin. Use it to select and reformat text.

4. **Hunt for the text you want to change.**

5. **Select the text.**

   Drag over the text you want to change — to "paint" it.

Voilà! The text is changed.

>> The Format Painter works with character and paragraph formatting, not with page formatting.

>> To change the formatting of multiple bits of text, double-click the Format Painter. That way, the Format Painter mouse pointer stays active, ready to repaint lots of text. Press the Esc key to cancel your Dutch Boy frenzy.

>> If you tire of the mouse, you can use the Ctrl+Shift+C key combination to copy the character format from one location to another. Use the Ctrl+Shift+V key combination to paste the character format.

>> You can sorta kinda remember to use Ctrl+Shift+C to copy character formatting and use Ctrl+Shift+V to paste, because Ctrl+C and Ctrl+V are the copy-and-paste shortcut keys. Sorta kinda.

>> Don't confuse the Format Painter with the highlighting tool, found in the Font group. See Chapter 26.

Automatic Formatting

Part of Word's AutoCorrect feature (covered in Chapter 7) is a tool named AutoFormat. Whereas AutoCorrect fixes typos and common spelling boo-boos, AutoFormat fixes formatting fumbles.

Enjoying automagical text

AutoFormat controls some minor text formatting as you type. All its settings are visible in the AutoCorrect dialog box's AutoFormat As You Type tab, as shown in Figure 17-2.

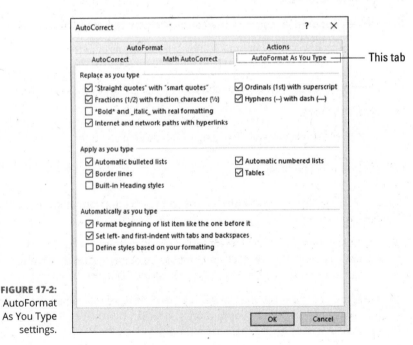

FIGURE 17-2:
AutoFormat As You Type settings.

To display the AutoCorrect dialog box and access the AutoFormat As You Type features, heed these steps:

1. **Click the File tab.**

2. **Choose Options.**

   The Word Options dialog box appears.

3. **Select Proofing from the left side of the window.**

4. **Click the button labeled AutoCorrect Options.**

   The AutoCorrect dialog box says, "Hello."

5. **Click the AutoFormat As You Type tab.**

   This part of the dialog box you see is where all the AutoFormat options dwell. (Well, aside from the AutoFormat tab, which is redundant.) Add or remove a check mark to turn an option on or off, respectively.

The best way to demonstrate the AutoFormat-as-you-type concept is to have a Word document on the screen and then type the examples in the following sections. Note that these samples demonstrate only a few of the tricks AutoFormat can perform.

Smart quotes

The quote characters on the keyboard are *tick marks:* " and ' . AutoFormat converts them into the more stylish open and closed curly quotes. Type hither:

```
He said, "Yes, I'm being honest. I really do love
you, but the monster is coming and you broke your
ankle, so I figured that you'd understand."
```

Both the single and double quotes are converted.

Real fractions

You can format a fraction by formatting the first value in superscript and the second value in subscript. Or you can let AutoFormat do it for you. Here's an example:

```
I spend twice the time doing ½ the work.
```

The characters 1/2 are converted into the single character ½. This trick works for some, but not all, common fractions. When it doesn't work, use superscript/subscript formatting, as described in Chapter 31.

Hyperlinks

Word can underline *and* activate hyperlinks that are typed in your document, such as:

> I've been to http://www.hell.com and back.

The website http://www.hell.com is automatically underlined, colored, and turned into an active web page link for you. (To follow the link, Ctrl+click the text.)

Ordinals

You're guessing wrong if you think that *ordinals* are a baseball team or a group of religious leaders. They're numbers that end in the letters *st, nd,* or *rd,* as this line demonstrates:

> There were two of us in the race; I came in 1st
> and Oglethorpe came in 3rd.

Word's AutoFormat feature automatically superscripts ordinal numbers, making them look oh-so-spiffy.

Em dashes

An *em dash* is the official typesetting term for a long dash, longer than the hyphen (or its evil twin, the en dash). Most people type two hyphens to emulate the *em dash.* Word fixes that problem:

> A red one is a slug bug—not a punch buggy.

After you type the - - ("dash dash") and then the word that follows, AutoFormat replaces it with the official em dash character.

>> The keyboard shortcut for typing an em dash is Ctrl+Alt+minus sign, where the minus sign (–) is the minus key on the numeric keypad.

>> The single hyphen is also converted into a en dash when you follow it with a word.

>> The keyboard shortcut for typing an en dash is Ctrl+minus sign.

>> The en dash is approximately the width of the letter *N.* Likewise, the em dash is the width of the letter *M.*

Formatting tricks for paragraphs

At the paragraph level, AutoFormat helps you quickly handle some otherwise irksome formatting issues. Some folks enjoy this feature, some despise it. The following sections provide a few examples of what AutoFormat is capable of.

Numbered lists

Anytime you start a paragraph with a number, Word assumes (through AutoFormat) that you need all your paragraphs numbered. Here's the proof:

```
Things to do today:
1. Get new treads for the tank.
```

Immediately after typing 1., you probably saw the infamous AutoCorrect Lightning Bolt icon and noticed your text being reformatted. Darn, this thing is quick! That's the AutoFormat feature guessing that you're about to type a list. Go ahead and finish typing the line; after you press Enter, you see the next line begin with the number 2.

Keep typing until the list ends or you get angry, whichever comes first. To end the list, press the Enter key twice to erase the final number and restore the paragraph formatting to Normal.

TIP

>> This numbering trick works also for letters (and Roman numerals). Just start something with a letter and a period, and Word picks up on the next line by suggesting the next letter in the alphabet and another period.

>> Bulleted lists can also be created in this way: Start a line by typing an asterisk (*) and a space to see what happens.

>> See Chapter 21 for more information on Word's numbering and bulleted list formats.

TECHNICAL STUFF

>> You don't press the Enter key twice to end a typical paragraph in a document, but pressing Enter twice to terminate an AutoFormat list is completely acceptable. Doing so doesn't add an empty paragraph to your document.

Borders (lines)

A line above or below a paragraph is typographically called a *rule*, but Word uses the term *border*. Most folks call them lines. Here's how to use AutoFormat to whip out a border:

```
- - -
```

Type three hyphens and press the Enter key. Word instantly transmutes the three wee hyphens into a solid line that touches the left and right paragraph margins.

>> To create a double line, type three equal signs and press Enter.

>> To create a bold line, type three underlines and press Enter.

>> Refer to Chapter 18 for details on borders and boxes around your text.

Undoing an AutoFormat

You have two quick ways to undo autoformatting. The first, obviously, is to press Ctrl+Z on the keyboard, which is the Undo command. That's easy.

You can also use the Lightning Bolt icon to undo autoformatting. Click the icon to display a drop-down menu, shown in Figure 17-3. Use the options displayed to control the AutoFormat options as you type.

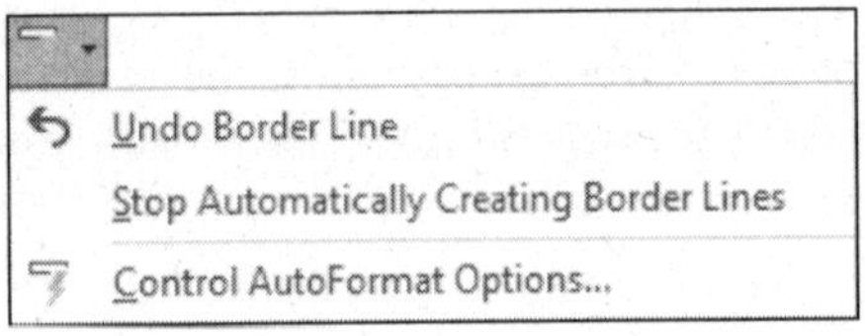

FIGURE 17-3:
AutoFormat
options.

Choosing the first option, Undo [whatever] (refer to Figure 17-3), is the same as pressing Ctrl+Z on the keyboard.

Selecting the second option, Stop Automatically [doing whatever], disables the specific AutoFormat feature so that it never happens again. People enjoy using this option.

Choosing the final option, Control AutoFormat Options, displays the AutoCorrect dialog box's AutoFormat As You Type tab, which is shown earlier, in Figure 17-2.

Also see Chapter 33 for more details on disabling AutoFormat features.

Center a Page, Top to Bottom

Nothing makes a document title nice and crisp like having it sit squat in the center of a page, as shown in Figure 17-4. The title is centered left to right, which is a paragraph formatting trick, but how can it be centered top to bottom on the page?

A Perfectly

Centered

Title

By Evan Middlebottom

FIGURE 17-4:
This title
is centered
on a page.

If you're thinking about whacking the Enter key 17 times in a row to center a title top to bottom, stop! Let Word do the math to make the title perfectly centered. Here's how:

1. **Press the Ctrl+Home key combination.**

   The insertion pointer jets to the start of the document.

2. **Type and format the document's title.**

   It can be on a single line or on several lines.

   To center the title, apply center paragraph justification: Press Ctrl+E. Apply any additional font or paragraph formatting as necessary.

   If the title is split between two or more lines, use Ctrl+Enter to break a line, which reduces the spacing.

REMEMBER

   Avoid the temptation to press the Enter key to add space above or below the title. Such space isn't needed, and would wreck Word's automatic centering powers.

3. **Position the mouse pointer at the end of the title.**

Press the End key on the last line of the title, or the author line. (Refer to Figure 17-4.)

4. **Click the Layout tab.**

5. **In the Page Setup group, choose Breaks ⇨ Next Page.**

A next-page section break is inserted into the document. The title now sits on its own page as its own section.

6. **Click the document's first page.**

You need to be on the page you want to format.

7. **Click the Layout tab.**

8. **Click the dialog box launcher in the lower right corner of the Page Setup area.**

The Page Setup dialog box appears.

9. **Click the Layout tab.**

10. **Click the Vertical Alignment drop-down list and choose Center.**

11. **Confirm that the Apply To drop-down list shows This Section.**

12. **Click OK.**

The first page of the document is centered from top to bottom. Because that page is its own section, the top-to-bottom centering applies only to that page and not the rest of the document.

>> Review Chapter 14 for more information on document sections.

>> Also see the book *Word 2016 For Professionals For Dummies* (Wiley) for many additional formatting tips, tricks, and suggestions.

4
Spruce Up a Dull Document

IN THIS PART . . .

Learn how to use borders, draw lines, and add color to a document's background.

Use tables in your documents.

Split your text into multiple columns.

Discover how to make several types of lists, including bulleted lists, numbered lists, and indexes.

Learn how you can insert images and captions into a document.

Chapter **18**

They're Called Borders

f you try to use any of these characters to draw a line or box in your text, your computer will explode: – = _ + |

Well, maybe not explode, but it will get angry with you. That's because Word hosts a collection of line-drawing tools to artfully place borders and boxes in and around your text. You have no need to pore over the keyboard and scout out the best character to highlight some chunk of text in your document. All you must know is that the text format is called a *border* and the graphical element is a *line*.

» This chapter covers the border, which is a linear graphical doojobbie applied to text.

» Lines are graphical elements that you can set in your document. See Chapter 22.

» To create a fill-in-the-blank underline, refer to Chapter 12.

» Terms aside, graphics designers refer to any line in your text as a *rule*.

The Basics of Borders

A border is a paragraph-level format. Yes, it's a line. People call it a line. But as a paragraph format, a *border* is coupled to a paragraph on the top, bottom, left, or right or some combination thereof. The line can be thick, thin, doubled, tripled, dashed, or painted in a variety of colors.

Like any paragraph style, a border sticks to the paragraph it's applied to: Add a border to the left of the current paragraph, press Enter, and the next paragraph inherits the same border.

Borders can also be part of a style, applied to text like any other format.

 To control the border format, click the Home tab. In the Paragraph group, look for the Borders button. The button reveals the current paragraph's border style, such as No Border, shown in the margin. Click this button to apply the format shown. To choose another border style, and view other options, click the triangle next to the button. The Borders menu is shown in Figure 18-1.

⊞	Bottom Border
⊞	Top Border
⊞	Left Border
⊞	Right Border
⊞	No Border
⊞	All Borders
⊞	Outside Borders
⊞	Inside Borders
⊞	Inside Horizontal Border
⊞	Inside Vertical Border
◪	Diagonal Down Border
◪	Diagonal Up Border
≝	Horizontal Line
⬚	Draw Table
⊞	View Gridlines
▯	Borders and Shading...

FIGURE 18-1:
The Borders and
Shading menus.

The final item on the Borders menu summons the Borders and Shading dialog box, covered in the later section "The Borders and Shading Dialog Box." Use that dialog box to gain more flexibility when formatting paragraph borders.

Other sections in this chapter describe how to use the Borders button to apply borders (lines) to paragraphs in a document.

Putting borders around a paragraph

To apply a border to any or all sides of a paragraph, follow these steps:

1. **Place the insertion pointer in a paragraph.**

2. **Click the Home tab.**

3. **In the Paragraphs group, click the triangle next to the Borders command button.**

The Borders menu appears.

4. **Choose a border style from the menu.**

For example, to place a line atop the paragraph, choose Top Border. Its icon is shown in the margin.

The border is applied using the line style, thickness, and color set in the Borders and Shading dialog box. See the later section "The Borders and Shading Dialog Box" for details.

TIP

To apply multiple lines, choose both border styles sequentially. For example, to add lines above and below a paragraph, first choose the Top Border command, and then click the Borders command again and choose Bottom Border.

>> Horizontal borders stretch between the paragraph's left and right margins. These margins are different from the page margins. See Chapter 11 for information on setting a paragraph's left and right margins.

>> A common use of paragraph borders is to set off a document title or heading. See the later section "Creating a fancy title" for formatting tips.

REMEMBER

>> When multiple paragraphs are selected, the border is applied to all paragraphs as a group. Therefore, a top or bottom border appears on only the first or last paragraph in the selected block.

>> To place lines between paragraphs, see the later section "Boxing multiple paragraphs."

>> If you press Enter to end the paragraph, the border formatting is applied to the following paragraph. For top and bottom borders, the effect is that only the first or last paragraph displays the border line.

Boxing multiple paragraphs

To stick a box around a paragraph, use the Outside Borders command, found on the Borders menu and shown in the margin. When multiple paragraphs are selected, the box wraps around the group.

If you desire to box several paragraphs in a row and keep lines between the paragraphs, use the All Borders command instead of Outside Borders. The All Borders icon is shown in the margin.

>> More and fancy options for boxing paragraphs can be found in the Borders and Shading dialog box. See the later section "The Borders and Shading Dialog Box."

>> Before you go paragraph-boxing crazy, what you might need in your document instead is a table. See Chapter 19 for information on tables.

Removing borders

To peel away the border format from one or more paragraphs of text, apply the No Border format: Select the paragraph(s), click the Borders button, and then choose No Border, as shown in the margin.

To remove specific parts of a border, use the Borders and Shading dialog box, covered . . . why, it's in the next section!

TIP

The Borders and Shading Dialog Box

To fully flex Word's border bravado, summon the Borders and Shading dialog box:

1. **Click the Home tab.**

2. **In the Paragraph group, click the triangle by the Borders button to display the Borders menu.**

3. **Choose the Borders and Shading command.**

The Borders and Shading dialog box appears, as shown in Figure 18-2.

Unlike the Borders menu, additional and custom border-setting options are available in the Borders and Shading dialog box. Most notably, you can set the border line style, thickness, and color.

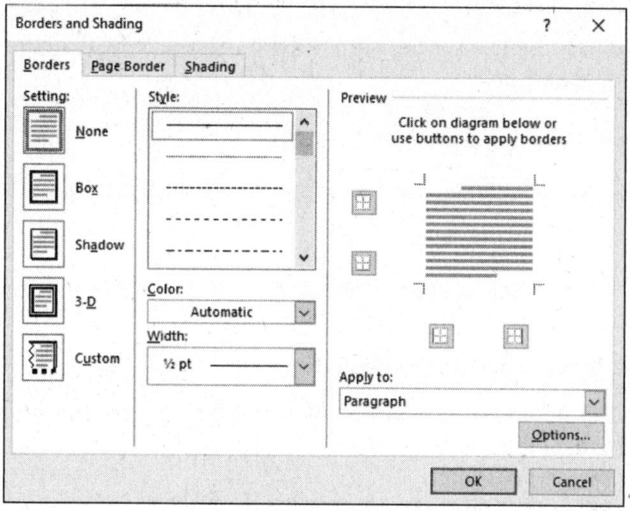

FIGURE 18-2:
The Borders and Shading dialog box.

>> The Borders and Shading dialog box also allows you to place a border around a page, which is covered in the later section "Applying a page border."

>> You can use the commands in the Borders and Shading dialog box to format a table. See Chapter 19 for information on tables in Word.

Creating a fancy title

To create custom titles for newsletters, documents, or anything else you want to pretend is super important, click to select a paragraph and then go nuts in the Borders and Shading dialog box. You may end up with results similar to what's shown in Figure 18-3.

Grockmeister
Government Consulting

869 Van Horn Road, Culpepper, MO, 63054 ~ (636) 555-6797

"Twice the fees for half the work"

FIGURE 18-3:
Fancy borders.

To properly apply a special border, follow these general steps in the Borders and Shading dialog box:

1. **Choose a line style in the Style list.**

   Scroll the list to view the full variety of styles. (Refer to Figure 18-2.)

2. **Set the color in the Color list.**

   The Automatic color uses black, or the standard color as set by the document's theme (usually black).

3. **Choose a width in the Width list.**

4. **Click in the Preview part of the dialog box to place the line: top, bottom, right, or left.**

To remove a line, click it in the Preview window.

TIP

To start out quickly, select a preset design from the list of icons on the right side of the dialog box. (Refer to Figure 18-2.)

Click the OK button to apply the customized border to your document's text.

Boxing text

The border is primarily a paragraph-level format, though you can also wrap borders around tiny tidbits of text. To do so, follow these steps:

1. **Select the text.**

2. **Summon the Borders and Shading dialog box.**

   Directions are found earlier in this chapter.

3. **Set the border style you desire.**

   Only the Box and Shadow options are available, although you can set the color and line thickness.

4. **Ensure that the Apply To menu shows Text and not Paragraph.**

5. **Click OK.**

Also see Chapter 10 for information on shading text. From a design point of view, I believe shading text is a better option than wrapping it in a box.

Applying a page border

One gem hidden in the Borders and Shading dialog box is the tool to place a border around an entire page of text. The border sits at the page's margins and is in addition to any paragraph borders you might apply.

Here are the secret directions to set a page border:

1. **Put the insertion pointer on the page you want to border.**

For example, you might put it on the first page in the document.

2. **Summon the Borders and Shading dialog box.**

3. **Click the Page Border tab.**

4. **Set the border style.**

Choose a preset style, line style, color, thickness.

TIP

Use the Art drop-down list to choose a funky pattern for the border.

5. **Click the Apply To menu button to select which pages you want bordered.**

Choose Whole Document to put borders on every page. To select the first page, choose the This Section – First Page Only item. Other options let you choose other pages and groups, as shown in the drop-down list.

And now, the secret:

6. **Click the Options button.**

The Border and Shading Options dialog box appears.

7. **In the Measure From drop-down list, choose the Text option.**

The Edge of Page option just doesn't work with most printers. Text does.

TIP

To add more "air" between the text and the border, increase the values in the Margin area.

8. **Click OK.**

9. **Click OK to close the Borders and Shading dialog box.**

To remove the page border, choose None under Settings in Step 4 and then click OK.

A page border is a page-level format. If you desire borders to sit on only certain pages, split the document into sections. Use the Apply To drop-down menu (refer to Step 5) to select the current section for the page borders. See Chapter 14 for more information on section formatting.

Stick a thick line between paragraphs

It's not a border, nor is it a paragraph-level format, but the Horizontal Line command can be used to break up paragraphs of text by sticking a line between them. To add such a horizontal line, follow these steps:

1. **Position the insertion pointer at the start or end of a paragraph, where you want the horizontal line to appear.**

2. **Click the Home tab.**

3. **In the Paragraph Group, click the Borders button.**

4. **Choose Horizontal Line.**

   Word inserts a line stretching from the left to right margins.

Click the line to adjust its size: Use the mouse to drag one of the six handles (top and bottom and the four corners) to set the line's width or thickness.

To format the horizontal line, double-click it. Use the Format Horizontal Line dialog box to set the width (as a percentage), height, color, and alignment.

To remove the horizontal line, click once to select it and then press the Delete key.

IN THIS CHAPTER

» **Understanding tables in Word**

» **Building a table**

» **Converting between text and a table**

» **Selecting items in a table**

» **Setting text alignment**

» **Adding or inserting rows and columns**

» **Applying table quick styles**

» **Putting a caption on the table**

Chapter **19**

Able Tables

Writing is a linear task. Characters flow into words, which flow into sentences, which form paragraphs. You start reading here and end up there. That's how it works, up until the information you're trying to organize is best presented in a grid. Then you must summon a table.

Put a Table in Your Document

A table presents information organized into rows and columns — a grid. In olden times, writers used the Tab key to build such a thing, setting various and clever tab stops and formatting the text accordingly. This approach worked, but Word offers something better: the Table menu and its array of table-making commands.

Word's table commands create a grid with a given number of cells organized into rows and columns. Each cell can be formatted with its own margins, spacing, or paragraph style. And into those formatted cells you can place text or graphics. Lines and background colors complete the table design. These feats are beyond the capabilities of the silly old Tab key.

Working with tables in Word

To begin your table-making journey, click the Ribbon's Insert tab. In the Tables group, the only item is the Table button. Click that button to see the Table menu, as shown in Figure 19-1.

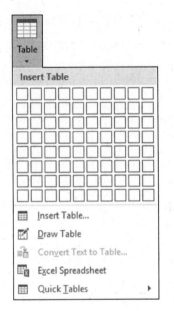

FIGURE 19-1:
The Table menu.

The Table menu features multiple methods for slapping down a table in the document, each of which is covered in the following sections. Or, if you already used the Tab key to create tabular text, you can convert its clumsy self into a nifty table; see the later section "Convert tab-formatted text into a table."

After the table is created, fill it in. See the later section "Typing text in a table" for details.

To help you modify the table and make it look pretty, two new tabs appear on the Ribbon: Table Tools Design and Table Tools Layout. Details about using the commands on these two table tabs are offered throughout this chapter.

Creating a table

Word offers multiple ways to create a table, from right brain to left brain to options between. The choices allow for more flexibility but also make this chapter longer than it would be otherwise.

TIP

» I recommend placing the table on a blank line by itself. Furthermore, add a second blank line *after* the table. That makes it easier to continue typing text below the table.

» Don't worry about getting the table dimensions wrong. You can easily add or remove rows or columns after creating the table. See the later section "Adding or removing rows or columns."

The quick way to create a table

The fastest way to make a table in Word is to use the grid on the Table button's menu, as shown earlier, in Figure 19-1. Follow these steps:

1. **Click the mouse at the location in the document where you want the table to appear.**

2. **Click the Insert tab.**

3. **Click the Table button.**

4. **Drag through the grid to set the desired number of rows and columns.**

   In Figure 19-2, a 4-column-by-3-row table is created. As you drag the mouse pointer on the menu, the table's grid magically appears in the document, as shown in the figure.

5. **Release the mouse button to begin working on the table.**

See the later section "Text in Tables" to continue the table-creation task.

The right-brain way to create a table

When dialog boxes make more sense than using menus and graphical goobers, follow these steps:

1. **On the Insert tab, click the Table button.**

2. **From the Table menu, choose the Insert Table command.**

   The Insert Table dialog box appears.

3. **Enter the number of rows and columns.**

4. **Click the OK button to plop down the table.**

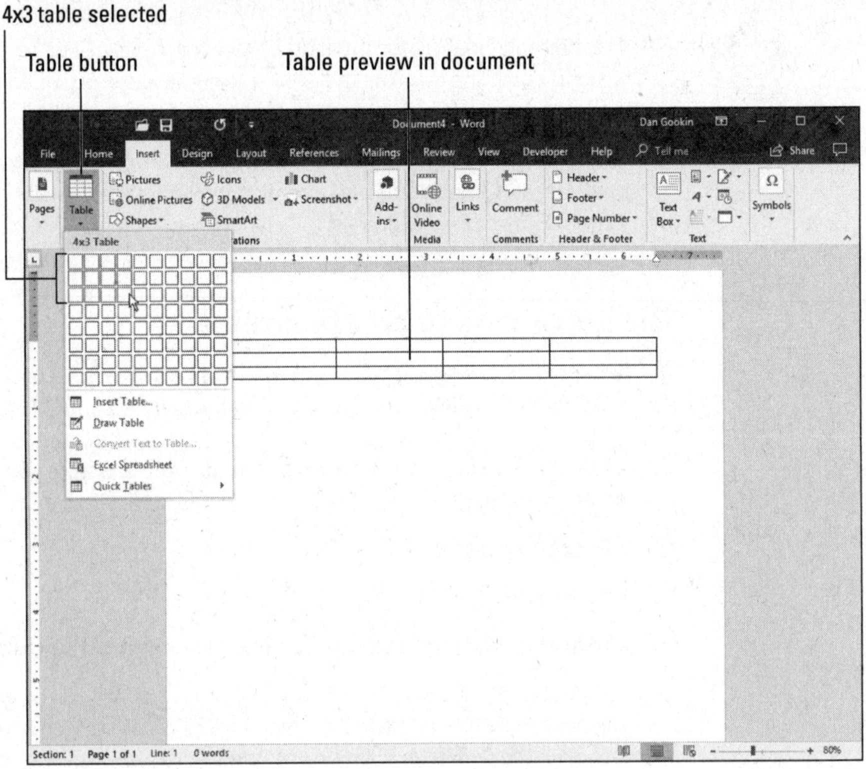

4x3 table selected

Table button   Table preview in document

FIGURE 19-2:
Creating a 4-by-3
table.

The left-brain way to create a table

Free your mind from the constraints of conventionalism, clutch a crystal, and use the mouse to draw a table inside your document:

1. **Click the Table button and choose Draw Table.**

   The mouse pointer changes to a pencil, as shown in the margin.

2. **Drag to draw the table's outline in the document.**

   Start in the upper left corner and drag to the lower right corner, which tells Word where to insert the table. You see an outline of the table as you drag down and to the right, as shown in Figure 19-3.

3. **Draw horizontal lines to create rows; draw vertical lines to create columns.**

   Refer to Figure 19-3 (on the right) for an example of drawing a row.

   As long as the mouse pointer looks like a pencil, you can use it to draw the rows and columns in the table.

4. **Press the Esc key when you've finished drawing the table.**

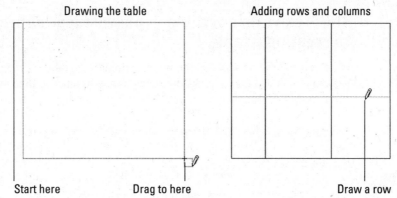

Drawing the table

Adding rows and columns

FIGURE 19-3:
Drawing a table
in a document.

Start here   Drag to here   Draw a row

Convert tab-formatted text into a table

If you've used the Tab key to create rows and columns of text, you can quickly snap that part of your document into an official Word table. Follow these steps:

1. Select the tab-formatted text.

If columns are separated by tabs, great. If not, each paragraph you select becomes a row in a single-column table.

2. Click the Insert tab.

3. Choose Table ➪ Convert Text to Table.

4. Confirm the values in the Convert Text to Table dialog box.

Ensure that the values Word has guessed for the proper number of columns and rows are correct. If the columns are separated by tabs, ensure that Tabs is chosen at the bottom of the dialog box. Word does a good job of getting the conversion settings correct, but it's polite enough to ask before it makes the conversion.

Use the mouse to move the Convert Text to Table dialog box so that you can better see the text in the document.

TIP

5. Click OK.

A table is born.

See the later section "Table Modification" for information on fixing the freshly created table.

The "I can't do anything — please help" approach to creating a table

Word comes with an assortment of spiffy predefined tables. Plopping one down in a document is as easy as using the Quick Tables submenu: Click the Table button, and from the menu, choose Quick Tables. Select a table type from the submenu.

After the table is inserted, you can add or edit the existing text, add more rows or columns, or otherwise modify the table. Refer to directions elsewhere in this chapter for specifics.

TIP

A Quick Table is the fastest way to create a calendar in Word.

Un-creating a table

At some point, you may surrender the notion of needing a table, and desire the text to be freed from the table's confines. To perform such a jailbreak, you convert the table back into plain text or even tab-formatted text. Obey these steps:

1. **Click inside the table you want to convert.**

Don't select anything — just click the mouse.

2. **Click the Table Tools Layout tab.**

3. **From the Table group, choose Select ⇨ Select Table.**

4. **From the Data group, choose Convert to Text.**

The Convert to Text dialog box appears. It guesses how you want the table converted, such as using tabs or paragraphs.

5. **Click OK.**

Bye-bye, table. Hello, ugly text.

Some post-table-destruction text clean-up might be necessary, but generally the conversion goes well. The only issue you may have is when a cell contains multiple paragraphs of text. In that case, undo the operation (press Ctrl+Z) and choose Paragraph Marks from the Convert to Text dialog box (before Step 5).

Deleting a table

To utterly remove the table from a document, text and all, heed these destruction directions:

1. **Click inside the table.**

2. **Click the Table Tools Layout tab.**

3. **In the Rows & Columns group, choose Delete ➪ Delete Table.**

   The table is blown to smithereens.

WARNING

Deleting the table deletes its contents as well. If you must save the contents, I recommend converting the table instead of deleting it. See the preceding section.

Text in Tables

Text fills a table on a cell-by-cell basis. A cell can be empty or contain anything from a single letter to multiple paragraphs. The cell size automatically changes to accommodate larger quantities of text.

>> Within a cell, text is formatted just as it is elsewhere in Word, including margins and tabs.

>> Although a single cell can deftly handle vast quantities of text, graphics artists don't put a lot of text into a single cell. Consider another way to present such information.

>> I don't recommend formatting text inside a cell with first-line indents. Although it's possible, such formatting can be a pain to manipulate.

TIP

>> Show the ruler when you work with formatting text in a table: Click the View tab, and in the Show group, place a check mark by the Ruler item.

>> You can also perform math in tables, similar to what Excel does but without all the heartburn. Refer to the book *Word 2016 For Professionals For Dummies* (Wiley) for details on table math, headings, sorting, splitting, and spiffing up tables in an expert way.

Typing text in a table

Text appears in whichever cell the insertion pointer is blinking. Type some text and it wraps to fill the cell. Don't worry if it doesn't look right; you can adjust the cell size after you type the text, as described in the later section "Adjusting row and column size."

>> To move to the next cell, press the Tab key.

>> To move back one cell, press Shift+Tab.

TIP

>> Pressing Tab at the end of a row moves the insertion pointer to the first cell in the next row.

>> Pressing the Tab key while the insertion pointer is in the table's lower right cell adds a new row to the table.

>> To produce a tab character within a cell, press Ctrl+Tab. Even so:

>> I don't recommend putting tabs into table cells. It makes the cell formatting all funky.

>> When you press the Enter key in a cell, you create a new paragraph in the cell, which probably isn't what you want.

>> Use the Shift+Enter key combination (a soft return) to break up long lines of text in a cell.

Selecting in a table

Selecting within a table refers to selecting text but also cells, rows, columns, and the entire table. Here are my suggestions:

>> Triple-click in a cell to select all text in that cell.

>> Select a single cell by positioning the mouse pointer in the cell's lower left corner. The pointer changes to a northeastward-pointing arrow, as shown in the margin. Click to select the cell, which includes the cell's text but also the cell itself.

>> Move the mouse pointer into the left margin and click to select a row of cells.

>> Move the mouse pointer above a column, and click to select that column. When the pointer is in the sweet spot, it changes to a downward-pointing arrow (shown in the margin).

>> Clicking the table's handle selects the entire table. The handle is visible whenever the mouse points at the table or when the insertion pointer blinks inside the table.

If you have trouble selecting any part of a cell, click the Table Tools Layout tab. In the Table group, the Select button's menu provides commands to select the entire table, a row, a column, or a single cell.

Aligning text in a cell

Text in a cell sports some special, table–specific alignment options. To adjust the position of text in a cell, follow these steps:

1. **Click in the cell's text.**

2. **Click the Table Tools Layout tab.**

3. **In the Alignment group, click an icon representing the desired alignment.**

The Alignment group features nine icons representing nine position combinations: left, center, and right with top, middle, and bottom.

 Click the Alignment group's Text Direction button (shown in the margin) to change the way text reads in a cell. Keep clicking the button to reset the orientation.

Table Modification

No table is perfect. You may need to add or remove a row or column, adjust the width or height, or otherwise fine-tune and format the table. The tools to help you are found on two special tabs on the Ribbon: Table Tools Design and Table Tools Layout. To summon these tabs, click anywhere in a table. Then start making your adjustments.

The best time to format and fix a table is *after* you add text.

TIP

Adding or removing rows or columns

You can not only add rows and columns to any of a table's four sides but also squeeze new rows, columns, and even cells inside a table. The secret is to click the Table Tools Layout tab. In the Rows & Columns group, use the Insert buttons to add new rows and columns.

To remove a row or column, click to position the mouse, and then click the Table Tools Layout tab. In the Rows & Columns group, choose the proper command from the Delete button menu.

>> Rows and columns are added relative to the insertion pointer's position: First click to select a cell, and then choose the proper Insert command to add a row or column relative to that cell.

>> Refer to the earlier section "Selecting in a table" for information on selecting a row or column. Make that selection before choosing a Delete command to ensure that the proper row or column is removed.

>> When you choose the Delete ⇨ Delete Cells command, you see a dialog box asking what to do with the other cells in the row or column: Move them up or to the left. Also see the later sections "Merging cells" and "Splitting cells."

>> A mousey way to add a new row is to position the mouse pointer outside the table's left edge. A Plus (+) button appears, as shown in the margin. Click that button to insert a new row.

>> Likewise, if you position the mouse pointer at the table's top edge, click the Plus (+) button, shown in the margin, to insert a new column.

Adjusting row and column size

After text is in the table, you should adjust row height and column width to best present the information. This process works best *after* you've added text.

To automatically adjust the column width, position the mouse pointer at the left side of the column, just on the vertical border. The mouse pointer changes to the icon shown in the margin. Double-click and the column width is adjusted.

TIP

To adjust all column widths, put the mouse pointer at the far left vertical border in the table. Double-click.

To evenly distribute row and column sizes, click the Table Tools Layout tab. In the Cell Size group, click the Distribute Rows and Distribute Columns command buttons.

To oddly distribute row and column sizes, click the Auto Fit button, also found in the Cell Size group on the Table Tools Layout tab. Use the commands on the Auto Fit menu to choose how to adjust a table's row and column size.

The most common way to adjust rows and columns in a table is to use the mouse: Position the mouse pointer at the vertical or horizontal border within a table. When the pointer changes to a left–right or up–down pointy thing, drag to the left, right, up, or down to change the border's position.

Merging cells

The completely rational way to combine two cells into one or to split one cell into two is to use the table drawing tools. Heaven have mercy on you should you decide to merge or split cells in any other fashion.

To combine two cells, erase the line that separates them. Follow these steps:

1. **Click the Table Tools Layout tab.**

2. **In the Draw group, click the Eraser tool.**

   The mouse pointer changes to a bar of soap, shown in the margin, but it's supposed to be an eraser.

3. **Click the line between the two cells.**

   The line is gone.

4. **Click the Eraser tool again to quit merging.**

   Or you can tap the Esc key.

To merge a clutch of cells, select them and click the Merge Cells button. This button is found on the Table Tools Layout tab, in the Merge group, and shown in the margin.

Splitting cells

The easy way to turn one cell into two is to draw a line separating the cell. Follow these steps:

1. **Click the Table Tools Layout tab.**

2. **In the Draw group, click the Draw Table button.**

   The mouse pointer changes to the pencil pointer.

3. **Draw a line in the table to split a cell.**

   You can draw horizontally or vertically.

4. **Click the Draw Table button again when you're done.**

Any text in the cell you split goes to one side of the drawn line.

You can also split cells by selecting a single cell, and then choosing the Split Cells command from the Table Tools Layout tab's Merge group. Use the Split Cells dialog box to determine how to best mince up the cell.

Making the table pretty

Unless you want your table to look like it was made from hog wire, I recommend applying some table formatting. You can set the line's thickness, color, and style and apply color to the various rows and columns. The commands necessary are found on the Table Tools Design tab; click anywhere within a table to summon that tab on the Ribbon.

TIP

Rather than get bogged down with details, you should know that the spiffiest way to spruce up a table is to choose a preset format from the Table Styles gallery: Click inside the table, and then position the mouse pointer at a thumbnail in the gallery to see a preview. Click the thumbnail to apply that format to the table.

>> More thumbnails are available in the Table Styles gallery than are shown on the Ribbon: Scroll through the list or click the down-pointing arrow (below the scroll bar on the left) to view the full gallery.

>> If you'd rather format the table in a more painful manner, use the Shading button as well as the commands located in the Borders group. These are the same borders applied to a paragraph, as revealed in Chapter 18.

TIP

>> To remove the table's borders, select the table and choose No Border from the Borders menu. If you choose that format, the borders vanish, and it makes working with the table more difficult. Therefore, I recommend that you also select the table and choose the View Gridlines command from the Borders menu. Unlike borders, gridlines show up in the document window, but they don't print.

Adding a table caption

The best way to stick a title or caption on a table is to use Word's Insert Caption command. Don't bother trying to find that command on any of the Table Tools tabs. Instead, follow these steps:

1. Click in the table you want to caption.

2. Click the References tab.

3. Click the Insert Caption button.

The Caption dialog box appears.

4. Type the table's caption in the Caption text box.

The text *Table 1* might already appear. You cannot remove this text, so type a space after it and continue typing the table's caption.

TIP

If the text says *Figure 1* instead of *Table 1*, click the Label menu and choose Table. Or you can click the New Label button and concoct your own label.

5. Click the Position menu and choose whether to place the caption above or below the table.

6. Click OK to set the caption.

A benefit of using Word's Insert Caption command is that you can easily create a list of tables for a document. See Chapter 21 for details on building such a list.

Chapter **20**

Columns of Text

I f someone asks about columns and you immediately think of something written in a magazine or newspaper, you're a writer. If you think Doric, Ionic, and Corinthian, you're a history nerd. And if you think of rows of marching soldiers or rolling tanks, you're a military buff. What you probably don't think of are columns of text in a document, despite Word sporting such a clever formatting tool.

All about Columns

You probably don't think of a document's text as being formatted into a column, but it is. Word places all text on a page into columns. It's just that when you see only a single column of text, you don't think of it as anything odd – until you want more columns.

To set the number of text columns on a page, use Word's Columns command: Click the Layout tab, and in the Page Setup group, click the Columns button. A menu appears, listing common column-formatting options, as shown on the left in Figure 20-1.

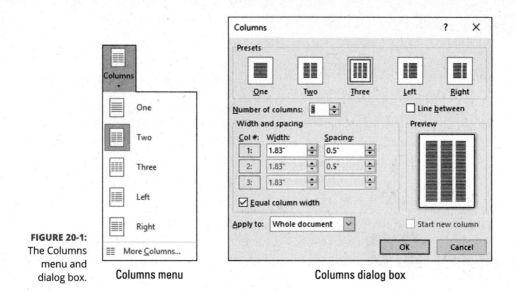

FIGURE 20-1:
The Columns menu and dialog box.

Columns menu   Columns dialog box

To be more specific with column layout, choose the More Columns command, at the bottom of the Columns menu. The Columns dialog box appears, as shown on the right in Figure 20-1.

The Columns dialog box helps you create and design multiple columns not available on the Columns menu: Use the Number of Columns box to set the quantity of columns desired. Use the Preview window to determine how the page is formatted. Click the OK button to apply the column format to the text.

TIP

>> When using multiple columns in a document, click the mouse to position the insertion pointer. That's because the keyboard's cursor-movement keys don't operate in a predictable manner when a document is formatted with more than one column of text.

>> The column is a page format. Choosing a column format from the Columns button menu affects the entire document, reformatting every page to the number of columns specified.

>> If you need to set different column formats on different pages, split the document into sections and apply the column format to only the current section. See Chapter 14 for more information on sections.

REMEMBER

>> When you're working with columns and notice that Word starts acting slow and fussy, *save your work!*

>> The maximum number of columns per page depends on the page size. Word's minimum column width is half an inch, so a typical sheet of paper can have up to 12 columns — not that such a layout would be appealing or anything.

>> Columns look best when using Print Layout view. Use this view when formatting columns. Columns don't show up well in Draft view.

Making 2-column text

When you desire to impress someone with your word processing prowess, I suggest putting two columns on the page. Any more columns and the text width would be too skinny and difficult to read. Two columns, however, is a great way to get fancy and remain legible, as shown in these steps:

1. **Click the Layout tab.**

2. **Click the Columns button and choose Two.**

You're done.

If the document already has text, it flows into two columns. If you create text after setting the number of columns, you see your scribblings flow down the left side of the page and then hop up to the upper right to start a new column.

TIP

>> To restore the document to one column, choose One from the menu (in Step 2).

>> Columns look best when full justification is applied to all paragraphs. The keyboard shortcut is Ctrl+J. See Chapter 11 for more information on paragraph alignment.

>> You can make specific column adjustments in the Width and Spacing area of the Columns dialog box. (Refer to Figure 20-1.)

>> If you want an attractive line to appear between the columns of text, visit the Columns dialog box and put a check mark in the Line Between box.

TECHNICAL
STUFF

>> The space between columns is called the *gutter*. Word sets a gutter width at 0.5" (half an inch). This amount of white space is pleasing to the eye without being too much of a good thing.

Building a trifold brochure

The 3-column text format works nicely on standard-size paper in Landscape mode. This method is how most trifold brochures are created. Obey these steps after you've written the document's text:

1. Click the Layout tab.

2. Choose Orientation ➪ Landscape.

The document's pages appear in landscape orientation, which is best for three columns of text and traditional for trifold brochures, programs, and documents.

3. Click the Columns button and choose Three.

Your trifold brochure is effectively formatted. Three columns are evenly spaced across the page, as illustrated in Figure 20-2.

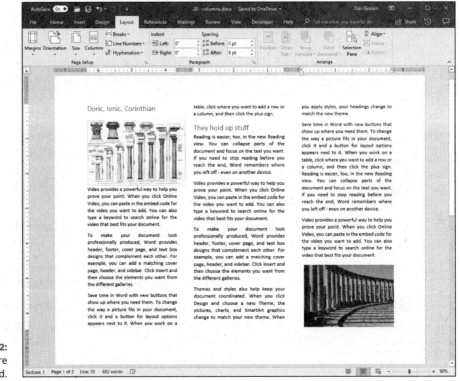

FIGURE 20-2:
Trifold brochure in Word.

For more sprucing up, use the Columns dialog box: On the Layout tab, click the Columns button and choose More Columns from the menu. In the dialog box, adjust the spacing between columns, add a line between, and perform other magic.

See Chapter 22 for information on sticking graphics into a document, such as those shown in Figure 20-2.

Giving up on columns

Converting a multicolumn document into a "normal," single-column document involves switching the page format back to one column:

1. **Click the Layout tab.**

2. **Click the Columns button and choose One.**

The document's text layout is restored.

When these steps don't work, summon the Columns dialog box (refer to Figure 20-1) and choose One from the list of presets. Ensure that Whole Document is chosen from the Apply To menu and then click the OK button. The columns are gone.

REMEMBER

» In Word, you don't remove column formatting as much as you choose the standard column format, One.

» Removing columns from a document doesn't remove sections or section breaks. See Chapter 14 for information on deleting section breaks.

Column Termination

You can stop the multicolumn format in one of several ways. For a newspaper column, the newspaper can go bankrupt. For Doric, Ionic, and Corinthian columns, civilization can collapse. For a military column, use a nuke. For a column of text, however, Word offers a number of tricks, none of which involves bankruptcy, revolution, or radiation.

Changing column formats

Your whole document need not sport a single column format. You can split things up so that part of the document is in one column and another part is in two columns and then maybe another part goes back to one column.

To change column formats at a specific spot in the text, follow these steps:

1. **Click to place the insertion pointer at the spot where you need the columns to change.**

2. **Click the Layout tab.**

3. **Click the Columns button and choose More Columns.**

   The Columns dialog box appears.

4. **Choose the new column format.**

   Click one of the presets or use the clicker thing to set a specific number of columns.

5. **From the Apply To drop-down list, choose This Point Forward.**

6. **Click OK.**

The text is broken at a specific point in the document (set in Step 1). Above that point, one column format is used; after that point, the format chosen in Step 4 is used.

TIP

>> To help you pull off this feat, Word inserts a continuous section break in the document.

>> If you really know section breaks, it's easier to add the section break first and then switch column formats. In the Columns dialog box, choose This Section from the Apply To drop-down list to apply the column format to the document's current section.

>> Refer to Chapter 14 for more information on section breaks.

Placing a column break

Just as you can break a page of text, in Word you can break a column. This *column break* works only on multicolumn pages. It forces the column's text to stop at some point down the page and then continue at the top of the next column.

In Figure 20-3, you see an example of a column break, inserted in the column on the left. That column break stops the left side column and continues the text at the top of the right column.

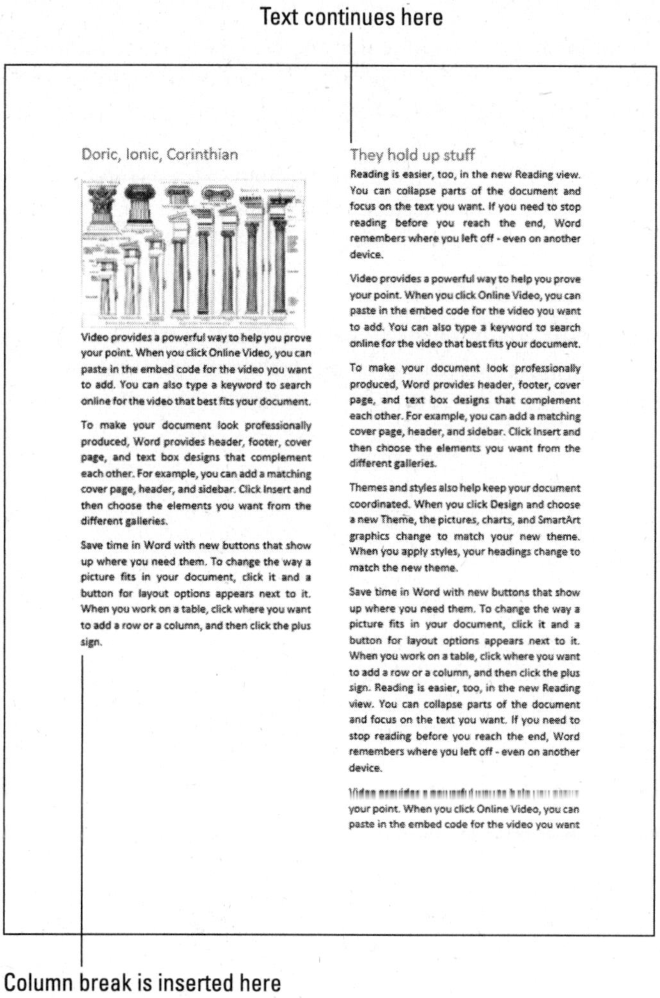

Text continues here

Doric, Ionic, Corinthian

They hold up stuff

Reading is easier, too, in the new Reading view. You can collapse parts of the document and focus on the text you want. If you need to stop reading before you reach the end, Word remembers where you left off - even on another device.

Video provides a powerful way to help you prove your point. When you click Online Video, you can paste in the embed code for the video you want to add. You can also type a keyword to search online for the video that best fits your document.

To make your document look professionally produced, Word provides header, footer, cover page, and text box designs that complement each other. For example, you can add a matching cover page, header, and sidebar. Click Insert and then choose the elements you want from the different galleries.

Themes and styles also help keep your document coordinated. When you click Design and choose a new Theme, the pictures, charts, and SmartArt graphics change to match your new theme. When you apply styles, your headings change to match the new theme.

Save time in Word with new buttons that show up where you need them. To change the way a picture fits in your document, click it and a button for layout options appears next to it. When you work on a table, click where you want to add a row or a column, and then click the plus sign. Reading is easier, too, in the new Reading view. You can collapse parts of the document and focus on the text you want. If you need to stop reading before you reach the end, Word remembers where you left off - even on another device.

Video provides a powerful way to help you prove your point. When you click Online Video, you can paste in the embed code for the video you want

Video provides a powerful way to help you prove your point. When you click Online Video, you can paste in the embed code for the video you want to add. You can also type a keyword to search online for the video that best fits your document.

To make your document look professionally produced, Word provides header, footer, cover page, and text box designs that complement each other. For example, you can add a matching cover page, header, and sidebar. Click Insert and then choose the elements you want from the different galleries.

Save time in Word with new buttons that show up where you need them. To change the way a picture fits in your document, click it and a button for layout options appears next to it. When you work on a table, click where you want to add a row or a column, and then click the plus sign.

FIGURE 20-3:
Column break.

Column break is inserted here

To break a column, heed these steps:

1. **Click to place the insertion pointer in your document.**

   The insertion pointer's location becomes the start of the next column.

2. **Click the Layout tab.**

3. **In the Page Setup group, click the Breaks button.**

   A menu appears.

4. **Choose Column.**

   The text hops to the top of the next column.

Column breaks don't end columns, switching from multicolumn text back to a single column. Instead, they split a column, ending text at a certain point on a page and starting the rest of the text at the top of the next column.

Use the Show/Hide command in the Home group (the Paragraph Mark button) to spy exactly where to place the column break. You might want to insert the column break *after* a paragraph mark (¶) to have the columns line up at the top of the page.

To remove a column break, switch to Draft view: Click the View tab and choose Draft. The column break appears in the text as a line by itself. Delete that line. Switch back to Print Layout view to examine your document's columns.

IN THIS CHAPTER

» **Automatically bulleting or numbering text**

» **Building a multilevel list**

» **Numbering lines on a page**

» **Adding a TOC to a document**

» **Creating an index**

» **Using footnotes and endnotes**

Chapter **21**

Lots of Lists

ists can be simple, such as a list of the various diets you've tried over the years. A list can be complex, such as a table of contents or an index or another, more professional, listy thing. In Word, you can type such lists manually, but it's better to use the proper tools. That way, a list of anything can be formatted automatically and updated as necessary. Add this tip to your list of timesavers.

Lists with Bullets and Numbers

Whenever you have more than two items to describe in a document, consider using one of Word's automatic list-formatting commands. These tools format the list in a way that draws attention, calling the items out from the rest of the text.

TIP

» Word's list commands are found on the Home tab, in the Paragraph group.

» You might find Word overly eager to format a list for you. The feature is called AutoFormat. See Chapter 33 for information on disabling this potentially annoying feature.

Making a bulleted list

In typesetting, a *bullet* is a graphical element, such as a ball or a dot, that highlights items in a list. The word *bullet* comes from the French word *boulette*, which has more to do with food than with round pieces of lead quickly exiting a firearm, like this:

» Bang!

» Bang!

» Bang!

To apply bullets to the text, drop the gun and select several paragraphs. On the Home tab, in the Paragraphs group, click the Bullets button, shown in the margin. Instantly, the text is not only formatted with bullets but also indented and made all neat and tidy.

TIP

» To choose a different bullet style, click the menu triangle next to the Bullets command. Select a new bullet graphic from the list, or use the Define New Bullet command to concoct your own bullet style.

» The bullet is a paragraph format. As such, bullets *stick* to the paragraphs you type until you remove that format.

» To remove bullets from the text, select the bulleted paragraphs and click the Bullet command button. You can stop applying bullets as you type by pressing the Enter key twice.

Numbering a list

To have word number a list, heed these directions:

1. **Write the text, the items in the numbered list.**

   Don't write the numbers at the start of each paragraph. Word does that for you in Step 3.

2. **Select the paragraphs as a block.**

3. **On the Home tab, in the Paragraph group, click the Numbering command button.**

   The button is shown in the margin. The Numbering command assigns a number to each paragraph, plus it formats the paragraphs with a hanging indent, which looks nice.

You can also click the Numbering command button and then type the list. Press the Enter key twice, or click the Numbering command button again to turn off automatic numbering.

As a bonus, if you insert or rearrange paragraphs in the list, Word automatically renumbers everything. This trick makes using the Numbering command better than trying to manually number and format the paragraphs.

>> To choose another numbering format, click the menu triangle next to the Numbering command button. You can choose letters or Roman numerals, or you can concoct a numbering scheme by choosing the command Define New Number Format.

>> The None number format removes numbering from a paragraph.

>> More details on numbering lists, including tips on resetting the starting number, can be found in the book *Word 2016 For Professionals For Dummies* (Wiley).

TIP

Creating a multilevel numbered list

A *multilevel* list consists of items and subitems all properly indented, similar to those presented in Figure 21-1. Word automatically formats such a list, but it's a tricky thing to do. Pay attention!

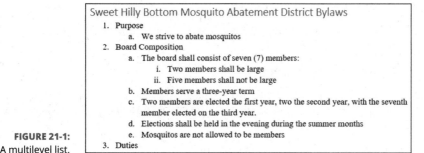

Sweet Hilly Bottom Mosquito Abatement District Bylaws
1. Purpose
    a. We strive to abate mosquitos
2. Board Composition
    a. The board shall consist of seven (7) members:
        i. Two members shall be large
        ii. Five members shall not be large
    b. Members serve a three-year term
    c. Two members are elected the first year, two the second year, with the seventh member elected on the third year.
    d. Elections shall be held in the evening during the summer months
    e. Mosquitos are not allowed to be members
3. Duties

FIGURE 21-1:
A multilevel list.

1. **Start typing the list.**

   Type the first, top-level item, such as the line that reads *Purpose* in Figure 21-1. You do not need to type the number (or letter) before this initial item.

2. **On the Home tab, in the Paragraph group, click the Multilevel List button.**

   The button is shown in the margin. Immediately, the first line grows one number or letter, depending on the list format.

3. **Continue typing the list.**

Press the Tab key to indent and create a sublevel. Press Shift+Tab to unindent and promote an item to a higher level. Word labels the paragraphs according to the multilevel list format.

You can also write the entire list in advance, select it, and then click the Multilevel List button to format it. As long as you use Tab and Shift+Tab to organize the topics, you don't break the format, and the list stays intact.

>> To change the list's format, select all paragraphs and then choose a new presentation from the Multilevel List menu.

>> Where you can get into trouble is when you try to edit the list, insert new items, or move items around. Unless you remember the trick about pressing Tab and Shift+Tab to format the list, things can get screwy. If so, reapply the multilevel list format, as explained in the preceding bullet.

TIP

>> If you're creating a complex, hierarchical list, use Word's Outline view instead of the multilevel list format. See Chapter 25.

Numbering lines on a page

Word lets you slap down numbers for every line on a page, a popular feature with those in the legal profession. Here's how it goes:

1. **Click the Layout tab.**

2. **In the Page Setup group, click the Line Numbers command button to display its menu.**

3. **Choose a numbering format.**

For example, to number lines on each page 1 through whatever, chose the Restart Each Page option. Or, to number all lines on all pages cumulatively, choose Continuous.

To remove the line numbers, choose None from the Line Numbers command button. Or choose Suppress for Current Paragraph if you don't want the selected paragraph numbered.

REMEMBER

Line numbering is a page-level format. It sticks to each page in the document. If you prefer to number only one page, set aside that page as its own section. See Chapter 14 for more information on sections.

Document Content Lists

One reason to obey some of Word's silly rules is that when things are done just so, you can easily construct a useful document content list. For example, when you use Word's heading styles (or properly created heading styles of your own), you can quickly create a table of contents. You can mark specific tidbits of text for inclusion in an instant index. And, if you bother with Word's Caption command, you can build a list of figures or tables. These feats would be excruciatingly difficult if attempted on your own in a manual manner.

Creating a table of contents

The trick to creating a quick table of contents, or TOC, for your document is to use Word's Heading styles. Use Heading 1 for main heads, Heading 2 for subheads, and Heading 3 for lower-level heads and titles. Word's Table of Contents command uses these formats to build a table-of-contents field, which reflects the heading names and their page numbers.

Providing that you've used the Heading (or equivalent) styles in your document, follow these steps to create a table of contents:

1. **Create a separate page for the TOC.**

    Word places the TOC field at the insertion pointer's location, though I prefer to have the thing on its own page. Refer to Chapter 13 for information on creating pages; a blank page near the start of the document is ideal for a TOC.

2. **Click the mouse to place the insertion pointer on the blank page.**

    The TOC field is inserted at that point.

3. **Click the References tab.**

4. **In the Table of Contents group, click the Table of Contents button.**

    The Table of Contents menu appears.

5. **Choose a format.**

    The TOC is created and placed in the document, page numbers and all.

A preset title may be applied, such as *Contents*. Feel free to edit the preset title to make it clever, such as *Table of Contents*. Do not format that title as a heading unless you want it included in the table of contents.

>> When the steps in this section don't produce the effect you intended, it usually means that the document doesn't use the Heading styles.

» If your document uses your own heading styles, ensure that the paragraph format specifies the proper outline level. See Chapter 15 for more information.

» If, instead of the TOC, you see a field such as **{ TOC \o "1-3" \h \z\ u }**, click the mouse in that ugly monster and press Alt+F9.

» The TOC field is static, so it doesn't reflect further edits in the document. To update the field, click once to select it. On the References tab, in the Table of Contents group, click the Update Table button. Use the Update Table of Contents dialog box to choose what to update. Click OK.

» Cool people in publishing refer to a table of contents as a *TOC*, pronounced "tee-oh-see" or "tock.")

» See Chapter 23 for more information about fields in a document.

Building an index

An index is yet another document reference or list, one that Word can help you build and format. The secret is to mark text in a document for inclusion in the index. Once words and phrases are marked, an index field is inserted, which displays the index.

Select index entries

To flag a bit of text for inclusion in an index, follow these steps:

1. **Select the text you want to reference.**

   The text can be a word or a phrase or any old bit of text.

2. **On the References tab in the Index group, click the Mark Entry button.**

   The selected text appears in the Mark Entry dialog box.

3. **If the entry needs a subentry, type that text in the Mark Index Entry dialog box.**

   The subentry further clarifies the main entry. For example, the word you select (the main entry) might be *boredom* and you type **In a waiting room** as the subentry.

4. **Click one of the buttons, either Mark or Mark All.**

   Click the Mark button to mark only the selected text. Click the Mark All button to direct Word to include all matching instances of the text in the document.

TECHNICAL STUFF

When you mark an index entry, Word activates the Show/Hide command, where characters such as spaces, paragraph marks, and tabs appear in the document. Don't let it freak you out.

Because Show/Hide is on, the Index code appears in the document. It looks something like this:

```
{·XE·"boredom"·}
```

5. **Continue scrolling the document and looking for items to mark for the index.**

   The Mark Index Entry dialog box remains open as you continue to build the index.

6. **Click the Close button when you're done, or just tired, to banish the Mark Index Entry dialog box.**

7. **Press Ctrl+Shift+8 to cancel the Show/Hide command.**

   Use the 8 key on the keyboard, not on the numeric keypad.

Place the index in the document

After you mark bits and pieces of text for inclusion in the index, the next step is to build and place the index. Do this:

1. **Position the insertion pointer where you want the index to appear.**

TIP

   If you want the index to start on a new page, create a new page in Word (see Chapter 13). I also recommend putting the index at the *end* of the document, which is what the reader expects.

2. **Click the References tab.**

3. **In the Index group, click the Insert Index button.**

   The Index dialog box appears. Here are my recommendations:

   - The Print Preview window is misleading. It shows how the index might look but doesn't use your actual index contents.

   - Use the Formats drop-down list to select a style for the index. Just about any choice from this list is better than the From Template example.

   - The Columns setting tells Word how many columns wide to make the index. The standard is two columns. I usually choose one column, which looks better on the page, especially for shorter documents.

   - I prefer to use the Right Align Page Numbers option.

4. **Click the OK button to insert the index into the document.**

   What you see is an index field, displayed using the information culled from the document. See Chapter 23 for more information on fields.

Review the index. Do it now. If you dislike the layout, press Ctrl+Z to undo and start over. Otherwise, you're done.

REMEMBER

If you modify a document, update its index: Click the index field. Then choose the Update Index command button from the Index group. Word updates the index to reference any new page numbers and includes freshly marked index entries.

>> Feel free to add a heading for the index, because Word doesn't do it for you.

>> Use a Heading style for the index header so that it's included in the document's table of contents. See the earlier section "Creating a table of contents."

>> Word uses continuous section breaks to place the index field in its own document section. Refer to Chapter 14 for more information on sections.

TECHNICAL
STUFF

Adding a list of figures

The References tab's groups help you insert other document lists, but only if you've created the list appropriately.

For example, you can create a table of figures, providing you've used the References tab's Caption button. To build the table of figures, click the Insert Table of Figures button. The process works similarly to inserting a table of contents or an index, but it works only when you've properly inserted the captions.

For full details on creating a list of figures, tables, or captions, obtain the book *Word 2016 For Professionals For Dummies* (Wiley).

Footnotes and Endnotes

Both footnotes and endnotes contain bonus information, clarifications, or asides to supplement text on a page. Each is marked by a superscripted number or letter in the text.[1]

---

[1] See? It orks!

The difference between a footnote and an endnote is in its placement: A footnote appears at the bottom of the *page*, and an endnote appears at the end of the *document*. Otherwise, both references are created in a similar way:

1. **Click the mouse so that the insertion pointer is to the immediate right of a word or some text that you want the footnote or endnote to reference.**

   There's no need to type the note's number; it's done automatically.

2. **Click the References tab.**

3. **From the Footnotes group, choose either the Insert Footnote or Insert Endnote command button.**

   A superscripted number is inserted into the text, and you're instantly whisked to the bottom of the page (footnote) or the end of the document (endnote).

4. **Type the footnote or endnote.**

5. **To return to where you last edited in the document, press Shift+F5.**

Here are some footnote/endnote notes:

>> The keyboard shortcut for inserting a footnote is Alt+Ctrl+F (F for *footnote*).

>> The keyboard shortcut for inserting an endnote is Atl+Ctrl+D (D for *da endnote*).

TECHNICAL STUFF

>> If you're curious, know that the keyboard shortcut Alt+Ctrl+E, which should be the Endnote command keyboard shortcut, actually enables and disables Word's Revision Marks feature, covered in Chapter 26.

>> The footnote and endnote numbers are updated automatically so that all footnotes and endnotes are numbered sequentially in the document.

>> To browse footnotes and endnotes, click the References tab. In the Footnotes group, use the Next Footnote button's menu to browse between footnote and endnote references.

>> You can preview a footnote's or endnote's contents by hovering the mouse pointer at the superscripted number in the document's text.

>> Use the Show Notes button (References tab, Footnotes group) to examine footnotes or endnotes as they appear on the page.

>> To delete a footnote or an endnote, highlight its reference number in the text and press the Delete key. Word magically renumbers any remaining footnotes or endnotes.

TIP

» To convert a footnote to an endnote, right-click the footnote's text at the bottom of the page. Choose the Convert to Endnote command. Likewise, you can convert endnotes to footnotes by right-clicking the endnote text and choosing the command Convert to Footnote.

» For additional control over footnotes and endnotes, click the Dialog Box Launcher button in the Footnotes group. Use the Footnote and Endnote dialog box to customize the reference text location, format, starting number, and other options.

Chapter **22**

Here Come the Graphics

t's sacrilege, of course. Word processing is about words. Images and words mix and mingle in the software realm of desktop publishing. Regardless, the mighty Microsoft Word allows you to slap down a picture, insert an object, edit images, and otherwise pretend it's some sort of graphics program. This trick might just save you 1,000 words, providing that you know how it works.

Graphical Goobers in the Text

The door to Word's graphical closet is found on the Insert tab. The command buttons nestled in the Illustrations group place various graphical goobers into the text. Here's how the process works for pictures and graphical images:

1. **Click the mouse at the spot in the text where you desire the image to appear.**

You don't need to be precise, because you can always move the image later.

2. **Click the Insert tab.**

3. **Use one of the command buttons to choose which type of image to add.**

   You can also paste a previously copied image, as described in the next section.

Figure 22-1 illustrates how a freshly added image looks, highlighting some of its features.

Image anchor   Rotation handle   Layout Options button

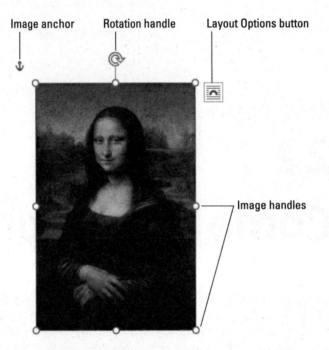

Image handles

FIGURE 22-1:
An image in a
document.

While the image is selected, a new tab appears on the Ribbon. For pictures, it's the Picture Tools Format tab; for other types of graphics, the Drawing Tools Format tab appears. Both tabs offer tools to help you perfect the recently inserted graphic. Later sections in this chapter cover using those tools, as well as the controls illustrated in Figure 22-1.

Beyond pictures and images, shapes are drawn on the page. In this case, they appear in front of or behind the text. Refer to the later section "Image Layout" for information on precise image placement.

>> To remove an image, click to select it and then tap the Delete key. If the graphical object, such as a shape, contains text, ensure that you've clicked the object's border before you tap the Delete key.

>> The more graphics you add in Word, the more sluggish it becomes. My advice: Write first. Add graphics last. Save often.

Copying and pasting an image

A simple way to stick an image into a document is to paste it in from elsewhere. Follow these steps:

1. **Select the image in another program or from the web.**

2. **Press Ctrl+C to copy the image.**

   For a web page image, right-click and choose the Copy or Copy Image command.

3. **Switch to the Word document window.**

   In Windows, press the Alt+Tab keyboard shortcut to deftly switch program windows.

4. **In Word, position the insertion pointer where you want the image to dwell.**

5. **Press Ctrl+V to paste the image into the document.**

If the image doesn't paste, it might be in a graphical format incompatible with Word.

 You can also obtain an image from the web directly, by performing a web image search from within Word: On the Insert tab, in the Illustrations group, click the Online Pictures button, shown in the margin. Use options in the Insert Pictures window to locate an online image, courtesy of Microsoft's Bing search engine.

Plopping down a picture

Your computer is most likely littered with picture files. No matter how the image was created, as long as it's found somewhere on your PC, you can stick it into your document. Follow these steps:

1. **Click the mouse in the text where you want the image to appear.**

2. **Click the Insert tab; in the Illustrations group, click the Pictures button.**

   After clicking the Pictures button, shown in the margin, the Insert Picture dialog box appears.

3. **Locate the image file on your PC's storage system.**

4. **Click to select the image.**

5. **Click the Insert button.**

   The image is slapped down in the document.

A nifty picture to stick at the end of a letter is your signature. Use a desktop scanner to digitize your John Hancock. Save the signature as an image file on your computer, and then follow the steps in this section to insert that signature picture in the proper place in the document.

Refer to the book *Word 2016 For Professionals For Dummies* (Wiley) for details on adding a caption to an image and creating a list of captions for the manuscript.

Slapping down a shape

Word comes with a library of common shapes ready to insert in a document. These include basic shapes, such as squares, circles, geometric figures, lines, and arrows — plus popular symbols. Graphics professionals refer to these types of images as *line art*.

To place some line art in a document, follow these steps:

1. **Click the Insert tab.**

2. **In the Illustrations group, click the Shapes button.**

   The button, shown in the margin, holds a menu that lists shapes organized by type.

3. **Choose a predefined shape.**

   The mouse pointer changes to a plus sign (+).

4. **Drag to create the shape.**

   The shape is placed into the document, floating in front of the text.

At this point, you can adjust the shape: Change its size, location, or colors. Use the Drawing Tools Format tab, conveniently shown on the Ribbon while the shape is selected, to affect those changes.

> » Instantly change the image by using the Shape Styles group on the Ribbon's Drawing Tools Format tab. Choose a new style from the Shape Gallery. Styles are related to the document's theme; see Chapter 16 for information on themes.

>> Other items in the Shape Styles group affect the selected shape specifically: Click the Shape Fill button to set the fill color; use the Shape Outline button to set the shape's outline color; choose an outline thickness from the Shape Outline button's menu, on the Weight submenu; use the Shape Effects button to apply 3D effects, shadows, and other fancy formatting to the shape.

TIP

>> To more effectively format a shape, click the Launcher in the lower right corner of the Shape Styles group. Use the Format Shape pane to manipulate settings for any selected shape in the document.

Sticking things into a shape

Shapes need not be clunky, colorful distractions. You can use a shape to hold text or a picture, which makes them one of the more flexible graphical goobers to add to a document.

To slip a smidgen of text into a shape, right-click the shape and choose the Add Text command. The insertion pointer appears within the shape. Type and format the text.

To place a picture into a shape, select the shape. Click the Drawing Tools Format tab. Click the Shape Fill button and choose the Picture menu item. Use the Insert Pictures window to hunt down an image to frame inside the shape.

>> Yes, it's possible to have both a picture and text inside a shape.

>> To further deal with text in a shape, click the shape and then click the Drawing Tools Format tab on the Ribbon. The Text group contains buttons to manipulate the shape's text.

>> To remove text from a shape, select and delete the text.

>> To remove a picture, select a solid color from the Shape Fill menu.

>> Also see Chapter 23 for information on text boxes, which are similar to shapes with text inserted.

Using WordArt

Perhaps the most overused graphic that's stuck into any Word document is WordArt. This feature is almost too popular. If you haven't used it yourself, you've probably seen it in a thousand documents, fliers, and international treaties. Here's how it works:

1. **Click the Insert tab.**

2. **In the Text group, click the WordArt button to display the WordArt menu.**

   The Word Art button is shown in the margin.

3. **Choose a style from the WordArt gallery.**

   A WordArt graphic placeholder appears in the document.

4. **Type the (short and sweet) text that you want WordArt-ified.**

Use the Word Art Styles group on the Drawing Tools Format tab to customize WordArt's appearance. If you don't see the Drawing Tools Format tab, first click the WordArt graphic.

TIP

Image Layout

To keep text and graphics living in harmony within a document, you must provide the proper layout options. These options control how the text and graphics interact, creating a visually impressive presentation where things don't look (to use graphics designer terminology) dorky.

In Word, layout options fall into three general categories:

>> **Inline:** The image is inserted directly into the text, just like a large, single character. It stays with the text, so you can press Enter to place it on a line by itself or press Tab to indent the image, for example.

>> **Wrapped:** Text flows around the graphic, avoiding the image like cheerleaders at a high school dance avoid the team from the chess club.

>> **Floating:** The image appears in front of or behind the text. Shapes (or line art) inserted in the document originally appear floating in front of the text.

To set image layout options, click to select an image and then click the Layout Options button. It appears to the upper right of a selected image (refer to Figure 22-1) and is shown in the margin. The Layout Options menu lists various layout settings, as illustrated in Table 22-1.

TABLE 22-1 ## Image Layout Options

Icon	Setting	What It Does
	Inline	The image acts like a character, moving with other text on the page.
	Square	Text flows around the image in a square pattern, regardless of the image's shape.
	Tight	Text flows around the image and hugs its shape.
	Through	Text flows around the image but also inside the image (depending on the image's shape).
	Top and Bottom	Text stops at the top of the image and continues below the image.
	Behind Text	The image floats behind the text, looking almost like the image is part of the paper.
	In Front of Text	The image floats on top of the text, like a photograph dropped on the paper.

Wrapping text around an image

For smaller images, or images that otherwise break up a document in an inelegant manner, choose one of the text-wrapping layout options. Heed these steps:

1. **Click to select the image.**

   A selected image appears with eight handles, as shown earlier, in Figure 22-1.

2. **Click the Layout Options button.**

   Word features four text-wrapping options, found in the With Text Wrapping area of the Layout Options menu. These options are Square, Tight, Through, and Top and Bottom, described in Table 22-1.

3. **Choose a text-wrapping option.**

Examine the image to see how text wraps around. If you're unpleased, repeat these steps and choose another layout option in Step 3.

To remove text wrapping, choose the Inline option from Step 3.

Floating an image

When you want an image to be placed in your document independently of the text, you float the image. The image can float in front of the text, like some little kid pasted a sticker on the page, or float behind the text, as if the image were part of the paper.

 To float an image, select it and then click the Layout Options button, as shown in the margin. Choose Behind Text or In Front of Text. Refer to Table 22-1 for the appropriate icons.

After choosing either Behind Text or In Front of Text, you see the image released from the confines of the text. The image floats freely, either behind or in front of the text.

Keeping an image with text

Graphics and images in Word belong to a specific paragraph in the text. It's as if the image is linked or anchored to a specific paragraph, which helps keep the document's graphics associated with the tidbit of text that references them.

 To see which paragraph belongs to an image, click to select the image. Then look for the Anchor icon, shown in the margin, next to a paragraph of text. To change paragraphs, drag this icon to another paragraph — hopefully, one that references the image. That way, if the paragraph moves to another page, the image moves with it.

To keep an image pasted to the same spot on a page, select the image and then click the Layout Options button. Choose the setting Fix Position on Page. The image becomes stuck on the page at a specific location regardless of how the text flows around it.

TIP

Image Editing

Word is not a graphics application or a photo-editor program. Yes, it's a word processor. Still, Word features a handful of commands to manipulate pictures and images in a document. For serious work, however, I recommend that you use an image-editing program or any application designed to manipulate graphics.

» Use Word's Undo command, Ctrl+Z, to undo any image editing boo-boos.

» When you're using a document theme, theme effects are automatically applied to any graphic inserted into your document. Refer to Chapter 16 for more information on themes.

Resizing an image

To make an image larger or smaller, heed these steps:

1. Select the image.

Click the image and it grows handles, as shown earlier, in Figure 22-1.

2. Drag one of the image's four corner handles inward or outward to make the image smaller or larger, respectively.

If you hold down the Shift key as you drag, the image is proportionally resized.

TIP

On the Picture Tools Format tab, in the Size group, you can use the Height and Width controls to nudge the image size vertically or horizontally or to type specific values for the image's size.

Cropping an image

In graphics lingo, *cropping* works like taking a pair of scissors to the image: You make the image smaller, but by doing so, you eliminate some content, just as an angry, sullen teen would use shears to remove his cheating scumbag former girl-friend from a prom picture. Figure 22-2 shows an example.

To crop an image in a document, put away those shears and obey these directions:

1. Click the image once to select it.

The Picture Tools Format tab appears on the Ribbon.

2. On the Picture Tools Format tab, in the Size group, click the Crop button.

The button is shown in the margin. After you choose this command, the image grows eight thick crop handles.

3. Drag one of the crop handles in or out to discard a portion of the image.

4. Press the Enter key to crop the image.

The portion of the image not contained within the crop handles is eliminated.

Portion discarded   Portion kept   Crop handles

FIGURE 22-2:
Cropping an
image.

I use the edge (left, right, top, or bottom) handles to crop. The corner handles never crop quite the way I want them to.

TIP

Rotating an image

You have two handy ways to rotate an image, neither of which involves turning the computer's monitor or craning your neck to the point of chiropractic necessity.

To freely rotate an image, use the mouse to grab the rotation handle at the top of the image. (Refer to Figure 22-1.) Drag the mouse to orient the image to any angle.

For more precise rotation, on the Picture Tools Format tab in the Arrange group, click the Rotate command button. From its menu, you can choose to rotate the image 90 degrees to the left or right or to flip the image horizontally or vertically.

Changing an image's appearance

To manipulate a selected image, click the Picture Tools Format tab and use the tools in the Adjust group. Specifically, use these tools: Corrections, Color, and Artistic Effects. As a bonus, each tool's button shows a menu full of options previewing how the image will be affected. To make the change, choose an option from the appropriate button's menu. Here are some suggestions:

» Brightness and contrast settings are made from the Corrections button menu.

» To wash out a picture you placed behind the text, click the Color button and choose the Washout color from the Recolor area.

» To convert a color image to monochrome (black and white), click the Color button and choose the first item in the menu, Saturation 0%.

» A slew of interesting, artistic brushstrokes and other effects are found on the aptly named Artistic Effects button menu.

Image Arrangement

Managing more than one image on a page can be toilsome, especially when the images overlap. You may find yourself unable to click an image to select it. Or maybe you prefer one image to be in front of the other, perfectly aligned, or you must move two images together. All these image-arranging tasks are made easier, thanks to special tools available in Word, providing you know where to find them and how they're used.

» To arrange images, click a graphic to summon the Picture Tools or Drawing Tools Format tab. For either tab, the tools you need are located in the Arrange group.

» To select multiple images, press and hold down the Shift key as you click each one.

TIP

Moving an image hither and thither

To relocate an image to a better spot, point the mouse at the image. The mouse pointer changes to a 4-way arrow, similar to what's shown in the margin. When you see this mouse pointer, drag the image nigh and yon.

» Point the mouse at the center of the image to drag. If you accidentally point at one of the image's handles, you resize the image.

» An image's layout options determine where and how you can move it. When an image floats behind the text, you may need to open up a spot in the text so that you can grab the image. To do so, position the mouse pointer by or on the same line as the image, and then whack the Enter key a few times. After moving the image, delete the extra blank paragraphs you created when you pressed the Enter key.

TIP

Aligning graphics

Image alignment is necessary to keep two or more graphical objects looking neat and tidy on the page. Especially when the images use a floating or wrapped layout, you want to ensure that they line up by the top edges, side to side, or centered.

To align graphics, follow these steps:

1. **Click the first image to select it.**

2. **Hold down the Shift key and click the rest of the images.**

3. **On the Picture Tools Format tab, in the Arrange group, click the Align Object button.**

   The button is shown in the margin. Click that button to display a menu of alignment choices.

4. **Choose an alignment command.**

   For example, choose Align Top to ensure that the top edge of both pictures will be aligned on the page.

If you'd rather eyeball the arrangement, activate Grid: Click the Align Object button and choose View Gridlines from the menu. Instantly, the page looks like it's a sheet of graph paper. Use the grid to help position multiple images. Choose the View Gridlines command again to hide the grid.

TIP The Distribute commands on the Align Object menu help you organize multiple images evenly across a page. For example, if you have three images left-to-right and you want to space them evenly, first align the images by choosing Align Middle. Then choose Distribute Horizontally to evenly space the images.

Shuffling images front or back

Graphics are plunked down on a page one atop the other. This arrangement is difficult to notice unless two images overlap, as shown in Figure 22-3. To change the order and shuffle images in front of or behind each other, click the Picture Tools Format tab, and in the Arrange group, use the Bring Forward or Send Backward commands.

To move one image in front of another, first click that image. Choose Bring Forward ⇨ Bring Forward to shuffle that image forward one position. To bring the image in front of all other images, choose Bring Forward ⇨ Bring to Front.

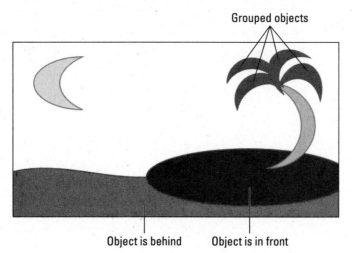

Grouped objects

Object is behind   Object is in front

Likewise, use the Send Backward⇨ Send Backward or Send Backward⇨ Send to Back commands to shuffle an image to the background.

Grouping images

When you use smaller shapes to cobble together a complex image, use the Group command to keep those items together. That way, you can move them as a single unit, copy and paste them, and apply image effects to the entire group.

 To group two or more graphical objects in a document, select the images: Click the first one, and then press and hold the Shift key as you click other images. When the group is selected, on the Picture Tools Format tab, in the Arrange Group, click the Group button and choose the Group command. The images are then treated as a unit, such as the palm tree shown earlier, in Figure 22-3, which is a collection of individual shapes.

To ungroup, click the grouped images and then choose the Ungroup command from the Group menu.

Chapter **23**

Insert Tab Insanity

Aside from formatting, everything from text to graphics that's put into a Word document is inserted. That makes me curious why the magicians at Microsoft sought to dedicate a tab on the Ribbon to the topic of Insert. What weird, wonderful, and wanted buttons could crowd that tab's various groups — especially those items not covered elsewhere in this book.

Characters Foreign and Funky

The computer's keyboard lets you type all 26 letters of the alphabet — plus numbers, a smattering of symbols, and punctuation thingies. Writers weave these characters into a tapestry of text heretofore unseen in literary history. As if that weren't enough, you can sprinkle even more characters into the document, those not directly found on a computer keyboard, spicing up your document like garlic in a salad.

Nonbreaking spaces and hyphens

The space and the hyphen characters are special in Word. They're used to wrap a line of text: The space splits a line between two words, and the hyphen (using hyphenation) splits a line between a word's syllables.

When you don't want a space or hyphen to split a line of text, you use one of the unbreakables:

>> The nonbreaking hyphen character is Ctrl+Shift+ – (hyphen).

>> The nonbreaking space is Ctrl+Shift+spacebar.

For example, if you don't want a phone number split between two lines, press Ctrl+Shift+– (hyphen) instead of the standard hyphen. And when two words must remain together in a paragraph, use Ctrl+Shift+spacebar to marry them.

Typing characters such as Ü, Ç, and Ñ

You can be boring and type *deja vu* or be all fancy and type *déjà vu* or *café* or *résumé*. Such tricks make your readers think that you know your stuff, but what you really know is how to use Word's diacritical mark keys.

Diacritical is not an urgent medical situation. Instead, it's a term that refers to symbols appearing over certain letters. Foreign languages use diacritical marks, such as the examples used in the preceding paragraph.

To create a diacritical mark in Word, you press a special Control-key combination prefix. The prefix somewhat represents the diacritical mark you need, such as Ctrl+' to produce the ' diacritical mark. The Ctrl-key combination is followed by the character that needs the new "hat," as shown in Table 23-1.

For example, to insert an é into a document, press Ctrl+' and then type uppercase E for É or lowercase e for é. This shortcut makes sense because the apostrophe (') is essentially the diacritical mark you're adding to the vowel.

REMEMBER

>> The apostrophe (or tick) and the accent grave (or back tick) are two different characters found at two different locations on the keyboard.

>> For the Ctrl+@, Ctrl+:, Ctrl+^, and Ctrl+~ key combinations, you must also press the Shift key. Therefore, Ctrl+~ is really Ctrl+Shift+`.

>> Word's AutoCorrect feature recognizes a few special characters. For example, when you type *café,* Word automatically sticks that whoopty-doop over the e.

TABLE 23-1 **Those Pesky Foreign Language Characters**

Prefix Key	Characters Produced
Ctrl+'	á é í ó ú
Ctrl+`	à è ì ò ù
Ctrl+,	ç
Ctrl+@	å
Ctrl+:	ä ë ï ö ü
Ctrl+^	â ê î ô û
Ctrl+~	ã õ ñ
Ctrl+/	ø

Inserting special characters and symbols

On the far right side of the Insert tab dwells the Symbols group. Two items reside in that group: Equation and Symbol. (If the window is too narrow, you see the Symbols button, from which you can choose Equation or Symbol.) Click the Symbol button to see some popular or recently used symbols. Choose a symbol from the menu to insert the special symbol directly into the text.

To see a horde of available symbols and characters, click the Symbol button and choose the More Symbols command. The Symbol dialog box appears, as shown in Figure 23-1. Choose a decorative font, such as Wingdings, from the Font menu to see strange and unusual characters. To see the gamut of what's possible with normal text, choose (normal text) from the Font drop-down list. Use the Subset drop-down list to see specific symbols and such.

To stick a character into the document from the Symbol dialog box, select the symbol and click the Insert button.

REMEMBER

You must click the Cancel button when you're done using the Symbol dialog box.

>> Click the Insert button once for each symbol you want to insert. For example, when you're putting three Σ (sigma) symbols into the document, you must locate that symbol on the grid and then click the Insert button three times.

>> Some symbols have shortcut keys, which appear at the bottom of the Symbol dialog box. (Refer to Figure 23-1.) For example, the shortcut for the degree symbol (°) is Ctrl+@, spacebar — press Ctrl+@ (actually, Ctrl+Shift+2) and then type a space.

Highlighted symbol

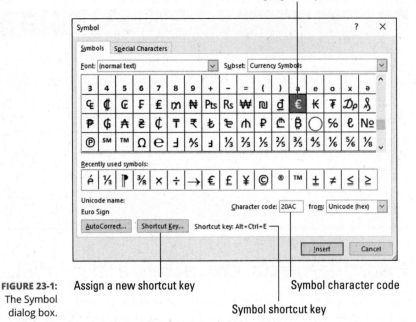

FIGURE 23-1:
The Symbol
dialog box.

Assign a new shortcut key

Symbol character code

Symbol shortcut key

**TECHNICAL
STUFF**

» You can insert symbols by typing the symbol's character code and then pressing the Alt+X keyboard shortcut. For example, the character code for Σ (sigma) is 2211: Type **2211** in the document and then press Alt+X. The number 2211 is magically transformed into the Σ character. The character code appears in the Symbol dialog box, as illustrated in Figure 23-1.

Spice Up a Document with a Text Box

A *text box* is a graphical element that contains — hold your breath, wait for it, wait — *text*. The text is used as a decorative element (commonly called a *pull quote* or *callout*) to highlight a passage of text on the page, or it can be an information box or an aside, such as those elements that litter the pages of *USA Today*. The primary purpose of the text box is to prevent your document from becoming what graphic designers refer to as the dreaded Great Wall of Text.

To shove a text box into a document, follow these steps:

1. Click the Insert tab.

2. In the Text group, choose Text Box.

3. **Choose a preformatted text box from the list.**

   The text box is splashed onto the current page in your document.

4. **Rewrite the text in the box.**

   La-di-da.

Even though it's stuffed with text, a text box is a graphical element. As such, when it first appears in your document, or any time it's selected, the Drawing Tools Format tab appears on the Ribbon. This tab hosts a garrison of text box formatting and style commands.

Other text in the document wraps around the text box. As such, you can drag the text box (by its edge) to any position on the page. You can set the layout options for the text box just as you would for any graphical goober in the document; options are presented in Chapter 22.

TIP

>> It's common to copy and paste text from the document into the box, which is how pull quotes work.

>> To change text orientation within the text box, click the box and then click the Drawing Tools Format tab. In the Text group, click the Text Direction button to peruse orientation options.

>> To delete a text box, click its edge (so that the box is selected, not its text) and press the Delete key.

Fun with Fields

What you write in Word isn't carved in stone — well, unless you have a cool printer I've not heard of. Still, the text you scribble remains static until you change it or until the computer screws up.

To liven things up a tad, Word lets you add *dynamic* elements to a document. Unlike the text you normally compose, dynamic text changes to reflect a number of factors. To add these dynamic elements to a document, you use a Word feature called *fields*.

Understanding fields

Word's dynamic field feature is part of the Quick Parts tools. To add a field to a document, click the Insert tab and in the Text group, click the Quick Parts button, shown in the margin. Choose the Field command to behold the Field dialog box, shown in Figure 23-2.

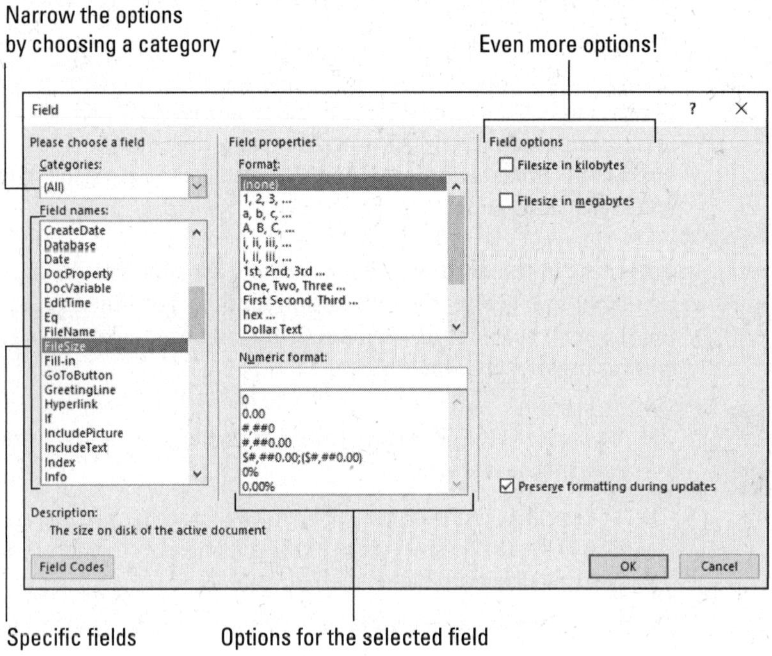

Narrow the options
by choosing a category

Even more options!

FIGURE 23-2:
The Field
dialog box.

Specific fields   Options for the selected field

The scrolling list on the left side of the Field dialog box shows categories. These represent various dynamic nuggets you can insert in a document. Choose a specific category to narrow the list of Field Names.

The center and right part of the dialog box contain formats, options, and other details for a selected field. (Examples are described in the sections that follow.)

To insert the field, click the OK button. The field appears just like other text, complete with formatting and such, but the information displayed changes to reflect whatever the field represents. For example, a page number field always shows the current page.

TIP

When the insertion pointer is placed inside a field, the text is highlighted with a dark gray background. It's your clue that the text is a field and not plain text. Also see the later section "Deleting fields."

Adding some useful fields

Word offers an abundance of fields you can thrust into a document. Of the lot, you might use only a smattering. My favorites are listed in this section.

These subsections assume that the Fields dialog box is open, as described in the preceding section.

Page numbers

To ensure that the document accurately reflects the current page number, insert a current page number field:

1. In the Field dialog box, select Numbering from the Categories drop-down list.

2. Select Page from the Field Names list.

3. In the Field Properties section of the Field dialog box, select a format for the page number.

4. Click OK.

The current page number appears in the document. No matter how you edit or modify the document, that number reflects the current page number.

Total number of pages

To insert the total number of pages in a document, heed these directions:

1. Select Document Information from the Categories drop-down list.

2. Select NumPages from the Field Names list.

3. Select a format.

4. Click OK.

Word count

Getting paid by the word? Stick an automatic word count at the end of the document:

1. From the Categories list, select Document Information.

2. Select NumWords from the Field Names list.

3. Click OK.

Document filename

Many organizations place the document's filename into a document header or footer. Rather than guess, why not use a field that contains the document's exact name? Do this:

1. From the Categories list, select Document Information.
2. Select FileName from the Field Names list.
3. In the field properties list, choose a text case format.
4. Optionally (though recommended), put a check mark by the option Add Path to Filename.
5. Click OK.

The FileName field always reflects the name of the file, even when you change it.

Updating a field

Not every field updates automatically, like the page number fields. For some fields, you must perform a manual update to keep the content fresh. To do so, right-click the field and choose the Update Field command. The field's text is refreshed.

REMEMBER

Printing fields update when you print the document. They don't need to be manually updated.

Changing a field

When you don't get the field's text quite right — for example, you desire a date format that displays the weekday name instead of an abbreviation — right-click the field and choose the Edit Field command. Use the Field dialog box to make whatever modifications you deem necessary.

Viewing a field's raw data

TECHNICAL STUFF

Just as those mutants at the end of *Beneath the Planet of the Apes* removed their human masks, you can remove a field's mask by right-clicking it and choosing the Toggle Field Codes command. For example, the FileSize field looks like this:

```
{ FILESIZE \* MERGEFORMAT }
```

To restore the field to human-readable form, right-click it again and choose the Toggle Field Codes command. The keyboard shortcut is Alt+F9. All praise be to the bomb.

THE MYSTERY OF CONTENT CONTROLS

Word's fields aren't the only dynamic text gizmos you can stick into a document. Another changing goober is the content control. It's not really a field, though it can be inserted and updated in a similar manner. The primary difference is how a content control looks, which is something like this:

$$V = \frac{4}{3}\pi r^3$$

Content controls are usually inserted by Word commands, such as those that automatically create headers or footers or insert page numbers. On the Insert tab, in the Text group, you can choose Quick Parts ⇨ Document Property to insert a property control. The Equation menu, found in the Insert tab's Symbols group, also inserts content controls.

For more information on content controls, including those fill-in-the-blanks items you frequently find in document templates, refer to the book *Word 2016 For Professionals For Dummies* (Wiley).

Deleting fields

Removing a field works almost like deleting text. Almost. The main difference is that you must press the Delete or Backspace key twice.

For example, when you press Backspace to erase a field, the entire field is highlighted. It's your clue that you're about to erase a field, not regular text. Press Backspace again to remove the field.

The Date and Time

With few exceptions, time travelers are the only ones who bother asking for the current year. Otherwise, people merely want to know the month and day or just the day of the week. Word understands those people (but not time travelers), so it offers a slate of tools and tricks to insert date-and-time information into a document.

Adding the current date or time

Rather than look at a calendar and type a date, follow these steps:

1. **Click the Insert tab.**

2. **In the Text group, click the Date and Time button.**

   The button may say Date & Time, or you may see only the icon, shown in the margin.

3. **Use the Date and Time dialog box to choose a format.**

4. **If desired, click the Update Automatically option so that the date-and-time text remains current with the document.**

   Setting the Update Automatically ensures that the date and time values are updated when you open or print the document.

5. **Click the OK button to insert the current date or time into the document.**

The keyboard shortcut to insert the current date is Alt+Shift+D. To insert the current time, press Alt+Shift+T.

Using the PrintDate field

TIP

The date field I use most often is PrintDate. This field reflects the current date (and time, if you like) when a document prints. It's marvelous for including in a letterhead template or in another document you print frequently. Here's how it works:

1. **Click the Insert tab.**

2. **In the Text group, click Quick Parts ⇨ Field.**

   The Field dialog box, which is covered earlier in this chapter, appears.

3. **Select Date and Time from the Categories drop-down list.**

4. **Select PrintDate from the Field Names list.**

5. **Choose a date-and-time format from the Field Properties area.**

6. **Click OK.**

The field looks odd until you print the document, which makes sense. Also, the field reflects the last day you printed the document. It's updated when you print again.

5

The Rest of Word

IN THIS CHAPTER

» **Working with more than one document at a time**

» **Comparing documents side by side**

» **Seeing one document in two windows**

» **Splitting the screen**

» **Opening a non-Word document**

» **Converting older Word documents**

Chapter **24**

Multiple Documents, Windows, and File Formats

Y ou need not limit your word processor usage to toiling with one document in a single window. Oh, no! You can open multiple documents, working on the lot and moving from window to window at your whim. You can even split a single document into two views in a single window, or open one document in two windows. Word does it all, plus it lets you work with documents in strange and alien non–Word formats.

Multiple Document Mania

It's not a question of whether Word can work on more than one document at a time. No, it's a question of how you open those documents. Let me count the ways:

> » **Keep using the Open command to open documents.** No official limit exists on the number of documents Word can have open, though if you open too many (say, more than 9) your computer's performance may suffer.

>> **In the Open dialog box, select multiple documents to open.** Press and hold the Ctrl key as you click to select documents. Click the Open button, and all the documents open like flowers, each in its own pot (window).

>> **From any folder window, select multiple Word document icons.** Lasso them with the mouse, or Ctrl+click to select multiple documents. Press the Enter key to open the lot.

Each document dwells in its own Word program window. To switch between windows, click one, or choose one by clicking the Word icon on the Windows taskbar.

TIP

To switch windows in Word, follow these steps:

1. **Click the View tab.**

2. **In the Window group, click the Switch Windows button.**

The Switch Windows button is shown in the margin.

3. **Choose a document from the menu.**

Because some folks are insane enough to have more than nine documents open at a time, the last command on the Switch Windows menu is More Windows. Choose this item to view the Activate dialog box, which lists *all* open document windows. Select a document from the window and click OK to switch to it.

WARNING

>> Should you spy any document in the list named Document1, Document2, or similar, that document is unsaved! Immediately switch to that window and save before it's too late!

>> Refer to Chapter 8 for details on opening and saving Word documents.

Arranging open document windows

To see two or more documents displayed on the screen at the same time, select the View tab and click the Arrange All button, shown in the margin. Immediately, Word organizes all its windows. They're arranged like the pieces of fabric in a quilt.

>> The Arrange All command works best when only a few documents are open. Otherwise, the document windows are too small to be useful.

>> Word doesn't arrange minimized windows.

>> Though you can see more than one document at a time, you can *work* on only one at a time. The document with the highlighted title bar is the one "on top."

REMEMBER

Comparing two documents side by side

A nifty way to review two documents is to arrange them side by side. Both documents are visible on the screen, and their scrolling is locked so that you can peruse both in parallel. Here's how to accomplish this trick:

1. **Open both documents.**

2. **On the View tab, in the Window group, click the View Side by Side button.**

    The View Side by Side button is shown in the margin. After you click this button, Word arranges both documents in vertical windows.

3. **Scroll either document.**

    Scrolling one document also scrolls the other. In this mode, you can compare two different or similar documents.

    You can disable synchronous scrolling by clicking the Synchronous Scrolling button, found in the Window group.

TIP

4. **When you're done, choose View Side by Side again.**

Also see Chapter 26, which covers reviewing changes made to a document.

Viewing one document in multiple windows

A handy document-viewing trick — especially for long documents — is to open a single document in two windows. This perspective makes writing and editing easier than hopping back and forth within the same document window and potentially losing your place.

To open a second window on a single document, obey these steps:

1. **Click the View tab.**

2. **In the Window group, click the New Window button.**

    After you click the New Window button, shown in the margin, a second window opens, showing the current document.

To confirm that the same document is open in two windows, check the title bar: The first window's filename is followed by :1, and the second window's filename is followed by :2.

When you no longer need the second window, simply close it. You can close either window :1 or :2; it doesn't matter. The document is still open and available for editing in the other window.

REMEMBER

» Don't be fooled by the two windows! You're still working on only one document. The changes you make in one window are updated in the second.

» This feature is useful for cutting and pasting text or graphics between sections of a long document.

» You can even open a third window by choosing the New Window command again, but that's just nuts.

Using the old split-screen trick

Splitting the screen allows you to view two parts of your document in the same window. No need to bother with extra windows here: The top part of the window shows one part of the document; the bottom part, another. Each half of the screen scrolls individually, so you can peruse different parts of the same document without switching windows.

To split a window, heed these directions:

1. **Click the View tab.**

2. **In the Window group, click the Split Window button.**

A line bisects the document, splitting it from side to side, as illustrated in Figure 24-1. If the ruler is visible, a copy appears for both document splits.

You can scroll the top or bottom part of the document independently. That way, you can peruse or edit different parts of the document in the same window.

To undo the split, choose the Remote Split command from the Window group. (This command replaces the Split command). Or, you can double-click the line separating the document.

TIP

The split line is adjustable; drag it up or down to change the split proportions.

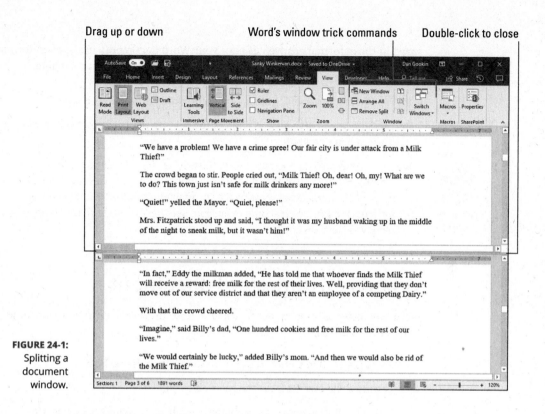

Drag up or down   Word's window trick commands   Double-click to close

FIGURE 24-1:
Splitting a
document
window.

Many, Many Document Types

Word begrudgingly recognizes that it's not the only word processor and that its document file type isn't the only one. As such, the program condescends to allow for the accommodation of lesser, mortal document formats. This feature allows you to read and edit non-Word documents as well as share documents with non-Word users, who aim to be blessed by Word's beneficence.

Understanding document formats

When you save a document, Word places the document's text, formatting, and other information into a file. To keep the information organized, Word uses a specific *file format*. The file format makes a Word document unique and different from other types of files languishing on your computer's storage system.

Word's document format is popular, but it's not the only word processing document format available. Other word processors, as well as document utilities such as Adobe Acrobat, use their own formats. Word permits you to open documents saved in those formats as well as save your Word documents in the alien formats. I'm not certain whether the software is pleased to do so, but it's capable.

>> Basic document opening and saving information is found in Chapter 8.

>> The best way to save a file in another format is to use the Export command, discussed in Chapter 9.

TECHNICAL STUFF

>> The standard Word document format uses the .docx filename extension. This extension is applied automatically to all Word documents you save, though it may not be visible when viewing files in a folder. The older Word document format used the .doc filename extension. See the later section "Updating an older Word document."

Opening a non-Word document

Word can magically open and display a host of weird, non-Word documents. Here's how it works:

1. **Press Ctrl+F12 to summon the traditional Open dialog box.**

2. **Choose a file format from the menu button.**

The menu button has no label, though it might say All Word Documents, as shown in Figure 24-2.

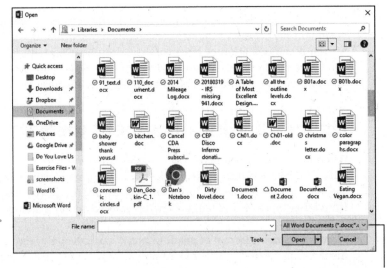

FIGURE 24-2: Change file types in the Open dialog box.

File type menu

When you choose a specific file format, Word narrows the number of files displayed in the Open dialog box; only files matching the specific file format are shown.

TIP

If you don't know the format, choose All Files from the drop-down list.

3. **Click to select the file.**

Or, work the controls in the dialog box to find another storage media or folder that contains the file.

4. **Click the Open button.**

The alien file appears onscreen, ready for editing, just like any other Word document — or not. Word tries its best to open other file formats, but it may not get everything 100 percent okey–doke.

>> For some document types, Word displays a file conversion dialog box. Use the controls to preview the document, though clicking the OK button is usually your best bet.

>> The Recover Text from Any File option is useful for peering into unknown files, especially from antique and obscure word processing file formats.

WARNING

>> Word *remembers* the file type! When you use the Open dialog box again, the same file type is already chosen from the Files of Type drop-down list. That means your regular Word document may be opened as a plain-text document, which looks truly ugly. Remember to check the Files of Type drop-down list if such a thing happens to you.

REMEMBER

>> Accordingly, when you open a Word document after opening an HTML document, or especially when using the Recover Text from Any File option, you *must* choose Word Documents from the list. Otherwise, Word may open documents in a manner that seems strange to you.

>> You may see a warning when opening a document downloaded from the Internet. Word is just being safe; the document is placed into Protected view. You can preview the document, but to edit it, you need to click the Enable Editing button.

>> Don't blame yourself when Word is unable to open a document. Many, many file formats are unknown to Word. When someone is sending you this type of document, ask the person to resend it using a common file format, such as HTML or RTF.

Updating an older Word document

Microsoft Word has been around for ages. It's used the same .doc file format since the early days, back when Word ran on steam-powered computers that took three people to hoist onto a table.

In 2007, Word changed its document file format. Gone was the .doc format, replaced by the .docx format. Because a lot of people still use older versions of Word, and given the abundance of older .doc files still available, it became necessary to work with and convert those older documents.

Working with an older Word document is cinchy: Open the document. You see the text *[Compatibility Mode]* after the filename at the top of the window. This text is a big clue that you're using an older Word document. Another clue is that a lot of Word's features, such as the capability to preview format changes and document themes, don't work when editing an older document.

To update an older document, follow these steps:

1. **Click the File tab.**

2. **On the Info screen, click the Convert button.**

   The Convert button is shown in the margin. After you click it, a descriptive dialog box appears. If not, skip to Step 5.

3. **In the Microsoft Word dialog box, click to place a check mark by the item Do Not Ask Me Again about Converting Documents.**

4. **Click the OK button.**

5. **Click the Save button to save the document.**

   Use the Save As dialog box as covered in Chapter 8. If you look at the File Type menu, you see that the chosen file format is Word Document (*.docx). The document is updated.

The older document isn't removed when you follow these steps, though you're free to delete it.

See Chapter 8 if you desire to save a current document in the older Word file format.

Chapter **25**

Word for Writers

The word processor is the best tool for writers since the ghostwriter. Of course, cobbling together words in a word processor doesn't make you a writer any more than working with numbers in a spreadsheet makes you an accountant. Even so, beyond its basic word processing capabilities, Word comes with an armada of tools for making a writer's job easier. Whether you're writing your first guest piece for the church newsletter or crafting your 74th horror-thriller, you'll enjoy Word's features for writers.

Organize Your Thoughts

Good writers use an outline to organize their thoughts. Back in the old days, an outline would dwell on a stack of 3-by-5 cards. Today, an outline is a Word document, which makes it easier to not confuse your outline with grandma's recipes.

Word's Outline view presents a document in a unique way. It takes advantage of Word's heading styles to help you group and organize thoughts, ideas, or plotlines in a hierarchical fashion. Outline tools make it easy to shuffle around topics, make subtopics, and mix in text to help organize your thoughts. Even if you're not a writer, you can use Word's Outline mode to create lists, work on projects, or look busy when the boss comes around.

Entering Outline view

To enter Outline view, click the View tab, and in the Views group, click the Outline button, shown in the margin. The document's presentation changes to show Outline view, and the Outlining tab appears on the Ribbon, as shown in Figure 25-1.

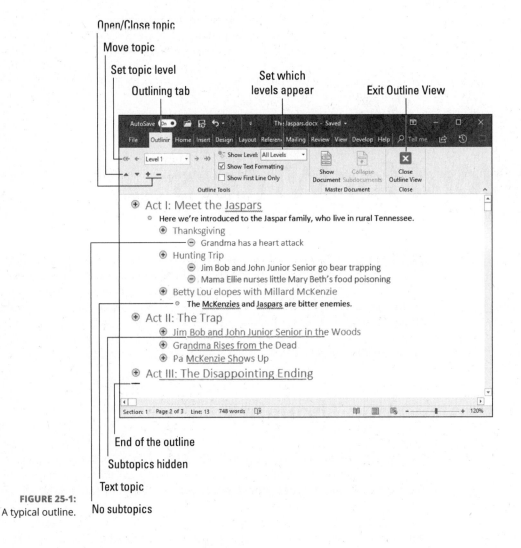

Open/Close topic

Move topic

Set topic level

Outlining tab

Set which levels appear

Exit Outline View

End of the outline

Subtopics hidden

Text topic

No subtopics

FIGURE 25-1:
A typical outline.

To exit Outline view, click the View tab and choose another document view. You can also click the big, honkin' Close Outline View button (labeled in Figure 25-1).

>> A squat, horizontal bar marks the end of the outline. You cannot delete that bar.

>> All basic Word commands work in Outline view. You can use the cursor keys, delete text, check spelling, save, insert oddball characters, print, and so on.

>> Don't worry about the text format in Outline view; outlining is not about formatting.

>> Word uses the Heading 1 through Heading 9 styles for the outline's topics. Main topics are formatted in Heading 1, subtopics in Heading 2, and so on.

>> Use the Body or Normal style to make notes or add text to the outline. See the section "Adding a text topic," later in this chapter.

REMEMBER

>> An outline isn't a special type of document; it's a different *view*. You can switch between Outline view and any other view and the document's contents don't change.

Typing topics in the outline

Outlines are composed of topics and subtopics. *Topics* are main ideas; *subtopics* describe the details. Subtopics can contain their own subtopics, going down to several levels of detail. The amount of detail you use depends on how organized you want to be.

To create a topic, type the text. Word automatically formats the topic using a specific heading style based on the topic level, as shown in Figure 25-2.

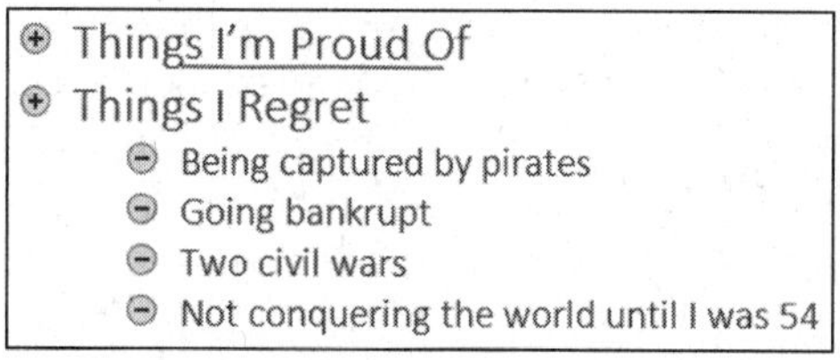

⊕ Things I'm Proud Of
⊕ Things I Regret
⊖ Being captured by pirates
⊖ Going bankrupt
⊖ Two civil wars
⊖ Not conquering the world until I was 54

FIGURE 25-2:
Topics in an
outline.

Keep the main topic levels short and descriptive. Deeper topics can go into more detail. Press the Enter key when you're done typing one topic and want to start another.

>> Use the Enter key to split a topic. For example, to split the topic Pots and Pans, replace the word *and* with a press of the Enter key.

>> To join two topics, press the End key to send the insertion pointer to the end of the first topic. Then press the Delete key. This method works just like joining two paragraphs in a regular document.

>> Don't worry about organizing the outline when you first create it. In Word's Outline view, you can rearrange topics as your ideas solidify. My advice is to start writing things down now and concentrate on organization later.

TIP

Rearranging topics

Outlines are fluid. As you work, some topics may become more important and others less important. To these changes, you can move a topic up or down:

>> Click the Move Up button (or press Alt+Shift+↑) to move a topic up a line.

>> Click the Move Down button (or press Alt+Shift+↓) to move a topic down a line.

You can also drag a topic up or down: Point the mouse pointer at the circle to the topic's left. When the mouse is positioned just right, the mouse pointer changes to a 4-way arrow. (See the margin.) I recommend using this trick only when you're moving topics a short distance; dragging beyond the current screen can prove unwieldy.

If you need to move a topic and all its subtopics, first collapse the topic. When the topic is expanded, only the topic itself is moved. See the later section "Expanding and collapsing topics."

TIP

Demoting and promoting topics

Outline organization also includes demoting topics that are really subtopics and promoting subtopics to a higher level. Making such adjustments is a natural part of working in Outline view.

>> Click the Demote button (or press Alt+Shift+→) to demote a topic into a subtopic.

>> Click the Promote button (or press Alt+Shift+←) to promote a topic.

New topics you type are created at the same level as the topic above (where you pressed the Enter key).

>> To instantly make any topic a main-level topic, click the Promote to Heading 1 button.

>> You can use the mouse to promote or demote topics: Drag the topic's circle left or right. I admit that this move can be tricky, which is why I use the keyboard shortcuts or buttons on the Ribbon to promote or demote topics.

REMEMBER

>> You don't really *create* subtopics in Word as much as you *demote* higher-level topics.

>> Promoting or demoting a topic changes the paragraph format. For example, demoting a top-level topic changes the style from Heading 1 to Heading 2. The subtopic also appears indented on the screen. (Refer to Figures 25-1 and 25-2.)

>> The Level menu in the Outlining tab's Outline Tools group changes to reflect the current topic level. You can also use this item's drop-down list to promote or demote the topic to any specific level in the outline.

TIP

>> Unlike with main topics, you can get wordy with subtopics. After all, the idea here is to expand on the main topic.

TECHNICAL STUFF

>> According to Those Who Know Such Things, you must have at least two subtopics for them to qualify as subtopics. When you have only one subtopic, either you have a second main topic or you've created a text topic. See the later section "Adding a text topic" for information.

Expanding and collapsing topics

A detailed outline is wonderful, the perfect tool to help you write that novel, organize a meeting, or set priorities. To help you pull back from the detail and see the Big Picture, you can collapse all or part of an outline. Even when you're organizing, sometimes it helps to collapse a topic to help keep it in perspective.

Any topic with subtopics shows a plus sign (+) in its circle. To collapse the topic and temporarily hide its subtopics, you have several choices:

>> Click the Collapse button on the Outlining toolbar (shown in the margin).

>> Press the Alt+Shift+_ (underline) keyboard shortcut.

>> Double-click the plus sign to the topic's left.

When a topic is collapsed, it features a fuzzy underline, in addition to a plus sign in the icon to the topic's left. To expand a collapsed topic, you have several choices:

>> Click the Expand button on the Outlining toolbar (shown in the margin).

>> Press Alt+Shift++ (plus sign).

>> Click the topic's plus sign.

THE JOY OF COLLAPSIBLE HEADERS

You may have seen a side effect of Word's Outline view when using the heading styles in a document: A tiny triangle button appears to the left of a heading-style paragraph when a document is shown in Print Layout view. Click that button to expand or collapse the heading and all its contents — including any subheadings. Using this trick is a great way to collapse parts of a document without having to switch to Outline view.

TIP

The fastest way to display an outline at a specific topic level is to choose that level from the Show Level drop-down list. To find that command, look on the Outlining toolbar, in the Outline Tools group.

For example, to show only Level 1 and Level 2 topics, choose Level 2 from the Show Level button's menu. Topics at Level 3 and higher remain collapsed.

To see the entire outline, choose Show All Levels from the Show Level menu.

When some of the subtopics get wordy, place a check mark by the Show First Line Only option. (Look on the Outlining tab in the Outline Tools group for this setting.) When it's active, Word displays only the first topic line of text in any topic.

Adding a text topic

TIP

Creating an outline can potentially be about writing text. When the mood hits you, write! Rather than write prose as a topic, use the Demote to Body Text command. Here's how:

1. **Press the Enter key to start a new topic.**

2. **On the Outlining tab, in the Outline Tools group, click the Demote to Body Text button (shown in the margin).**

    The keyboard shortcut is Ctrl+Shift+N, which is also the keyboard shortcut for the Normal style.

These steps change the text style to Body Text. That way, you can write text for a speech, some instructions in a list, or a chunk of dialogue from your novel and not have it appear as a topic or subtopic.

Printing an outline

Printing an outline works just like printing any other document in Word but with one big difference: Only visible topics are printed.

OUTLINE-MANIPULATION SHORTCUT KEYS

I prefer using Word's shortcut keys whenever possible. Especially when working an outline, when I'm typing more than mousing, it helps to know these outline-manipulation shortcut keys:

Key Combo	What It Does
Alt+Shift+→	Demotes a topic
Alt+Shift+←	Promotes a topic
Alt+Shift+↑	Moves a topic up one line
Alt+Shift+↓	Moves a topic down one line
Ctrl+Shift+N	Demotes a topic to body text
Alt+Shift+1	Displays only top-level topics
Alt+Shift+2	Displays first- and second-level topics
Alt+Shift+n	Displays all topics up to Level n, such as Alt+Shift+4 for Level 4
Alt+Shift+A	Displays all topics
Alt+Shift++ (plus sign)	Displays all subtopics in the current topic
Alt+Shift+_ (underline)	Hides all subtopics in the current topic

To control visible topics, use the Show Level menu, as discussed earlier, in the "Expanding and collapsing topics" section. For example, to print the entire outline, choose All Levels from the Show Level menu and then print.

To print only the first two levels of an outline, choose Level 2 from the Show Level drop-down list and then print.

>> Word uses the heading styles when it prints the outline, although it does not indent topics.

>> See Chapter 9 for more information on printing documents in Word.

Large Documents

The first novel I wrote (and never published, of course) was several hundred pages long. It was saved as a single document. Word documents can be *any* length, but putting everything into one document can be impractical. Editing, copying and pasting, searching and replacing, and all other word processing operations become less efficient the larger the document grows.

A better solution for long documents is to keep each chapter, or large chunk, as its own file. You can then take advantage of Word's Master Document feature to group everything together when it comes time to print or publish.

TIP

>> The *master document* stitches together all individual documents, or subdocuments, even continuing page numbers, headers, footers, and other ongoing elements. The result is a large document that you can print or publish.

>> What qualifies as a large document? Anything over 100 pages qualifies, as far as I'm concerned.

>> When writing a novel, create each chapter as its own document. Keep all those chapter documents in their own folder. Further, use document filenames to help with organization. For example, I name chapters by using numbers: The first chapter is 01, the second is 02, and so on.

>> This book is composed of several dozen individual Word documents — one for each chapter, each part introduction, the front matter, the index, and all that junk.

Creating a master document

Word's Master Document feature helps you collect and coordinate individual documents — called *subdocuments* — and cobble them into one large document. When you have a master document, you can assign continuous page numbers to your work, apply headers and footers throughout the entire project, and take advantage of Word's Table of Contents, Index, and other list-generating features.

To create a big, whopping document from many smaller documents — to create a master document — obey these steps:

1. **Start a new, blank document in Word.**

Press Ctrl+N to quickly summon a new, blank document.

2. **Save the document.**

Yeah, I know — you haven't yet written anything. Don't worry: By saving now, you get ahead of the game and avoid some weird error messages.

3. **Switch to Outline view.**

Click the View tab, and then click the Outline button.

4. **On the Outlining tab in the Master Document group, click the Show Document button.**

   The Master Document group is instantly repopulated with more buttons. One of these is the Insert button, used to build the master document.

5. **Click the Insert button.**

6. **Use the Insert Subdocument dialog box to hunt down the first document to insert in the master document.**

   The documents must be inserted in order. I hope you used a clever document-naming scheme, as recommended in the preceding section.

7. **Click the Open button to stick the document in the master document.**

   The document appears in the window, but it's ugly because Outline view is active. Don't worry: It won't be ugly when it is printed!

   If you're asked a question about conflicting styles, click the Yes to All button. It keeps all subdocument styles consistent with the master document. (Although it's best when all documents use the same document template.)

   Word sets itself up for you to insert the next document:

8. **Repeat Steps 5–7 to build the master document.**

9. **Save the master document when you've finished inserting all subdocuments.**

At this point, the master document is created. It's what you use to print or save the entire, larger document.

You can still edit and work on the individual documents. Any changes you make are reflected in the master document. In fact, the only time you really need to work in the master document is when you choose to edit the headers and footers, create a table of contents, or work on other items that affect the entire document.

TIP

» When you're ready, you can publish the master document just as you publish any individual document. See Chapter 9 for information on publishing a document.

» Use the Collapse Subdocuments button to hide all subdocument text. For example, if you need to create a table of contents or work on the master document's headers and footers, collapsing the subdocuments makes the process easier.

» See Chapter 21 for more information on creating a table of contents and an index for the document.

>> Alas, the master document method isn't perfect. It's good for printing, but for creating an eBook, it's better to use a single large document instead of multiple documents poured into a master document.

Splitting a document

Splitting a document isn't a part of creating a master document, but it might be the way you start. If you write your novel as one long document, I recommend that you split it into smaller documents. A simple shortcut doesn't exist; instead, you have to cut and paste to create smaller documents out of a huge one.

Here's how to split a document:

1. **Select half the document — the portion you want to split into a new document.**

   Or, if you're splitting a document into several pieces, select the first chunk that you want to plop into a new document. For example, split the document at the chapter breaks or a main heading break.

2. **Cut the selected block.**

   Press Ctrl+X to cut the block.

3. **Summon a new, blank document.**

   Ctrl+N does the trick. Or, if you're using a template (and you should be), start a new document with that template. See Chapter 16.

4. **Paste the document portion.**

   Press Ctrl+V to paste. If the text doesn't paste in with the proper formatting, click the Home tab, and in the Clipboard group, click the Paste button (shown in the margin). Click the Keep Source Formatting command button.

5. **Save the new document.**

Continue splitting the larger document by repeating these steps. After you've finished splitting the larger document, you can safely delete it.

Dan's Writing Tips

Nothing beats advice from someone who has been there and done that. As a professional writer, I'm excited to pass along my tips, tricks, and suggestions to any budding scrivener.

Choosing the best word

When two words share the same meaning, they're said to be *synonyms* — for example, *big* and *large*. Synonyms are helpful in that they allow you to find better, more descriptive words and, especially, to avoid using the same tired old words over and over. Obviously, knowing synonyms is a handy skill for any writer.

To find a word's synonym, right-click the word in your document. From the pop-up menu, choose the Synonyms submenu to see a list of words that have a similar meaning. Choose a word from the menu and it replaces the word in your document.

>> To see more word alternatives, right-click a word and choose Synonyms ⇨ Thesaurus. The Thesaurus pane appears, listing multitudinous alternative words.

>> To use a word from the Thesaurus pane, right-click the word and choose the Insert command. The word is placed in the document at the toothpick cursor's location.

>> *Antonyms,* or words that mean the opposite of the selected word, might also appear on the Synonyms submenu.

>> For more research on a specific word, right-click and choose the Smart Lookup command. The Insights pane appears, which lists sources from online references to help you determine whether you're using the best word

Counting every word

You pay the butcher by the pound. The barkeep is paid by the drink. Salespeople keep a percentage of their sales. Writers? They're paid by the word.

If you're lucky enough to be paid for your writing, you know that word count is king. Magazine editors demand articles based on word length. "I need 350 hilarious words on tech-support phone calls," an editor once told me. And novel writers typically boast about how many words are in their latest efforts. "My next book is 350,000 words," they say in stuffy, nasal voices. How do they know how many words they wrote?

The best way to see how many words dwell in a document is to view the status bar. The word count appears by the *Words* label, and the count is updated as you type.

If you don't see the word count at the bottom of the window, right-click the status bar and choose Word Count.

To obtain more than a word count, click the Review tab. In the Proofing group, click the Word Count button (shown in the margin). The detailed Word Count dialog box appears, listing all sorts of word-counting trivia.

Also see Chapter 25 for information on inserting a Word Count field in a document.

Writing for writers

Here's a smattering of tips for any writer using Word:

>> You'll notice that, thanks to AutoFormat, Word fixes ellipses for you. When you type three periods in a row, Word inserts the ellipsis character (. . .). Don't correct it! Word is being proper. When you don't use the ellipsis character, be sure to separate the three periods with spaces.

>> You can format paragraphs by separating them with a space or by indenting the first line of each paragraph. Use one or the other, not both.

>> Keep the proper heading formats: Heading 1, Heading 2, and so on. Or, create your own heading styles that properly use the Outline Level format. That way, you can easily create a table of contents as well as use other Word features that display headings in your documents.

>> Use Outline view to collect your thoughts. Keep working on the outline and organizing your thoughts. When you find yourself writing text-level topics, you're ready to write.

>> Use the soft return (Shift+Enter) to split text into single lines. I use the soft return to break up titles and write return addresses, and I use it at other times when text must appear one line at a time, such as in a chapter heading or title.

>> Word is configured to select text one word at a time. This option isn't always best for writers, where it's often necessary to select text by character. To fix that setting, from the File tab menu, choose Options. In the Options dialog box, click the Advanced item. Remove the check mark by the When Selecting, Automatically Select Entire Word item. Click OK.

Chapter **26**

Let's Work This Out

Writing isn't a team sport, but it can be. Eventually, writers encounter collaboration, welcome or not. Often it comes in the form of an editor, after the writing is done. In today's connected society, collaboration can happen at any time with just about anyone. Word recognizes this challenge and, to help you cope, provides some useful work-it-out-together tools.

Comments on Your Text

Perhaps the least aggressive method of collaboration is to add a comment to a document's text. In olden times, you would scrawl your remarks by using a different text color or ALL CAPS or by surrounding your observations with triple curly brackets. Instead of using such awkward and silly methods, consider clicking the Review tab and being prepared to use some tools abiding in the Comments group.

Adding a comment

To adroitly thrust a comment into a document, follow these steps:

1. **Select the chunk of text upon which you desire to comment.**

    Be specific. You may be tempted to select an entire phrase, but only the first few words are necessary.

2. **Click the Review tab.**

3. **In the Comments group, click the New Comment button.**

The New Comment button is shown in the margin. Click it to see the Comments box appear to the right of the current page, similar to what's shown in Figure 26-1. The side of the page where the comment appears is called the *markup area.*

Original comment

FIGURE 26-1:
Comments on a
text passage.

A comment on the comment

4. **Type a comment.**

Jot down your thoughts. I'm not sure how long a comment can be; if you want to blab, send an email instead. For some reason, text formatting can be applied to the comment.

5. **Press the Esc key when you've finished typing the comment.**

Or you can click in the document's text.

Replying to a comment

Comments aren't intended to hang in space — unless you just want to ignore them. Otherwise, you have two choices for dealing with a comment.

To reply to a comment, click the Reply button, illustrated in the margin. Your name appears in the comment box (refer to Figure 26-1), and you're offered the opportunity to jot down a counterpoint, rebuttal, or curse.

When the commented issue is no longer an issue, mark the comment as resolved: Click the Resolve button for the comment, which is illustrated in the margin. The original comment is dimmed, which allows collaborators to still read it. And, if further issues arise, click the Reopen button (which still looks like what's shown in the margin) to continue adding comments.

Showing or hiding comments

The markup area (to the right of your text) appears whenever a document features comments. To hide this area, click the Review tab. In the Tracking group, click the Display for Review button, shown in the margin. The four available options set how comments, as well as other document revisions (covered elsewhere in this chapter), are displayed:

Simple Markup: Chose this item to display the markup area and view limited comments and revisions.

All Markup: Choose this item to display the markup area, where all comments and revisions are shown, along with lines referencing their locations in the text.

No Markup: Choose this item to hide the markup area. Comments don't appear, and any revisions are hidden in the text.

Original: Choose this item to hide the markup area as well as any revisions made to the document. With regard to comments, this item is identical to No Markup.

I recommend working with document comments in Print Layout view, which works best. If you choose Draft view, the comments appear as bracketed initials highlighted with a specific background color. For example, my comments look like [DG1], where *DG* is my initials and the 1 represents Comment 1. Position the mouse pointer at that text to view the comment in a pop-up bubble.

TIP

» See Chapter 1 for more information on Word's different document views.

» To view all comments, no matter which document view is chosen, summon the Reviewing pane: On the Review tab, in the Tracking group, click the Reviewing Pane button. Choose either the horizontal or vertical display to summon the Reviewing pane and peruse comments as well as text revisions.

» See the later section "Tracking changes as they're made," for information on revisions.

Perusing comments one at a time

To get an idea of how commenting goes, don't just randomly scroll through your document trying to find the next gripe or compliment. Instead, use the Next Comment and Previous Comment buttons. These buttons are found on the Review tab, in the Comments group.

Click the Next Comment button to jump to the next comment in the document.

Click the Previous Comment button to jump to the previous comment in the document.

Clicking either the Next Comment or Previous Comment button activates All Markup view, as covered in the preceding section.

Printing comments (or not)

Yes, it's horrible, but comments print with your document. This output is probably not what you intended, so follow these steps:

1. **Press Ctrl I P.**

   The Print screen appears.

2. **Click the Print All Pages button to view its menu.**

3. **Choose the Print Markup command.**

   This setting controls whether comments, as well as other text markup covered in this chapter, print. Remove the check mark to suppress comments on the hard copy.

   The Print Preview window confirms whether comments and other markup print.

   TIP

4. **Make any other settings in the Print window as needed.**

5. **Click the big Print button to print the document.**

You must follow these steps every time you print the document otherwise, the comments print.

REMEMBER

See Chapter 9 for more information on printing documents in Word.

Deleting comments

Not only is the comment's issue resolved, but you also don't want to be reminded of the comment ever again. Work these steps:

1. **Click the Review tab.**

2. **Click the Next Comment or Previous Comment button to locate the offending comment.**

   Upon success, the comment is highlighted in the markup area.

3. **In the Comments area, choose Delete ➪ Delete.**

The Delete button is shown in the margin. It's one of those menu button icon-things that you must click to access the commands.

4. **Repeat Steps 2 and 3 to remove additional comments.**

Or just keep repeating Step 2 until you find a comment worthy of obliteration.

To delete all comments from a document in a single act of massive retaliation, use the Delete Comment button's menu: Choose Delete ➪ Delete All Comments in Document.

The Yellow Highlighter

Word comes with a digital pen that lets you highlight and colorize the text in a document without damaging the computer's monitor. To highlight text, abide by these steps:

1. **Click the Home tab.**

2. **In the Font group, click the Text Highlight button.**

The mouse pointer changes to a — well, I don't know what it is, but the point is that Word is now in Highlighting mode.

3. **Drag the mouse over the text you want to highlight.**

The text becomes highlighted — just as though you used a highlighter on regular paper but minus the felt-pen smell.

4. **Click the Text Highlight button again to return the mouse to normal operation.**

Or press the Esc key to exit Highlighting mode.

The highlight need not be yellow. Click the menu button to the right of the Text Highlight button, and choose a different highlighter color from the palette displayed.

To remove highlighting from the text, highlight it again in the same color. If that doesn't work, choose None as the highlight color and then drag the mouse over any color of highlighted text to remove the highlight.

> » To highlight multiple chunks of text, double-click the Text Highlight button. The mouse pointer stays in Highlighting mode until you click the Text Highlight button again or press the Esc key.

>> To highlight a block of text, mark the block and then click the Highlight button that appears on the mini toolbar.

>> Highlighting isn't the background color, nor is it a text format. See Chapter 10 for information on setting the text background color.

Look What They've Done to My Text, Ma

All good writers should enjoy feedback. Still, I'd like to know what's been done to my text, not only to see the effect but also to learn something. Word's revision-tracking tools make such a review possible.

Comparing two versions of a document

You have the original copy of your document — the stuff you wrote. You also have the copy that Brianne, the soulless automaton from the legal department, has worked over. Your job is to compare them to see exactly what's been changed from the original. Here's what to do:

1. **Click the Review tab.**

2. **In the Compare group, choose Compare ⇨ Compare.**

   The Compare Documents dialog box shows up.

3. **Choose the original document from the Original Document drop-down list.**

   The list shows recently opened or saved documents. Choose one, or use the Browse item to summon the Open dialog box and hunt down the document.

4. **Choose the edited document from the Revised Document drop-down list.**

   Choose the document from the list, or use the Browse item to locate the changed, altered, or mangled document.

5. **Click OK.**

Word compares the two documents. The changes are displayed in a quadruple-split window, as illustrated in Figure 26-2. This presentation is actually a third document, titled Compare Result.

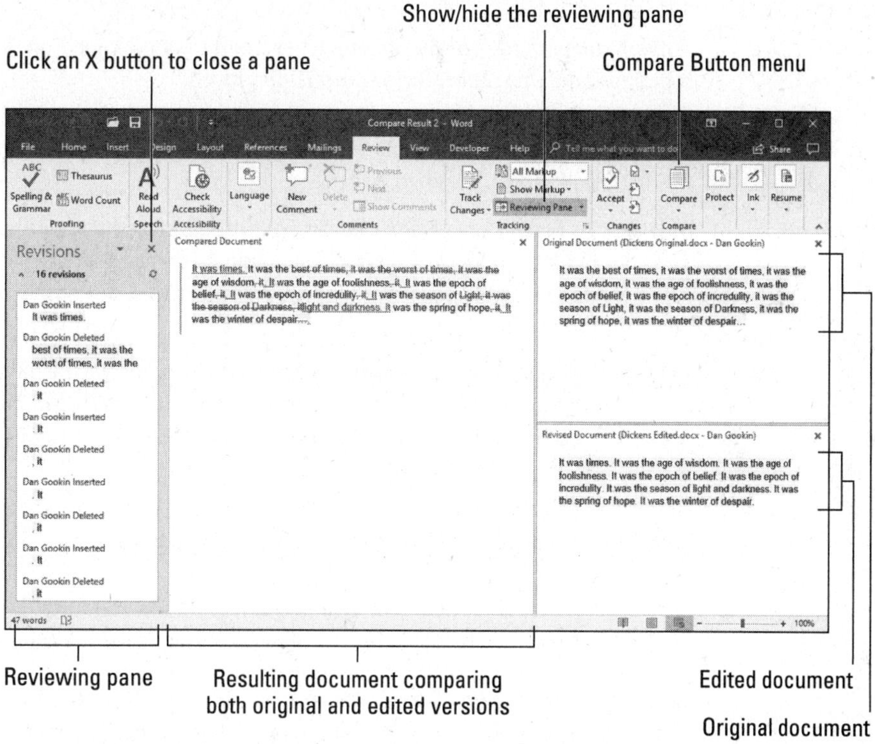

Show/hide the reviewing pane

Click an X button to close a pane

Compare Button menu

FIGURE 26-2:
The shameful
changes show up
here.

Reviewing pane

Resulting document comparing
both original and edited versions

Edited document

Original document

Look it over! Peruse the changes made to your pristine prose by the barbarian interlopers: Scrolling is synchronized between all three documents: original, edited, and compared. Click a change in the reviewing pane (shown on the left in Figure 26-2) to quickly see which part of your document was folded, spindled, or mutilated.

>> Changed text is highlighted in two ways: Added text is underlined. Removed text is shown in strikethrough style.

>> You can confirm or reject the changes in the Compare Result document, just as you would when tracking changes manually. See the upcoming section "Reviewing changes."

Tracking changes as they're made

To be a kind and gentle collaborator, activate Word's Tracking feature *before* you make changes to someone else's text: Click the Review tab, and in the Tracking group, click the Track Changes button, shown in the margin. From that point on, any changes made to the document are color coded based on who is making the changes and what level of markup is displayed:

» For Simple Markup, a color-coded bar appears to the left of a paragraph, indicating that a change was made.

» For All Markup, new text is color coded, depending on who made the changes. Added text appears underlined, and deleted text appears as strikethrough. These text highlights are called *revision marks*. They are not text-formatting attributes.

» For No Markup, the changes are tracked but not displayed in the document. This is a great setting to choose for the least amount of distraction. (The revision marks can be seen by choosing All Markup instead of No Markup.)

Refer to the earlier section "Showing or hiding comments," for information on the Simple Markup, All Markup, and No Markup settings.

Word continues to track changes and edits in the document until you turn off Track Changes. To do so, click the Track Changes button again.

TIP

Although the Track Changes button appears highlighted while the feature is active, a better way to check — and use — this feature is to activate the Track Settings option on the status bar. To set this option, right-click the status bar and choose Track Changes. As a bonus, you can click this item on the status bar to activate or deactivate revision marks in the document.

Reviewing changes

After your poor, limp document is returned to you, the best way to review the damage inflicted is to use the commands on the Review tab, located in the Changes group. These commands are illustrated in Figure 26-3; depending on the window size, you may or may not see text explaining what each one does.

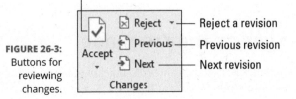

FIGURE 26-3:
Buttons for reviewing changes.

To review changes throughout the document, click the Next or Previous buttons. Click a button to hop from one change in the text to the next change.

Click the Accept button when you tolerate the change. To reject a change, click the Reject button. After clicking either button, you instantly see the next change in the document, until all the changes are dealt with.

TIP

>> The Accept and Reject buttons host menus with commands that accept or reject all changes in your document in one fell swoop. The only thing missing is the "swoop!" sound when you use these commands.

>> You can view a summary of changes by summoning the Revisions pane: On the Review tab, in the Tracking group, click the Reviewing Pane button. The Revisions pane doesn't show the changes in context, but it lists each one. Click an item in the Revisions pane to hop to each change in the document.

>> To see changes in the text, ensure that you choose the All Markup command from the Display for Review menu button.

>> When you goof while approving or rejecting a change, press Ctrl+Z to undo.

>> You can also right-click any revision mark to accept or reject it.

Collaborate on the Internet

Most document changes are made sequentially: You write something, save, and then someone else works on the document. If that chaos isn't enough for you, Word allows you to invite people to edit a document while you're working on it. This collaboration feature is called Sharing, probably because a better name wasn't available or Microsoft was pressed for time.

To make document sharing work, save your document to the *cloud*, or Internet storage. Specifically, the document must be saved to Microsoft's OneDrive storage. See Chapter 8 for details on OneDrive.

Sharing a document

After saving a document to OneDrive online storage, follow these steps to make the document available for collaboration:

1. **Click the Share button.**

The Share button is shown in the margin. Locate it above the Ribbon, near the upper right part of the document's window.

Upon success, the Share pane appears. Upon failure, you see a prompt asking you to save the document to OneDrive.

2. **Type an email address to invite a collaborator.**

   If you use Outlook as your computer's address book, click the Address Book icon to the right of the Invite People box to automatically add people.

3. **Choose whether the collaborators can edit.**

   Choose Can View from the menu, and the people you invite can read the document. Choose Can Edit, and they can make changes.

4. **Type a message in the Include a Message box.**

5. **Click the Share button.**

   The invites are sent.

Eventually, the recipients receive the email invite. To access the shared document, they click the link in the email address. Their web browser program opens and displays the document. If they want to edit the document, they click the link Edit in Browser. At that point, their web browser displays the document as it appears in Word, complete with a customized version of the Ribbon. Hack away.

Checking updates

To determine whether someone has edited your shared document, open the shared document and click the Share button found near the upper right corner of the document window. The Share pane lists all collaborators and whether they're currently editing. Collaborators who are currently editing show avatar icons to the left of the Share icon atop the document window. If they're actively editing, you see a color-coded insertion pointer appear in your document, showing where the collaborator is working.

If collaborators have changed the document, save your copy to view updates: Click the Save icon on the Quick Access toolbar, or press Ctrl+S. Any changed content appears in the document with a colored overlay, similar to how revision marks are displayed, as covered earlier in this chapter.

TIP

To check to see whether updates are pending, click the File tab, and on the Info screen, look for and click the button titled Document Updates Available.

IN THIS CHAPTER

» **Understanding mail merge**

» **Building the main document**

» **Conjuring up a recipient list**

» **Making a recipient list**

» **Inserting fields into the main document**

» **Previewing the results**

» **Merging (the final act)**

Chapter **27**

Mail Merge Mania

H ere's a little quiz. What do these things have in common? Rocket science. Quantum mechanics. Brain surgery. Levitation. The answer: They're all a lot easier to accomplish than attempting mail merge in Word.

It's not that mastering mail merge is impossible. True, it's an ancient word processing tradition — something that just about everyone toys with at one time or another. Yet the way Word handles mail merge has been consistently frustrating. That's why I wrote this chapter.

About Mail Merge

The term *mail merge* is given to the process of opening a single document, stirring in a list of names and other information, and then combining (*merging*) everything. The result is a sheaf of personalized documents. Sounds useful, right? Peruse this section before attempting the process on your own.

Understanding Word's mail merge jargon

Like me, you probably have your own delightful, descriptive terms for the steps required and pieces necessary to complete a mail merge. Word's terms are different. Before taking the mail merge plunge, I recommend that you review the following jargon:

Main document: This document is just like any other document in Word, complete with formatting, layout, and all the fancy stuff that goes into a document. The document also contains various fill-in-the-blanks items, which is what makes it the main document.

Recipient list: This list contains the information that creates the customized documents. It's a type of *database*, with rows and columns of information used to fill in the form letters.

Field: Each of these fill-in-the-blanks items inside the main document is a placeholder that will be filled in by information from the recipient list. Fields are what make the mail merge possible.

Getting these three elements to work together is the essence of mail merge. All the commands necessary are located on the Mailings tab. In fact, the Mailings tab's five groups are organized from left to right in the order you use them. The remainder of this chapter describes the details.

REMEMBER

>> The key to mail-merging is the recipient list. If you plan to create a mail merge as part of your regular routine, build a recipient list that you can use again and again.

>> A mail merge document can have as many fields as it needs. In fact, any item you want to change can be a field: the greeting, a banal pleasantry, gossip, whatever.

>> Fields are also known as *merge fields.*

TECHNICAL STUFF

>> You can use information from the Outlook program, also a part of Microsoft Office, as a recipient list for a mail merge in Word. This trick works best, however, when you're in a workplace environment that features Microsoft Exchange Server. Otherwise, making Outlook and Word cooperate is a frustrating endeavor.

MAIL MERGE DOCUMENT TYPES

In addition to a form letter, the main document in a mail merge can be an email message, an envelope, a set of labels, or anything else that can be mass-produced. Here are the official Word mail merge document types:

Letter: The traditional mail merge document is a letter, a document in Word.

Email messages: Word can produce customized email messages, which are sent electronically rather than printed.

Envelopes: You can use mail merge to create a batch of customized envelopes, each printed with its own address.

Labels: Word lets you print sheets of labels, each of which is customized with specific information from the mail merge. See Chapter 28 for specifics.

Directory: A directory is a list of information, such as a catalog or an address book.

Reviewing the mail merge process

The typical mail merge involves five steps. These steps are presented in more detail throughout this chapter:

I. Build the main document.

Choose the document type, usually a letter, though other document types are listed in the nearby sidebar, "Mail merge document types." As you create the document, you decide which fields are needed. That way, you can build an effective recipient list.

II. Create the recipient list — the data for the mail merge.

The recipient list is a table, consisting of rows and columns. Each column is a field containing information to go into the fill-in-the-blanks parts of the main document. Each row represents a different custom document created by the mail merge process.

III. Insert fields into the main document.

The fields are placeholders for information that is eventually supplied from the recipient list.

IV. **Preview the merge results.**

You don't just merge; first, you must preview how the document looks. That way, you can clean up any formatting, check for errors, and make other corrections.

V. **Merge the information from the recipient list into the main document.**

The final mail merge process creates the customized documents. They can then be saved, printed, emailed, or dealt with however you like.

The rest of this chapter covers the specifics.

WARNING

Mail merge involves coordination between multiple documents and various Windows technologies. When you open a mail merge document that you've already created, you may see an alert dialog box. You're informed that opening the document also runs an SLQ command. This command is what links the recipient list to the main document. Click Yes to proceed.

Using the Mail Merge Wizard

If all this mail merge malarkey is just too intense for you, consider an alternative: Word offers the Mail Merge Wizard, which guides you through the entire ordeal one step at a time.

To run the wizard, click the Mailings tab and choose Start Mail Merge ⇨ Step-by-Step Mail Merge Wizard. You see the Mail Merge pane on the right side of the document's window. Answer the questions, choose options, and click the Next link to proceed.

The rest of this chapter assumes that you're crazy enough to do mail merge the macho way.

The Main Document

Mail merge begins with the *main document.* It's the prototype for all the individualized documents you eventually create, so it contains only common elements.

The following sections discuss different types of main documents. Read the section that relates to the type of mail merge you're attempting, and then proceed with the later section "II. The Recipient List."

Creating a mail merge form letter

The most common thing to mail merge is the standard, annoying form letter. Here's how you start that journey:

1. **Start a new, blank document.**

Press Ctrl+N.

2. **Click the Mailings tab.**

3. **In the Start Mail Merge group, choose Start Mail Merge ⇨ Letters.**

4. **Type the letter.**

You're typing only the common parts of the letter, the text that doesn't change for each copy.

REMEMBER

5. **Type the fields you need in ALL CAPS.**

This step is my idea, not Word's. For text that changes for each letter, type in ALL CAPS. For example, FIRST NAME or HAT SIZE. Use short, descriptive terms. Figure 27-1 shows an example.

6. **Save the main document.**

If you already saved the document as you were writing it, give yourself a cookie.

After you create the letter, the next step is to create or use a recipient list. Continue with the section "II. The Recipient List," a little later in this chapter.

Creating mail merge email messages

To spew out custom email messages, use Word's E-Mail option for mail merge. This option works only when you configure the Microsoft Outlook program on your computer. After that's done, you start the main document for your email merge by obeying these steps:

1. **Press Ctrl+N to create a fresh document.**

2. **On the Mailings tab, choose Start Mail Merge ⇨ E-Mail Messages.**

Word changes to Web Layout view, used for creating Internet documents in Word.

3. **Create your mail message.**

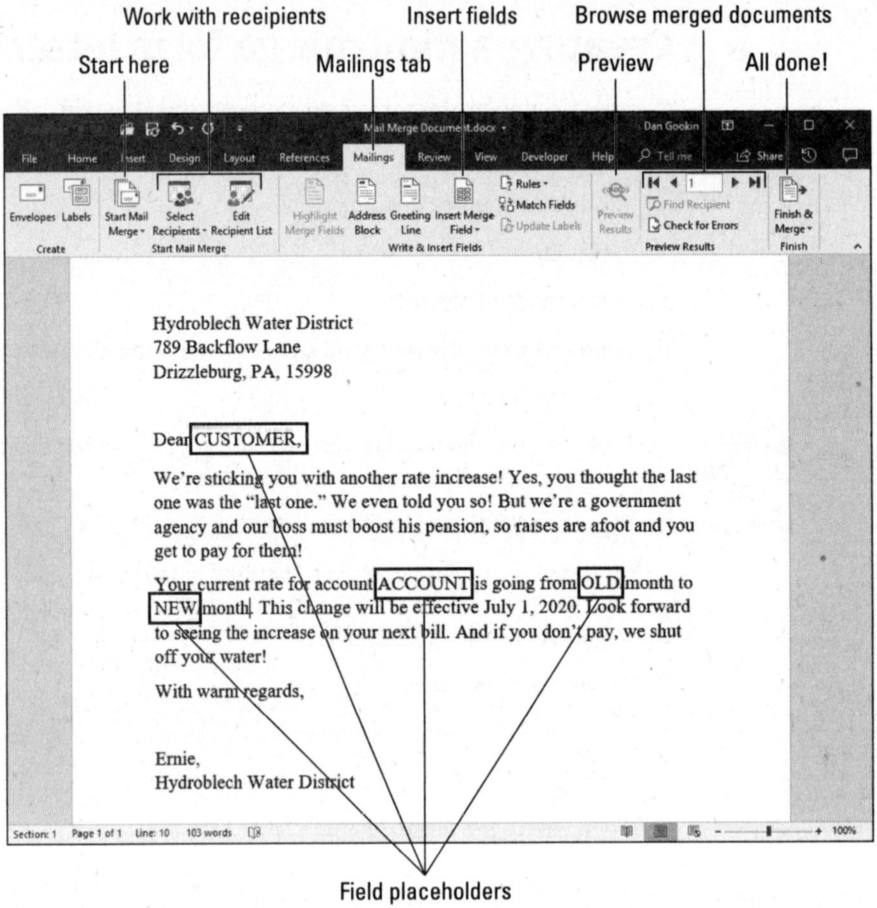
Work with receipients
Insert fields
Browse merged documents
Start here
Mailings tab
Preview
All done!
Field placeholders
Hydroblech Water District
789 Backflow Lane
Drizzleburg, PA, 15998
Dear CUSTOMER,
We're sticking you with another rate increase! Yes, you thought the last one was the "last one." We even told you so! But we're a government agency and our boss must boost his pension, so raises are afoot and you get to pay for them!
Your current rate for account ACCOUNT is going from OLD month to NEW month. This change will be effective July 1, 2020. Look forward to seeing the increase on your next bill. And if you don't pay, we shut off your water!
With warm regards,
Ernie,
Hydroblech Water District

FIGURE 27-1: A mail merge main document.

4. **If you anticipate inserting fields in the message, type them in ALL CAPS.**

   An email mail merge isn't required to have fields in the document. Instead, email addresses are used to send out multiple copies of the message. If you plan to add fields, refer to Step 5 in the preceding section.

5. **Save your document.**

The primary field you use when merging an email document is the recipient's email address. You can't email-merge without it. Continue your mail merge adventure in the later section, "II. The Recipient List."

Creating mail merge envelopes

To create a stack of mail merge envelopes, which is far classier than using peel-and-stick mailing labels, abide by these steps:

1. **Start a new document.**

2. **On the Mailings tab, choose Start Mail Merge ⇨ Envelopes.**

   The Envelope Options dialog box appears. You can set the envelope size and font options, if necessary.

3. **Click OK.**

   Word's window changes to reflect a typical envelope, a size specified in the Envelope Options dialog box (from Step 2).

4. **Edit or create the return address.**

   If you desire a return address and one isn't added automatically, type it in.

   Press Shift+Enter to place a soft return at the end of a line in the return address. The soft return keeps the lines in the return address tightly together.

   TIP

5. **Save the envelope.**

That's pretty much it for a mail merge envelope. Not readily visible in the envelope document is a large text box (lower center). This location is where fields for the recipient's name are inserted.

Your next task is to use the recipient list to gather the information for your mailing. Keep reading in the next section.

The Recipient List

To make mail merge work, you need a list of items to merge, rows and columns, as in a database. This information, called the *recipient list,* contains the field data used to create the individual documents, email messages, envelopes, and so on.

Your options include building a new recipient list, reusing an existing list, and pulling in information from the Outlook program.

Building a new recipient list

I enjoy writing a mail merge main document. I do not look forward to building the recipient list. It's time-consuming, data-input drudgery. Still, it beats creating multiple individual documents, which is the point of a mail merge.

Four steps are involved to build a recipient list:

1. **Create the new list.**
2. **Add the desired fields.**
3. **Remove the undesired fields.**
4. **Type in the recipient data.**

The last step is the most time-consuming. If you're an intern at a major organization, Step 4 is why you were given the mail merge task.

Create the new recipient list

Before you can create a new recipient list, you must have created and saved the main document. Specific steps are provided in the earlier section "I. The Main Document." Creating the recipient list works the same, no matter which mail merge document type you created. Follow these steps:

1. **Click the Mailings tab.**
2. **In the Start Mail Merge group, choose Select Recipients ➪ Type a New List.**

   You see the New Address List dialog box.

Add any new fields you need

The New Address List dialog box comes prestocked with fields, which you see marching atop the dialog box (Title, First Name, Last Name, and so on). If you can use these, great! Otherwise, you must add fields not already present.

Follow these steps in the New Address List dialog box:

1. **Click the Customize Columns button.**

   The Customize Address List dialog box appears.

2. **Click the Add button.**

   The teeny Add Field dialog box pops into view.

3. **Type the field name and click the OK button.**

   Follow these rules for naming fields:

   - Name the field to reflect the kind of information in it; for example, Snake Bite Location.

   - No two fields can have the same name.

- Field names can contain spaces but cannot start with a space.

- Field names can be quite long, though shorter is best.

- The following characters are forbidden in a field name: . ! ` [ ].

4. **Repeat Steps 2 and 3 for each new field you need in the main document.**

   The list of fields should match with the list of ALL CAPS text in the main document (if you chose to create them). Don't worry if it doesn't — you can add fields later, though it takes more time.

5. **Click OK.**

   You now see customized fields as column headings in the New Address List dialog box.

Remove any fields you don't need

Removing unnecessary fields is optional, but I include it out of spite: The New Address List dialog box comes with a basic assortment of fields. If you don't need them, remove them. Or you can skip ahead to the next subsection, "Add recipient data."

To remove extra fields from the New Address list dialog box, heed these steps:

1. **Click the Customize Columns button.**

   The Customize Address List dialog box appears, displaying fields that Word assumes you need. Such foolishness cannot be tolerated.

2. **Click to select a field that you *do not* need.**

   When you're merging an email message, you need the E-mail Address field, whether it appears in the message body or not. Word uses this field so that it knows where to send the message. Don't delete the field!

REMEMBER

3. **Click the Delete button.**

4. **Click Yes in the confirmation dialog box.**

   The keyboard shortcut for the Yes button is the Y key.

5. **Repeat Steps 2–4 for each field you don't need.**

   Be careful not to remove any fields you added!

When you're done, the New Address List dialog box should contain only those fields you need, those for which placeholders are found in the main document.

Rather than delete all fields, you can rename some fields to match what you need: Select a field and click the Rename button. For example, I renamed *First Name* to *First*; *Last Name* to *Last*; and so on.

Add recipient data

After customizing the fields, your final job is to fill in the recipient list. You need to input records, one for each document you plan to create. Perform these steps in the New Address List dialog box:

1. **Type the first record's data.**

Type the information that's appropriate to each field: name, title, evil nickname, planet of origin, and so on.

2. **Press Tab to move to the next field.**

After filling in the last field, you'll probably want to add another record:

3. **To add a new record, press the Tab key after typing in the last field.**

When you press the Tab key in the last field in a record, a new record is automatically created and added on the next line. Keep filling in data!

4. **Review your work when you're done.**

Figure 27-2 shows a completed recipient list.

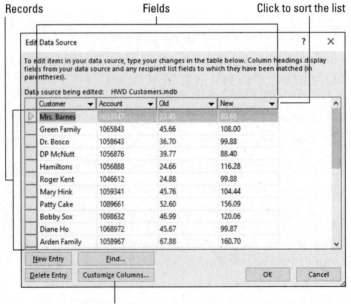

FIGURE 27-2:
Making a
recipient list.

To edit any field, click to select it.

If you accidentally add a blank record at the end of the list, click to select it and then click the Delete Entry button. You do this because blank records are still processed in a mail merge, which results in wasted paper.

5. **Click OK.**

   The Save Address List dialog box pops up, allowing you to save the recipient list.

   The recipient lists dwell in the folder named My Data Sources, found in the Documents or My Documents folder. Word automatically chooses (or creates) this folder.

6. **Type a name for the address list.**

   Descriptive names are best. After all, you might use the same recipient list again.

7. **Click the Save button.**

   You return to the main document.

The next step in your mail merge agony is to stir the fields from the recipient list into the main document. Refer to the section "III. Fold in the Fields," later in this chapter.

MAKING A RECIPIENT LIST DOCUMENT

Here's a secret: You can create a document in Word and use it as a data source for a mail merge. The document contains a single element: a table. The table must have a header row, formatted in bold text, which identifies all the fields. Every row after that becomes a record in the recipient list database.

Using a table as a recipient list provides an easy way to import information into Word and use it for a mail merge. For example, you can copy information from the Internet or a PDF file and then paste that information into Word. Edit the information into a typical Word table, add a table heading row, and save the document. Ta-da! You have a recipient list.

Follow the steps outlined in the nearby section "Using an already created recipient list" to use the table document as your recipient list. Also see Chapter 19 for more information on tables in Word.

Using an already created recipient list

To use an existing recipient list for your mail merge, follow these steps after creating the main document:

1. **From the Mailings tab, choose Select Recipients ➪ Use an Existing List.**

   The Select Data Source dialog box appears. It works like the Open dialog box, though it's designed to display recipient lists that Word can use or that you previously created and saved.

   Look for recipient lists in the My Documents folder, in the My Data Sources subfolder.

2. **Choose an existing recipient list from the displayed files.**

   I hope you used a descriptive name when you first saved the recipient list, which I recommend in the preceding section.

3. **Click the Open button.**

That's it: The recipient list is now associated with the main document.

Refer to the later section "III. Fold in the Fields" for information on inserting fields into your document, which is the next step in the mail merge nightmare.

You can tell when a recipient list is associated with the main document because the Insert Merge Field button is available. Look on the Mailings tab in the Write & Insert Fields group for this button.

Grabbing a recipient list from Outlook

Assuming that you use Microsoft Outlook, and further that you have access to Exchange Server, you can follow these steps to create a recipient list:

1. **On the Mailings tab, in the Start Mail Merge group, choose Select Recipients ➪ Choose from Outlook Contacts.**

2. **If necessary, select your profile from the Choose Profile dialog box.**

3. **Click OK.**

4. **In the Select Contacts dialog box, choose a contact folder.**

   Contact folders are created in Outlook, not in Word.

5. **Click OK.**

6. **Use the Mail Merge Recipients dialog box to filter the recipient list.**

   If the list isn't too long, remove the check marks by the names of the individuals you don't want in the list. You can also click the Filter link in the dialog box to do more advanced filtering, which I'm loathe to describe right now.

7. **Click OK when you're done culling the recipient list.**

Editing a recipient list

If you were sloppy when you created it, or new information has been acquired, you may need to edit the recipient list. Heed these directions:

1. **On the Mailing tab, in the Start Mail Merge group, click the Edit Recipient List button.**

   The button isn't available unless you're working on a main document and it has been associated with a recipient list: Click the Select Recipients button and choose Use an Existing List.

2. **Select the data source.**

   In the lower left corner of the Mail Merge Recipients dialog box, click the data source filename.

3. **Click the Edit button.**

   You can now use the Data Form dialog box to edit each record in the recipient list, to add or remove fields, and to perform other chaos:

   - Click the Delete button to remove the current record.

   - Click the Add New button to create a new record.

   - Click the Customize Columns button to add or remove fields.

4. **Click the Close button when you're done editing.**

5. **Click the OK button to dismiss the Mail Merge Recipients dialog box.**

This process may not be without its hiccups. The file may be "in use" or unavailable to edit. You may be prompted to save the recipient list before editing.

You can edit the recipient list file directly by opening it as a Word document and modifying the table. If you're adept at using Microsoft Access, the file can be manipulated within that application as well.

Fold in the Fields

Now that you have the main document and the recipient list ready to go, you must replace your silly placeholders with the actual mail merge fields. Obey these directions:

1. **Position the mouse pointer where you want the field to appear in the main document.**

   If you followed my advice from the earlier section "Creating a mail merge form letter," select a placeholder, such as FIRST NAME.

2. **On the Mailings tab, click the Insert Merge Field button.**

   When the Insert Merge Field button isn't available, a recipient list isn't associated with the document. See the earlier section "II. The Recipient List."

3. **Choose the field to add to the main document.**

   For example, choose the First Name field to stick it into the document.

   After the field is inserted, you see its name hugged by angle brackets, similar to this:

   ```
   «First_Name»
   ```

   If the field doesn't look like this, press Alt+F9 to toggle the field codes from the raw format to the angle bracket presentation.

4. **Repeat Steps 1–3 to add fields to the document.**

   When adding fields to an address, press Shift+Enter to end each line.

TIP

5. **Save the main document.**

   Always save! Save! Save! Save!

The next step in your journey is to preview the results and fix any mistakes. Keep reading and continue with the next section.

Preview the Merged Documents

Rather than just plow ahead with the merge, take advantage of the buttons in the Mailing tab's Preview Results group. That way, you can peruse the merged documents without wasting a lot of paper.

To preview, click the Mailings tab, and in the Preview Results group, click the Preview Results command button, shown in the margin. The fields in the main document vanish! They're replaced by information from the first record in the recipient list. What you see on the screen is how the first customized mail merge document appears. I hope everything looks spiffy.

Use the left and right triangles in the Preview Results group to page through each document. As you page, look for these problems:

>> Formatting mistakes, such as text that obviously looks pasted in or not part of the surrounding text

>> Punctuation errors and missing commas or periods

>> Missing spaces between or around fields

>> Double fields or unwanted fields, which happen when you believe that you've deleted a field but haven't

>> Awkward text layouts, strange line breaks, or margins caused by missing or long fields

To fix any boo-boos, leave Preview mode: Click the Preview Results button again. Edit the main document to correct the mistakes. Then repeat the preview process.

Once everything looks up to par, you're ready to perform the merge, covered in the next section.

Mail Merge, Ho!

The final step in the mail merge ordeal is to create personalized documents. The gizmo that handles this task is the Finish & Merge command button (shown in the margin), which is the sole item in the Finish group on the Mailings tab. This section describes how to use that button to complete the mail merge.

Merging to a new set of documents

When you want to save merged documents and print them, follow these steps:

1. **Choose Finish & Merge ➪ Edit Individual Documents.**

   The Merge to New Document dialog box appears.

2. **Ensure that the All option is selected.**

3. **Click OK.**

   Word creates a new document — a huge one that contains all merged documents, one after the other. Each document copy is separated by a Next Page section break. (See Chapter 14 for more information on section breaks.)

4. **Save the document.**

At this point, you can print the document, close it and edit it later, or do anything else you like.

Merging to the printer

The most common destination for merged documents is the printer. Here's how it works:

1. **Choose Finish & Merge ⇨ Print Documents.**

   A dialog box appears, from which you can choose records to print.

2. **Choose All from the Merge to Printer dialog box to print the entire document.**

   Or specify which records to print.

3. **Click OK.**

   The traditional Print dialog box appears.

4. **Click the OK button to print your documents.**

5. **Save and close the main document.**

See Chapter 9 for more information on printing documents in Word.

When merging and printing envelopes, use the printer's envelope slot or other special feeding mechanism. You may have to monitor the printer to insert the envelopes.

Merging to email

To send out multiple email messages, abide by these steps:

1. **Choose Finish & Merge ⇨ Send Email Messages.**

   The Merge to E-Mail dialog box appears.

2. **Choose the email address field from the To drop-down list.**

   Your document's recipient list must include an email address field, though the field doesn't need to be set within the document. If the recipient list doesn't contain the email address field, go back and edit it to include the email address field.

3. **Type a message subject line.**

4. **Fill in any other fields in the Merge to E-Mail dialog box.**

5. **Click OK.**

   It looks like nothing has happened, but the messages have been placed in the Outlook outbox.

6. **Open Outlook.**

   After you open Outlook, the queued messages are sent, or they sit ready to be sent when you give the command. (Whether the messages are sent right away depends on how you configured Outlook.)

Yes, this trick works only with Outlook, not with any other email programs.

WARNING

Unsolicited email is considered spam. Sending spam may violate the terms of your Internet service provider's or email service agreement, and they can terminate your account. Send mass email only to people who have cheerfully agreed to receive such things from you.

Chapter **28**

Labels and Envelopes

S tretching the notion of what a word processor is capable of doing, Word features commands that let you print labels and envelopes. After all, a sheet of labels or an envelope is simply a different type of paper. Rather than conjure a hack to perform the task, Word offers ready-made label- and envelope-printing commands.

Labels Everywhere

Word's label powers include printing sheets of identical labels or creating individual labels for a mass mailing. This process works because the labels, at their core, are merely cells in a table. So, to create a batch of labels in Word, you use special commands to muster a specially formatted table and then print that document on a sheet of sticky labels.

>> Label printer paper can be found wherever office supplies are sold. Avery is considered the top brand. Other brands use the Avery numbering scheme to describe different types of labels (size, rows, and columns).

>> Buy label paper that's compatible with your printer. Laser printers need special laser printer labels. Some inkjet printers require special, high-quality paper to soak up the ink.

Printing sheets of identical labels

It might seem impractical to print a sheet of identical labels, yet I use such a sheet for my return address. This peel–and–stick trick is convenient for other types of labels as well. Word deftly handles the chore. Just follow these steps:

1. **Click the Mailings tab.**

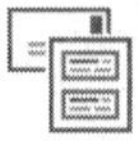

2. **In the Create group, click the Labels button.**

   The Envelopes and Labels dialog box appears, with the Labels tab ready for action, as shown in Figure 28-1.

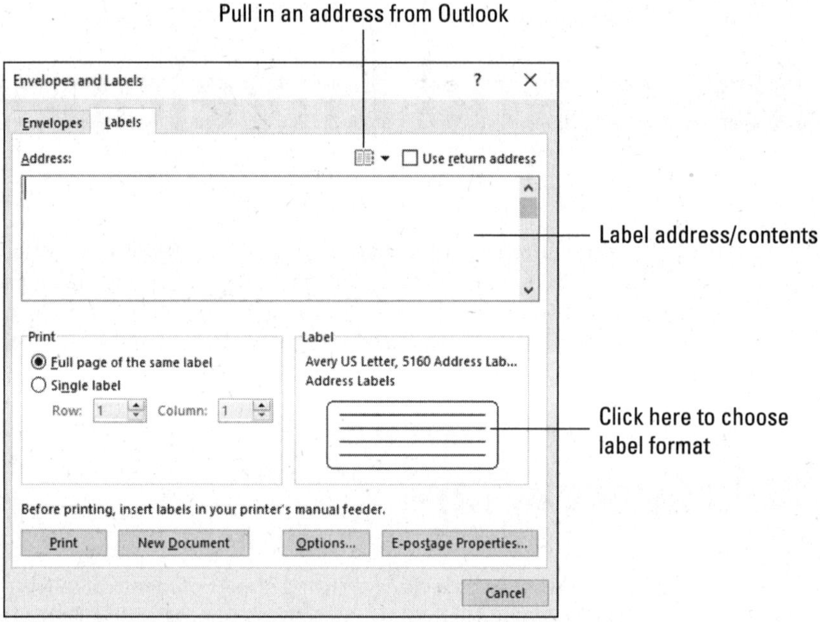

Pull in an address from Outlook

Label address/contents

Click here to choose label format

FIGURE 28-1:
The Labels side of the Envelopes and Labels dialog box.

3. **In the Address box, type the text you want printed on the label.**

   Press the Enter key at the end of each line. The paragraph format is single-spaced.

   You can apply some simple formatting at this stage: Ctrl+B for bold, Ctrl+I for italic, or Ctrl+U for underline, for example. If you right-click in the Address box, you can choose Font or Paragraph from the pop-up menu to further format the label.

4. **Click the Full Page of the Same Label radio button.**

5. **To choose a new label type, click in the Label area.**

   The Label Options dialog box appears.

6. **Choose a label vendor.**

   For some reason, Microsoft is chosen as the default, which is weird because I've never seen Microsoft-branded labels in any office supply store. Instead, choose Avery, which is the category leader. Most other label manufacturers use Avery's numbering system anyway.

7. **Choose the proper stock number.**

   For example, Avery US Letter 5160 (refer to Figure 28-1) is the standard address sticky label most folks use.

8. **Click the New Document button.**

   By placing the labels in a new document, you can further edit them, if you like. Plus, you can save the document for use (and printing) later.

TIP

9. **Print the labels.**

   Ensure that the sheet of label paper is loaded into the printer proper side up. Use the Ctrl+P command to print the labels as you do for any document. See Chapter 9 for details on printing in Word.

On my PC, I have a folder full of label documents I print from time to time. For example, one document holds my return address, one is for the IRS, and another has my lawyer's address. They all come in quite handy.

Printing an address list

To print a sheet of different labels, such as an address list, you encroach upon the terrifying territory of mail merge. This topic is covered in Chapter 27, so refer to that chapter for specific information. This section deals with printing one or more sheets of different labels.

Before getting started, you must have available a recipient list file. Refer to Chapter 27 for information on creating a recipient list. If you're fortunate enough to use the Outlook program as your digital address book, you can use it instead.

To print a list of names on a sheet of labels, follow these steps:

1. **Start a new document in Word.**

2. **Click the Mailings tab.**

   All commands and buttons mentioned in the remaining steps are found on the Mailings tab.

3. **Click the Start Mail Merge button, and from the menu, choose Labels.**

The Label Options dialog box appears.

4. **Choose the label vendor and product number representing the sheet of labels on which you're printing.**

For example, to print on a sheet of standard Avery address labels, use Avery catalog number 5160.

5. **Click OK.**

Word builds a table in the document, one with cells perfectly aligned to match the labels on the sheet you selected. (The gridlines may be hidden, but the table is still there.)

Do not edit or format the table! It's perfect.

WARNING

6. **Click the Select Recipients button and choose Use an Existing List.**

7. **Use the Select Data Source dialog box to choose the list.**

8. **Click Open.**

The document is updated with all cells filled in except the first. The remaining cells feature the field titled «Next Record». Your job is to create the first record, which sets the pattern for all labels.

The mouse pointer should be blinking in the first cell. If not, click that cell.

9. **Click the Insert Merge Field button.**

10. **Choose a field to place into the document.**

For example, choose the First Name field to set the placeholder for the label's first name.

11. **Repeat Steps 9 and 10 to continue adding fields.**

Don't worry about it looking messy; you can edit the field's layout later.

12. **Format the first label.**

Add spaces between the fields to separate them. Press Shift+Enter to create multiple lines. Add a comma between the city and state.

When you finish adding fields, the document should look similar to what's shown in Figure 28-2.

13. **In the Write & Insert Fields group, click the Update Labels button.**

Word populates the remaining cells in the table with the same fields and text placed into the first cell.

If you make a mistake, press Ctrl+Z to undo. Fix the first cell. Repeat Step 13.

TIP

«First_Name» «Last_Name» «Address» «City», «State» «ZIP»	«Next Record»	«Next Record»
«Next Record»	«Next Record»	«Next Record»
«Next Record»	«Next Record»	«Next Record»

FIGURE 28-2:
The first label dictates how other labels are formatted.

14. Ensure that the proper label sheet is in the printer.

And that you have enough of them.

15. Click the Finish & Merge button and choose Print Documents.

16. Ensure that the All radio button is chosen in the Merge to Printer dialog box.

17. Click the OK button.

The traditional Print dialog box appears. Ensure that you have enough of the proper label paper in the printer and that the labels are correctly oriented.

18. Click the OK button in the Print dialog box.

The address labels print.

I recommend saving the document when you're done. That way, you can more easily perform the merge again or use the same document again to print a fresh batch of labels.

Instant Envelope

Suddenly you need an envelope! Don't revert to the last century and use your fist to scribble text on that envelope. Join the digital realm and let Word do the task for you. Obey these steps:

1. Click the Mailings tab.

2. Click the Envelopes button.

The Envelopes and Labels dialog box appears with the Envelopes tab forward, as shown in Figure 28-3.

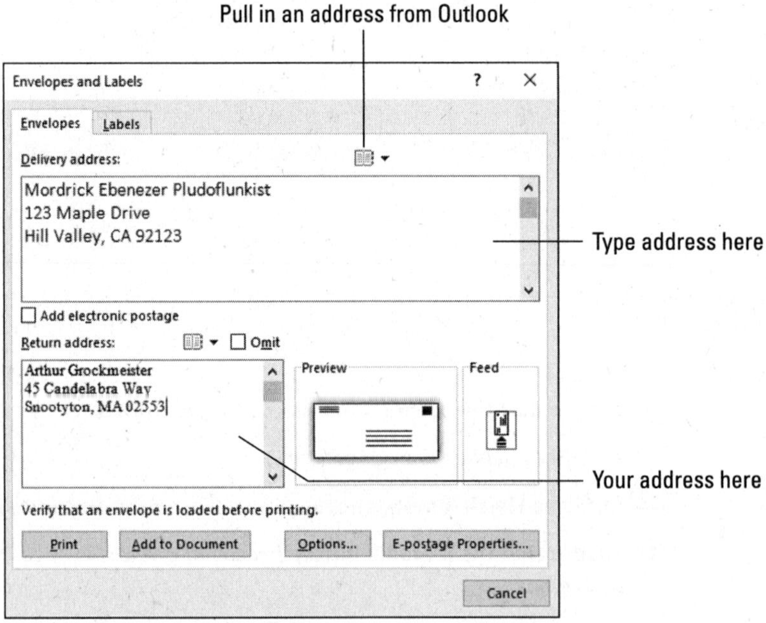

Pull in an address from Outlook

Envelopes and Labels　　　　　　　　　　　　　　　? 　×

Envelopes　Labels

Delivery address:

> Mordrick Ebenezer Pludoflunkist
> 123 Maple Drive
> Hill Valley, CA 92123

— Type address here

☐ Add electronic postage

Return address:　☐ O_mit

> Arthur Grockmeister
> 45 Candelabra Way
> Snootyton, MA 02553

Preview　　　Feed

— Your address here

Verify that an envelope is loaded before printing.

Print　　Add to Document　　Options...　　E-postage Properties...

Cancel

FIGURE 28-3:
The Envelopes
side of the
Envelopes and
Labels dialog box.

3. **Type the recipient's address in the Delivery Address box.**

Press Enter to separate the lines in the address. Word stacks each line atop the other, so don't fret over weird line spacing on the envelope.

If you use Outlook as your computer's address book, click the Address Book button to fetch the delivery address info.

TIP

4. **Ensure that an envelope is queued in the printer and ready to print.**

Most printers prompt you to manually enter envelopes. A guide on the printer's manual feed mechanism describes how to orient and insert the envelope.

5. **Click the Print button.**

You might need to press the printer's OK button or Ready button to print, though some printers may instantly consume the envelope.

If you want to print the envelope again, save it: Before Step 5, click the Add to Document button. Word inserts a new first page into your document, which is the formatted letter. (The page size is specific to the type of envelope.) When that's done, you can save the document so that you can reuse the envelope.

The Add to Document button's official purpose is to add an envelope to a letter. If you haven't written a letter in Word, you don't need the second (blank) page. To delete it, click that page and press the Backspace key. The page is removed, leaving only the envelope.

» The return address is supplied by Word. If the field is blank, type your address. Word asks whether you want to save the return address when the Envelopes and Letters dialog box closes. Click Yes.

» If the delivery address is already typed in the document, select it before you summon the Envelopes and Labels dialog box. Word automatically grabs the selected text and sets it as the delivery address.

» If you have trouble remembering which way the envelope feeds into the printer, draw a picture of the proper way and tape it to the top of the printer for reference.

» In the United States, Size 10 is the common envelope paper size.

» To change the envelope size, click the Envelope icon in the Preview area of the Envelopes and Labels dialog box. (Refer to Figure 28-3.) Use the Envelope Options dialog box to choose the proper envelope size.

» The Envelopes button merely creates a special Word document (or a single page). The paper size is set to an envelope. A text box is placed in the center of the page, into which you type the delivery address. The return address is text typed at the start of the page. You can use various Word commands to create such a page, but the Envelopes command saves you the trouble.

Chapter **29**

A More Custom Word

'm not one to customize things. Despite available options, I survive with the stock Windows desktop and background. I don't modify my phone's appearance. And I've only ever put one bumper sticker on my car. Still, I'm all in favor of having the ability to modify things if I so choose. Customization seems to be a part of everything, and Word is no exception.

A Better Status Bar

Lurking at the bottom of the Word window is an extremely useful gizmo, the status bar. Chapter 1 introduces the status bar but only hints at its potential. Now it's time to reveal all: Right-clicking the status bar produces the helpful Customize Status Bar menu, shown in Figure 29-1.

The Customize Status Bar menu does two things: First, it controls what you see on the status bar (informational tidbits as well as certain controls). Second, it lets you turn on or off certain Word features.

From Figure 29-1, as well as on the screen, you can see the current status for many optional settings. A check mark indicates that an item is either visible or appears when necessary. To add a check mark, click an item; clicking a check-marked item removes the check.

Customize Status Bar	
Formatted Page Number	1
✓ Section	1
✓ Page Number	Page 1 of 1
Vertical Page Position	3.7"
✓ Line Number	20
Column	2
✓ Word Count	65 words
Character Count (with spaces)	434 characters
✓ Spelling and Grammar Check	No Errors
Language	English (United States)
Signatures	Off
Information Management Policy	Off
Permissions	Off
Track Changes	Off
Caps Lock	Off
Overtype	Insert
✓ Selection Mode	
Macro Recording	Not Recording
Upload Status	
✓ This document has been updated. To refresh the document, click Save.	No
✓ View Shortcuts	
✓ Zoom Slider	
✓ Zoom	100%

FIGURE 29-1:
The Customize
Status Bar menu.

Check marks indicate visible items

Current setting information

Here are my thoughts:

>> Choosing an item from the menu doesn't cause the menu to disappear, which is handy. To make the menu go away, click the mouse elsewhere in the document window.

>> The topmost items on the menu display information about the document. To have that information displayed on the status bar, choose one or more of those items.

>> The Selection Mode option directs Word to display the text *Extend Selection* on the status bar when you press the F8 key to select text. Refer to Chapter 6 for more information on selecting text.

>> The Overtype item places the Insert/Overtype button on the status bar. You can click this button to easily switch between Insert and Overtype modes. However, most Word users prefer to use Insert mode all the time.

>> The last three items on the menu control whether the View buttons or Zoom shortcuts appear on the status bar.

The Quick Access Toolbar

Back in the old days, you could seriously mess with how the Word window looked. You could add toolbars, remove toolbars, modify toolbars, create your own toolbars, and generally use the word *toolbars* over and over again until it lost its meaning. Today, Word isn't quite as flexible as it once was, but you're still allowed to customize a toolbar.

The Quick Access toolbar is illustrated in Figure 29-2. It's found in the upper left corner of the window.

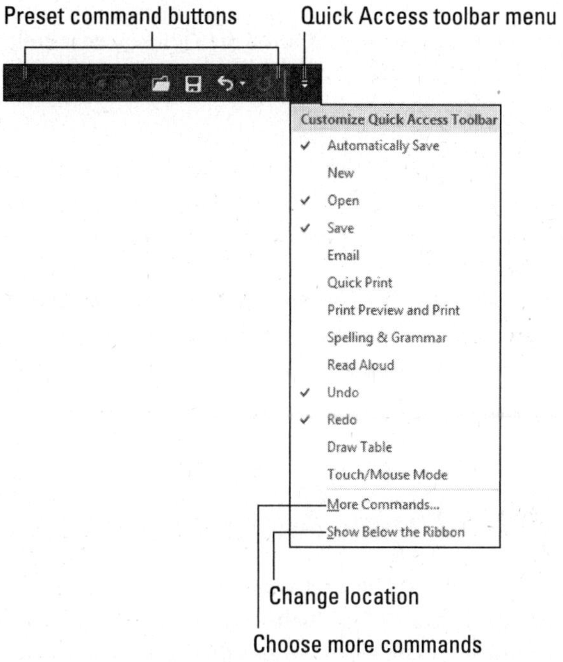

Preset command buttons   Quick Access toolbar menu

Customize Quick Access Toolbar

✓	Automatically Save
	New
✓	Open
✓	Save
	Email
	Quick Print
	Print Preview and Print
	Spelling & Grammar
	Read Aloud
✓	Undo
✓	Redo
	Draw Table
	Touch/Mouse Mode
	More Commands...
	Show Below the Ribbon

Change location

Choose more commands

FIGURE 29-2:
The Quick Access toolbar.

Click a wee icon on the Quick Access toolbar to activate a feature. You can customize the toolbar by removing icons you don't use and adding icons you do.

TIP

» When the Quick Access toolbar grows too many custom buttons and it begins to crowd into the document's title, place it below the Ribbon: Choose the Show Below the Ribbon command from the toolbar menu. (Refer to Figure 29-2.) To move the Quick Access toolbar back atop the Ribbon, choose the Show Above the Ribbon command.

>> Word is configured to show several buttons on the Quick Access toolbar: AutoSave (for documents saved to OneDrive), Open, Save, Undo, and Redo. If you have a touchscreen PC, another button appears, Touch/Mouse Mode.

Adding buttons to the Quick Access toolbar

When you enjoy using a Word command so much that you see the command button icon when you close your eyes, consider adding the command to the Quick Access toolbar.

To quickly add a common command to the Quick Access tollbar, click the menu button as illustrated in Figure 29-2. Choose a command from the menu to add it to the Quick Access toolbar.

TIP

For other commands, those that don't appear on the Quick Access toolbar menu, locate the command button on the Ribbon. Right-click the command button and choose Add to Quick Access toolbar from the shortcut menu that pops up.

>> Word remembers the Quick Action toolbar's commands. They show up again the next time you start Word, in every document window.

>> Some commands place buttons on the toolbar, and others place drop-down menus or text boxes.

Editing the Quick Access toolbar

If your adoration of the Quick Access toolbar turns into an obsession, you can go hog-wild modifying the thing: Choose More Commands from the Quick Access toolbar's menu. You see the Word Options dialog box with the Quick Access Toolbar area shown, as illustrated in Figure 29-3.

Use the list on the left to choose a new command to add to the Quick Access toolbar.

The list on the right shows items currently on the toolbar. Use the up or down buttons (refer to Figure 29-3) to move items up or down (left or right) on the Quick Access toolbar.

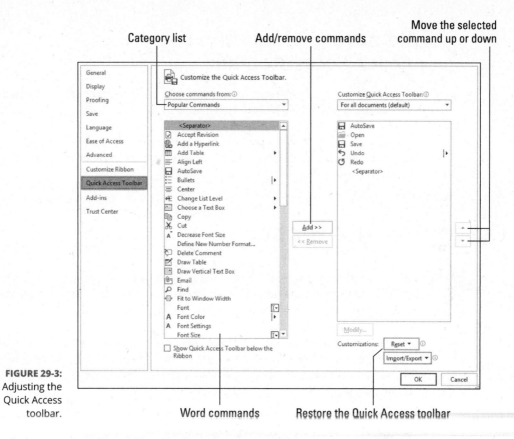

Category list   Add/remove commands   Move the selected
command up or down

Word commands   Restore the Quick Access toolbar

FIGURE 29-3:
Adjusting the
Quick Access
toolbar.

Click the OK button when you finish editing.

TIP

>> Choose the All Commands item from the Choose Commands From menu
(refer to Figure 29-3) to view every possible command in Word. Sometimes, a
missing command that you think could be elsewhere ends up being available
in the All Commands list — for example, the once-popular Save All command
or the Tabs command, which quickly displays the Tabs dialog box.

>> When the command list grows long, consider organizing it. Use the <Separator>
item to help group similar commands. This item appears as a vertical bar on
the Quick Access toolbar.

>> Yes, some commands lack specific graphics on their buttons; they show up as
large dots on the toolbar.

>> To return the Quick Access toolbar to the way Word originally had it, choose
Reset ➪ Reset Only Quick Access toolbar from the Word Options window.
(Refer to the lower right corner in Figure 29-3.)

Removing items from the Quick Access toolbar

To remove a command from the Quick Access toolbar, right-click its command button and choose Remove from Quick Access toolbar.

Likewise, you can choose a command with a check mark from the Customize Quick Access Toolbar menu. Or you can use the Word Options dialog box, as described in the preceding section, to remove items.

Customize the Ribbon

TECHNICAL STUFF

Word doesn't let you alter the basic tabs and groups on the Ribbon, which is probably a good thing for the sake of consistency. What Word does let you do, however, is create your own tab on the Ribbon or a new group on an existing tab.

Figure 29-4 shows the My Commands tab that I've added to the Ribbon, along with the groups named File Commands, Views, and Browse. This custom tab was created by using the Word Options dialog box. Follow these steps to access the proper location:

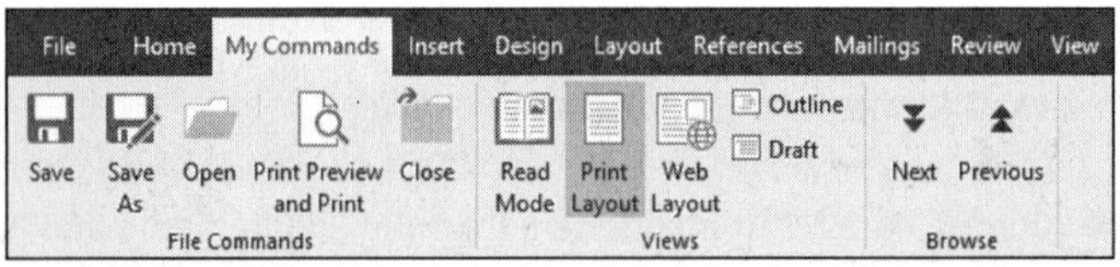

FIGURE 29-4:
A custom tab and groups on the Ribbon.

1. **Click the File tab.**

2. **Choose Options.**

3. **In the Word Options window, choose Customize Ribbon.**

    The Word Options window changes its appearance. Tabs on the Ribbon are listed on the right, and Word commands are shown on the left. The Ribbon is your oyster.

The commands in the Word Options dialog box, in the Customize Ribbon area, let you craft your own, unique tab as well as mess with the Ribbon in other ways. For full details on the fun and potential hazards available, refer to the book *Word 2016 For Professionals For Dummies* (Wiley).

TIP

If you mess around to create your own tab and goof things up horridly, click the Reset button found in the lower right corner of the Word Options window, in the Customize Ribbon area. Choose the Reset All Customizations command.

6

The Part of Tens

Chapter **30**

The Ten Commandments of Word

admit that I look nothing like Charlton Heston. Though I'm only guessing, I probably look nothing like Moses, either. Still, I feel compelled to descend from Mount Sinai with some basic codes for word processing. I call them my Ten Commandments of Word.

Thou Shalt Remember to Save Thy Work

Save! Save! Save! Always save your stuff. Whenever your mind wanders, have your fingers dart over to the Ctrl+S keyboard shortcut. Savest thy work.

Thou Shalt Not Use Spaces Unnecessarily

Generally speaking, you should never find more than one space anywhere in a Word document. The appearance of two or more spaces in a row is a desperate cry for a tab. Use single spaces to separate words and sentences. Use tabs to indent or to align text on a tab stop. To organize information into neat rows and columns, use a table.

>> Refer to Chapter 12 on setting tabs.

>> Refer to Chapter 19 for creating tables.

Thou Shalt Not Abuse the Enter Key

Word wraps text. As you type and your text approaches the right margin, the words fall to the next line. Therefore, there's no need to press the Enter key, unless you desire to begin a new paragraph. An exception is a 1-line paragraph, in which case pressing the Enter key at the end of the line is okay.

If you're pressing the Enter key to add "air" after a paragraph, modify the paragraph format to add padding. Refer to Chapter 11 for information on the Space After format.

TIP

When you don't want to start a new paragraph but you need to start a new line, such as when typing a return address, press Shift+Enter, the *soft* return command.

Thou Shalt Not Neglect Keyboard Shortcuts

When you type text in a word processor, your fingers are poised over the keyboard. As such, it pays to use keyboard shortcuts rather than grope for the mouse.

Word is rife with handy and memorable keyboard shortcuts. For example, stab the Ctrl+S key combo to quickly save a document. Press Ctrl+P to print or Ctrl+O to open a document. You need not know all the keyboard commands, but memorizing a few helps.

TIP

>> See Chapter 31 for information on keyboard accelerators to speed up access to the Ribbon.

>> Refer to this book's online Cheat Sheet for a full-on list of keyboard shortcuts mentioned in this book. You can find the Cheat Sheet at www.dummies.com. Search for Word 2019 Cheat Sheet.

Thou Shalt Not Manually Number Thy Pages

Word has an automatic page-numbering command. Refer to Chapter 13 for details on how to use it.

Thou Shalt Not Force a New Page

When you need to start text at the top of a new page, you use the *manual page-break* command. Its keyboard shortcut is Ctrl+Enter. That's the best and most proper way to start a new page. Also see Chapter 13.

The worst way to start a new page is to brazenly whack the Enter key a couple of dozen times. The result may look okay for now, yet this strategy guarantees nothing; as you continue to edit the document, the cluster of empty paragraphs wanders, creating an ugly hole in the text.

Thou Shalt Not Forget Thy Undo Command

Press Ctrl+Z to undo any unwanted change to your document. A shortcut to the Undo command is also found roosting on the Quick Access toolbar.

Honor Thy Printer

Before you print anything, verify that the printer is on, healthy, stocked with ink and paper, and ready to print before you direct Word to print something.

WARNING

Using the Print command a second time when it fails the first doesn't fix the problem. Instead, Word now tries to print *two* copies of the document, despite whatever issue prevents the first from printing.

Thou Shalt Have Multiple Document Windows Before Thee

In Word, as in most Windows applications, you can work on more than one document at a time. In fact, you can have as many document windows open as your pitiful PC can stand. Word even lets you view a single document in multiple windows. Refer to Chapter 24 to see how to conjure such alchemy.

REMEMBER

>> You need not close one document to open and view another.

>> You don't have to quit Word to run another program, either. In Windows, you can run multiple programs at a time. Don't quit Word when you plan to start it again in just a little while.

Neglecteth Not Windows

Word is a program. Windows is an operating system. Word is designed for productivity; it's word processing software. Windows is designed to control a computer and to drive human beings crazy. Word and Windows are two different things.

Word creates document files. Windows manages those files. If you need to rename a file, copy the file to a thumb drive, move the file to another folder, or recover the file from the Recycle Bin, you use Windows, not Word. They work together.

Verily I tell ye, know both Word and Windows and ye shalt be truly rewarded.

Chapter **31**

Ten Cool Tricks

When it comes down to it, just about everything Word does can be considered a cool trick. I still marvel at how word-wrap works and how you can change margins after a document is written and all the text quickly jiggles into place. Everything in this book can be considered a cool trick, but when it came down to the wire, I found ten cool tricks barely (or not) mentioned anywhere else and then listed them here.

Side-to-Side Page Movement

In Print Layout view, you can arrange the document window to display pages side-to-side, as illustrated in Figure 31-1. Workflow moves down the left page and then hops up to the top of the right page. This arrangement takes full advantage of widescreen computer monitors.

Page Management group

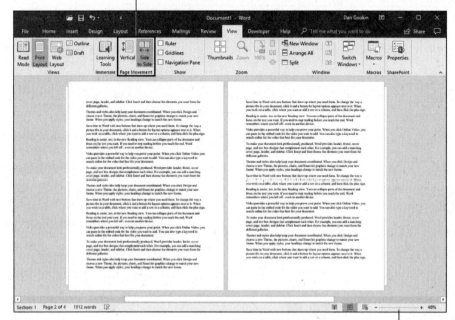

FIGURE 31-1:
Working on a
document
side-to-side.

Zoom is relative to window size

To enter Side-by-Side view, click the View tab and in the Page Movement group, choose Side-to-Side, shown in the margin. You may need to adjust the Word window to enlarge the document presentation; the Zoom command is disabled when you activate Side-to-Side page movement. So, the wider you can make the document window, the better things look.

In the Side-to-Side presentation, the horizontal scroll bar becomes more useful. Use it to page through the document. The pages automatically flip as you edit and create text.

To restore traditional document presentation, click the Vertical button. You can also switch document views, though when you return to Print Layout, Side-to-Side presentation is restored.

Automatic Save with AutoRecover

Someday, you will sing the praises of Word's AutoRecover feature. It periodically saves your document, even when you neglect to do so. In the event of a computer crash or some other mishap, Word recovers your document from a supersecret safety copy it secretly made for you. How nice.

To ensure that AutoRecover is active, heed these directions:

1. **Click the File tab.**
2. **On the File screen, choose Options.**

   The Word Options dialog box appears.
3. **Choose Save.**
4. **On the right side of the dialog box, ensure that a check mark appears by the item Save AutoRecover Information Every 10 Minutes.**

   You can change the time, though 10 minutes seems good.
5. **Click OK to close the window.**

   Whew! You're safe.

Most of the time, you never notice AutoRecover. On that rare, terrifying occasion that something goes awry, you see the document recovery pane when you restart Word. Information about unsaved documents appears in the document recovery pane, along with directions on how to recover a document.

REMEMBER

The best way to avoid accidentally losing stuff is to *save now* and *save often!*

Accelerate the Ribbon

Word has always been a mouse-based program, even when it ran in Text mode on old DOS PCs. Still, the keyboard remains a fast and effective way to access commands, especially given that in a word processor, your fingers are hovering over the keyboard most of the time.

If you're willing to learn, eschew the mouse and instead use some keyboard accelerators to access commands on the Ribbon.

The secret is to use the Alt key: Tap Alt and you see letters in boxes appear on the Ribbon, like tiny square freckles. Within each box are one or two letters, which are the accelerator keys. Tap a letter or the two letters in sequence to "click" a specific part of the Ribbon.

For example, to change the page orientation to Landscape mode, you press Alt, P, O to display the Orientation menu. Press the down-arrow key to choose Landscape. Press Enter to choose that menu item.

>> If you accidentally tap the Alt key, press it again to exit Accelerator mode.

>> You can also press the F10 key to access the Ribbon accelerators.

Ancient Word Keyboard Shortcuts

Before the Ribbon rode into town and freaked out all the townsfolk, Word relied upon keyboard commands. These ancient Word keyboard shortcuts still work in Word today. They're handy, though not too memorable.

F4: The F4 key is the Repeat key, exactly the same as Ctrl+Y, the Repeat key.

Shift+F4: Another repeat key, but this one is the Repeat Find command. It works even when the Find dialog box (or navigation pane) isn't visible.

Shift+F5: This key combo is the Go Back command, which returns to the spot you last edited. See Chapter 3 for details.

Shift+F8: The Shrink Selection key is the opposite of the Selection key, F8. For example, when the entire document is selected, press Shift+F8 to select only the current paragraph. Press Shift+F8 again to select only the current sentence. Press it again to select only the current word. Press Shift+F8 one more time to deselect the word. Refer to Chapter 6 for more text-selection tricks.

F12: Tap this key to quickly summon the Save As dialog box. I use this key a lot because it's quicker than wading through the Backstage to summon the Save As dialog box.

Ctrl+F12: This key does for the Open dialog box what F12 does for the Save As dialog box. It's not redundant to the Ctrl+O command, which conjures the Backstage. Ctrl+F12 always brings up the good ol' Open dialog box.

Build Your Own Fractions

Word's AutoCorrect feature builds common fractions for you, replacing your clumsy text with fraction characters. Sadly, Word has only a few of these fraction characters. When you need your own, custom fraction, such as $3/_{64}$, create it this way:

1. **Press Ctrl+Shift+= (the equal sign), the keyboard shortcut for the super-script command.**

2. **Type the *numerator* — the top part of the fraction.**

   For example, type **3** for $\frac{3}{64}$.

3. **Press Ctrl+Shift+= again to disable superscript.**

4. **Type the slash character (/).**

5. **Press Ctrl+= to activate subscript.**

6. **Type the *denominator* — the bottom part of the fraction.**

   For example, type **64** for $\frac{3}{64}$.

7. **Press Ctrl+= to turn off subscript.**

There's your fraction.

Electronic Bookmarks

When you must find your place in a document, you can write text like WORK HERE, or you can take advantage of Word's Bookmark command. The bookmark is invisible, but Word knows where it is. You can use the bookmark to return to a page for editing, to add a cross-reference, or to perform a bunch of other handy tricks written about in *Word 2016 for Professionals For Dummies* (Wiley). For this book, set a bookmark by following these steps:

1. **Place the insertion pointer where you want to insert the bookmark.**

2. **Click the Insert tab.**

3. **In the Links group, click the Bookmark button.**

   The Bookmark dialog box appears.

4. **Type a name for the bookmark in the Bookmark dialog box.**

   Try to keep the bookmark name to one word, letters only.

5. **Click the Add button.**

   The bookmark is created.

To hop to bookmarks in your document, use the Go To command: Press Ctrl+G to summon the Find and Replace dialog box, with the Go To tab forward. Choose

Bookmark from the Go to What list. Select the bookmark name from the list on the right side of the dialog box. Click the Go To button to visit that bookmark's location. Click the Close button or tap the Escape key to dismiss the dialog box.

Lock Your Document

When you really, *really* don't want anyone messing with your sweet text, you can lock the document. Several levels of protection are available, but you start the journey by following these steps:

1. Click the File tab.

2. Choose Info.

3. Click the Protect Document button.

Of the several choices, I recommend these options:

Mark as Final: The document is flagged as *final,* which means that further editing is disabled. Still, you can easily override it by clicking the Edit Anyway button that appears.

Encrypt with Password: The document is encrypted and a password is applied. To open the document in Word, you must enter the password. You cannot remove a password after it's applied.

Restrict Editing: You can limit whether a user can edit a document or whether all changes are tracked or restrict that person to make only comments.

4. Choose an option and answer the questions in the dialog boxes that appear.

5. Click OK.

The document protection you've chosen is applied.

WARNING

Locking your document is a serious decision! No one can help you if you forget a password or are otherwise unable to remove the restrictions you've applied to the document.

The Drop Cap

A *drop cap* is the first letter of a report, an article, a chapter, or a story that appears in a larger and more interesting font than the other characters. Figure 31-2 shows an example.

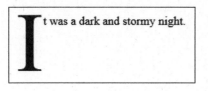

I t was a dark and stormy night.

To add a drop cap to a document, follow these steps:

1. **Select the first character of the first word at the start of the text.**

   For example, select the *I* in *It was a dark and stormy night*. (Refer to Figure 31-2.)

2. **Click the Insert tab.**

3. **In the Text group, click the Drop Cap button.**

4. **Choose a drop cap style.**

   And there's your drop cap.

It helps if the drop cap's paragraph is left justified and not indented with a tab or any of the tricky formatting operations discussed in Part 3.

To remove the drop cap, choose None in Step 4.

TIP

Map Your Document

Whenever I'm writing, I show the navigation pane on the left side of the document window. This pane lets me see the Big Picture, an overview of my document based on the heading styles. I can use it to quickly hop to a specific header. As a bonus, it also shows the handy Search Document text box, as illustrated in Figure 31-3.

To summon the navigation pane, follow these steps:

1. **Click the View tab.**

2. **In the Show group, click to put a check mark by the Navigation Pane item.**

To close the navigation pane, click its X Close button.

The navigation pane replaces a popular but long-gone Word feature called the Document Map.

TECHNICAL
STUFF

Search box

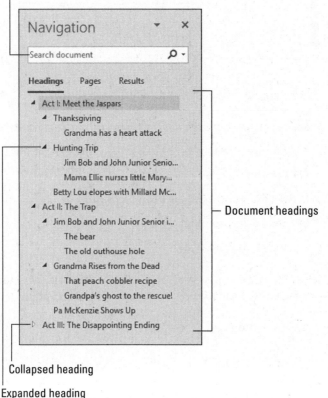

Document headings

FIGURE 31-3:
The navigation
pane document
map.

Collapsed heading

Expanded heading

Sort Your Text

Sorting is one of Word's better tricks, though it's surprising how few people know about it. You can use the Sort command to arrange text alphabetically or numerically. You can sort paragraphs, table rows and columns, and more.

Save your document before sorting. It's just a good idea.

REMEMBER Sorting isn't difficult. First, arrange whatever needs to be sorted into several lines of text, such as

```
Lemon
Banana cream
Apple
Cherry
Rhubarb
Tortilla
```

After you know what you're going to sort, obey these steps:

1. **Select the lines of text (or parts of a table) as a block.**

2. **Click the Home tab.**

3. **In the Paragraph group, click the Sort button.**

   The Sort Text dialog box appears. It's most useful when sorting multicolumn items, which is where the Then By parts of the dialog box are most useful.

4. **Choose Ascending or Descending to sort the text from A to Z or from Z to A, respectively.**

5. **Click the OK button.**

As if by magic, the selected text is sorted.

Chapter **32**

Ten Bizarre Things

f Word were only about word processing, this book would end at Chapter 17. Fully half the text references things more relevant to the topics of desktop publishing or graphics. These tasks are done far better by using other software, but Word doesn't stop there with its unique and weird features. Welcome to the *Twilight Zone,* Word edition.

Equations

Microsoft must recognize that a vast majority of Word users hold degrees in astrophysics and quantum mechanics. If you're one of them, or perhaps you dabble in rocket science or brain surgery, you'll appreciate Word's Equation tools. These tools sate your desire to place a polynomial equation or quantum calculation in your document without having to endure the tedium of building the thing yourself.

To place a premade equation into your third doctoral thesis from MIT, click the Insert tab. In the Symbols group, click the Equation button menu and choose a preset mathematical monster from the list. Or you can choose the Insert New Equation command to share your own brilliance by crafting the equation yourself.

>> An equation *content control* is inserted in a document at the insertion pointer's location. When selected, the Equation Tools Design tab appears on the Ribbon.

>> No, Word won't solve the equation.

Video in Your Document

Seriously? I'm guessing that Word's capability to stick a video into a document doesn't translate well when the page is printed. That's just a guess — I haven't tried it, though I think I'm probably correct.

 When you're been up late and the alcohol in your bloodstream is flirting with every neuron in your brain, click the Insert tab. Use YouTube or choose another video-searing option in the Insert Video window. After way too much time passes, the video appears as a large graphical goober in the document. You can play it right there on the screen. Amazing.

 Videos are best viewed when a Word document is presented in Read mode — which in and of itself is yet another bizarre thing. To enter Read mode, click the Read Mode button on the status bar (shown in the margin); or, on the View tab, choose Read Mode from the Views group.

Hidden Text

One text format not covered in Chapter 10 is hidden text. I mean, why bother? Hidden text doesn't appear in a document. It doesn't print. It's just not there!

If you desire to write hidden text so that you can put it on your résumé for application to the CIA, select the text and press Ctrl+Shift+H. The same keyboard shortcut deactivates this format. The following text is hidden:

The only way you know that hidden text exists in a document is to use the Show/Hide command: Click the Home tab, and in the Paragraph group, click the Show/Hide button, which looks like the Paragraph symbol. The hidden text shows up in the document with a dotted underline.

The Developer Tab

Computer users love secrets, especially when no one else knows about them. One such secret in Word is the Developer tab. Shhh!

The Developer tab plays host to some of Word's advanced and cryptic features. These commands don't make creating a document any easier, and they open a can of worms that I don't want to cover in this book. Still, you're reading this text, so follow these steps to summon the mysterious Developer tab:

1. **Click the File tab.**

2. **Choose the Options command to display the Word Options dialog box.**

3. **Choose the Customize Ribbon item on the left side of the dialog box.**

4. **Under the Customize Ribbon list on the right side of the dialog box, place a check mark by the Developer item.**

5. **Click OK.**

The Developer tab is aptly named; it's best suited for people who either use Word to develop applications, special documents, and online forms or are hellbent on customizing Word by using macros. Scary stuff, but it's covered in the book *Word 2016 For Professionals For Dummies* (Wiley). Now you know the secret.

Hyphenation

Hyphenation is an automatic feature that splits a long word at the end of a line to make the text fit better on the page. Most people leave this feature disabled because hyphenated words tend to slow down the pace at which people read. However, if you want to hyphenate a document, click the Layout tab and then the Page Setup group, and choose Hyphenation⇨Automatic.

REMEMBER

Automatic hyphenation works only on paragraphs formatted with full justification alignment. If the paragraph is otherwise formatted, the Hyphenation command button is dimmed. See Chapter 11 for information on paragraph alignment.

Document Properties

Word merrily tracks lots of details about the documents you craft, stuff that you normally wouldn't pay attention to if you didn't know about the Document Properties feature.

To view a document's properties, click the File tab and choose the Info item. The Properties are on the right, showing document size, pages, word count, and other trivia. To view or set other options, click the Properties button and choose Advanced Properties.

Document Version History

You write, you save, you write you save. These different document versions can be recovered if you enable the Windows File History feature. Within Word, however, you can peruse a document's revision history, providing you've saved the document to OneDrive.

To check out previous editions of a document, click the document name, top and center of the window. From the menu, choose See All Versions. The Version History pane appears. If you click and don't see a menu, the document was saved locally or to cloud storage that's better than OneDrive.

The Version History pane lists all major document revisions by date, time, and author. To see a revision, click the Open Version link. The selected revision appears in a new window.

Collect-and-Paste

I hope the word processing concept of copy-and-paste is simple for you. What's not simple is taking it to the next level by using Word's collect-and-paste feature.

Collect-and-paste allows you to copy multiple chunks of text and paste them in any order or all at once. The secret is to click the dialog box launcher in the lower right corner of the Clipboard group on the Home tab, right next to the word *Clipboard.* The clipboard pane appears on the screen.

With the clipboard pane visible, you can use the Copy command multiple times in a row to collect text. To paste the text, simply click the mouse on that chunk of text in the clipboard pane. Or you can use the Paste All button to paste into the document every item you've collected.

Even more bizarre: You can actually select multiple separate chunks of text in a document. To do so, select the first chunk, and then, while holding down the Ctrl key, drag over additional text. As long as the Ctrl key is held down, you can drag to select multiple chunks of text in different locations. The various selected chunks work as a block, which you can cut, copy, or delete or to which you can apply formatting.

Click-and-Type

A feature introduced in Word 2002, and one that I don't believe anyone ever uses, is click-and-type. In a blank document, you can use *click-and-type* to stab the mouse pointer anywhere on the page and type information at that spot. *Bam!*

I fail to see any value in click-and-type, especially when it's a more positive aspect of your Word education to learn basic formatting. But click-and-type may bother you when you see any of its specialized mouse pointers displayed; thus:

Those weird mouse pointers indicate the click-and-type feature in action. The mouse pointer itself tries to indicate the paragraph format to be applied when you click the mouse.

See Chapter 33 for information on disabling this feature.

Translations

Allora, hai il desiderio di scrivere il tuo testo l'italiano? Rather than get bored trying to learn Italian in school or waste precious time vacationing in Italy, you can use Word's Translate feature to magically create Italian or any other foreign language text. The secret lies on the Review tab, in the Language group.

To translate a chunk of text in a document, follow these steps:

1. **Write the text you want to translate.**

I came. I saw. I conquered.

2. **Select the text.**

3. **On the Review tab, in the Language group, click the Translate button and choose Translate Selection.**

The Translate command button is shown in the margin.

4. **Click the Turn On button if prompted to activate Intelligent Services.**

The translator pane appears on the right side of the document window. It automatically detects the language selected, which I assume is English for this book.

5. **Choose a target language from the To menu.**

Alas, Latin isn't one of them, at least as this book goes to press.

6. **Review the translation.**

If you know a smattering of the selected language, consider fixing it up. For example, the Italian sentence at the start of this section was originally translated with the second person plural instead of second person singular.

7. **Click the Insert button to set the translated text into the document.**

Bello.

8. **Close the Translate pane.**

Click the X button to close.

As with all computer translations, what you get is more of an approximation of what a native speaker would say. The text is generally understandable, but nothing truly substitutes for a knowledge of the language — or a month in Italy.

Chapter **33**

Ten Automatic Features Worthy of Deactivation

You need not put up with it. You know what I'm referring to: those annoying things that Word does. Those features you might dislike but tolerate simply because no one has told you how to turn them off. Until now.

Bye-Bye, Start Screen

I prefer to see a blank page when I start Word, not a screen full of options. The Word Start screen can easily be disabled. Follow these blessed steps:

1. **Click the File tab.**

2. **Choose Options.**

   The Word Options dialog box appears with the General category chosen for you.

3. **Remove the check mark by the item Show the Start Screen When This Application Starts.**

   This item is found in the Start-Up Options section.

4. **Click OK.**

After completing these steps, Word starts with a blank document, or whichever document you've opened.

Restore the Traditional Open and Save Dialog Boxes

When you use the Ctrl+O or Ctrl+S commands, you're thrust into the Open or Save As screens, respectively. These screens are referred to as the Backstage, and I find them one more annoying step in a process that eventually ends up at the traditional Open and Save dialog boxes.

To dismiss the Backstage, follow these steps:

1. **Click the File tab and choose Options to bring up the Word Options dialog box.**

2. **Choose the Save category on the left side of the dialog box.**

3. **Place a check by the item Don't Show the Backstage When Opening or Saving Files.**

   This item is found in the Save Documents section.

4. **Click OK.**

One advantage of the Backstage is that it does show recent files. It also lets you pin popular files so that they're easy to find. Refer to Chapter 8.

REMEMBER

Turn Off the Mini Toolbar

When you use the mouse to select text, Word displays the mini toolbar, which looks like Figure 33-1. You may find its assortment of commands useful, or you may just want to set the thing on fire. If the latter, you can disable the mini toolbar by following these steps:

1. **Click the File tab and choose Options.**

   The General category is automatically chosen for you.

2. **Remove the check mark by the item Show Mini Toolbar on Selection.**

   This item is located below the heading User Interface Options. It's right up top.

3. **Click OK.**

If you would rather not eternally banish the mini toolbar, note that it hides itself whenever you move the mouse pointer beyond the selected chunk of text.

Select Text by Letter

When you're selecting more than a single word, the mouse grabs text a full word at a time. If you want Word to select text by characters rather than by words (which is what I prefer), follow these steps:

1. **Click the File tab and choose Options to display the Word Options dialog box.**

2. **Choose Advanced.**

3. **Remove the check mark by the item labeled When Selecting Automatically Select Entire Word.**

   This item is located below the Editing Options heading.

4. **Click OK.**

You can still select text a word at a time: Double-click to select a word, but keep the mouse button down. As you drag, text is selected one word at a time.

Disable Click-and-Type

Click-and-Type is that feature where you can click anywhere in a document and start typing. The feature is evident by an odd-looking mouse pointer and strange lines around the insertion pointer in your text (refer to Chapter 32). To mercifully disable this Click-and-Type, follow these steps:

1. **Click the File tab menu and choose Options.**

The Word Options dialog box appears.

2. **Choose Advanced.**

3. **Remove the check mark by Enable Click and Type.**

This option is located below the Editing Options heading.

4. **Click the OK button.**

Seriously: Who uses this feature? For the past few editions of this book, I've asked readers to send me an email if they use Click-and-Type. So far, nothing.

Paste Plain Text Only

When you copy and paste text from one part of a document to another, the format is retained. Similarly, the format is kept when you copy and paste text from another document. If you like, you can direct Word to paste only plain text or attempt to paste formatted text. Heed these directions:

1. **Click the File tab and choose Options.**

2. **In the Word Options dialog box, choose Advanced.**

Four text-pasting options are listed under the Cut, Copy, and Paste heading. These options tell you how text is pasted based on its source.

3. **Change the paste settings according to how you prefer text to be pasted.**

In most cases, keeping the source formatting is what you want. I prefer to choose the option Keep Text Only because it doesn't mess up my document's formatting.

4. **Click OK.**

REMEMBER

You can use the Paste Special command at any time to override your decision: Click the Home tab and, in the Clipboard group, click the Paste button to choose whether or not to keep the formats. See Chapter 6 for details.

Disable AutoFormat Features (×4)

The final four items worthy of deactivation fall under the domain of the AutoCorrect dialog box. Specifically, the overeager AutoFormat feature, which aggressively interrupts your writing with jarring suggestions you probably don't want to see.

Start your disabling binge by summoning the AutoCorrect dialog box. Follow these steps:

1. **Click the File tab and choose Options.**

2. **In the Word Options dialog box, click the Proofing category.**

3. **Click the AutoCorrect Options button.**

   The AutoCorrect dialog box shows up.

4. **Click the AutoFormat as You Type tab.**

   You've arrived.

Here are four annoying features you can disable:

Automatic Bulleted Lists: This feature assumes that whenever you start a paragraph with an asterisk (*) you really want a bulleted list, so it changes the format.

Automatic Numbered Lists: This feature works like Automatic Bullet Lists, but does the same annoying thing for any paragraph you start numbering.

Border Lines: Type three dashes in a row and you see this feature activated. Use the Borders paragraph format instead. See Chapter 18.

Format Beginning of List Item Like the One Before It: This feature assumes that just because the first word of the preceding paragraph is in bold or italics that you desire all other paragraphs to start that way as well.

Deselect each of these items. Oh, and while you're at it, look for other things to disable in the AutoCorrect dialog box. Some of those features may bother you more than they bother me.

Index

D

slicing into sections, 163–167

split-screen, 280–281

splitting, 294

terminology for, 83–84

updating, 89, 284

version history of, 358

video in, 356

viewing in multiple windows, 279–280

Don't Save button, 17

double-spacing, 26, 126, 132

double-underline, applying, 112

downward-pointing triangle, 13

Draft view, 15, 27

drafts, recovering, 94

Draw Table button, 224, 231

drawing tables, 224–225

drop cap, 350–351

Dropbox, 84

E

editing

graphics, 258–261

PDF files, 106

Quick Access toolbar, 336–337

recipient lists, 319

text, 41–48

electronic bookmarks, 349–350

electronic publishing, 104–106

Elevator button, 34–35

ellipsis character (. . .), 296

em dashes, 206

email messages

creating for mail merge, 311–312

merging to, 322–323

en dash, 206

End key, 37

endnotes, 248–250

Enter key, 22, 26, 342

entering Outline view, 286–287

envelopes, creating, 312–313, 329–331

Envelopes and Labels dialog box, 330

equations, 355–356

Eraser tool, 231

erasing text, 26

even headers/footers, 173

Even Page section break, 166

Expand button, 289

expanding topics, 289–290

exporting documents, 106

Extend Selection mode, 64

F

F1 key, 16

F4 key, 348

F8 key, 64

Field dialog box, 269–270

fields

about, 269–270

adding, 271–272, 314–315

changing, 272

defined, 308

deleting, 273

inserting in mail merge, 320

removing, 315–316

restoring, 272

updating, 272

viewing raw data from, 272

file format, 281–282

File screen, accessing, 2

File tab, 13

filenames, 89

files, 84

Find and Replace dialog box, 51–52, 56–57

Find command, 50–51, 53

finding

case-sensitive text, 52

formatting, 54–55

special characters, 53–54

styles, 178–179

text, 50–51

word variations, 53

words, 52

Finish & Merge command button, 321, 329

First Line Indent control, 131

first-page options, headers/footers on, 174

fixing misspelled words, 72–73

floating images, 256, 258

folders, 84

follow-me style, 184

Font Color command button, 116

Font dialog box, 118–120

font theme, 199

fonts

resizing, 115

selecting, 110–112

footers

creating custom, 170–172

defined, 169

even, 173

on first page, 174

multiple, 173–175

odd, 173

removing, 175

sections and, 174–175

using preset, 170

footnotes, 169, 248–250

foreign language characters, 267

forgetting to save, 90

form letters, creating for mail merge, 311

Format Painter, 203–204

Format Painter command button, 203

formats, for documents, 281–282

numbered lists
  about, 207
  automatic, 365
  multilevel, 243–244
numbering
  lines on pages, 244
  lists, 242–243
  pages manually, 343
Numbering command button, 242–243
numeric keypad, 23

O

Object button, 93
odd headers/footers, 173
Odd Page section break, 166
Online Pictures button, 253
online version, of Ribbon, 14
onscreen keyboard, 23
Open command, 91–93
Open dialog box, 91, 362
Open screen, 91
opening
  documents, 84–85, 90–94, 277–278
  Navigation pane, 351
  non-Word documents, 282–283
  PDF files, 106
  Reveal Formatting pane, 180
  Word documents, 9
ordinals, 206
orientation, changing, 150–151
Orientation button, 151
Original, 299
orphans, 28
outdents, 129–130
Outline button, 286
Outline view
  about, 15
  entering, 286–287
  exiting, 287

outlines
  printing, 290–291
  typing topics in, 287–288
Outlook, 308, 318–319

P

page borders, applying, 219
Page Break command button, 159
page breaks, 27–28, 343
Page Color button, 160
page formatting
  about, 149
  adding automatic page numbers, 155–156
  adding cover pages, 168
  adding watermarks, 161–162
  backgrounds, 160–162
  changing orientation, 150–151
  coloring pages, 160
  creating custom headers/footers, 170–172
  creating sections, 165–166
  first-page, 167–169
  footers, 169–175
  headers, 169–175
  inserting blank pages, 159
  inserting cover pages manually, 168–169
  multiple-page options, 154
  numbering pages, 155–158
  numbering with Roman numerals, 157
  Page Setup dialog box, 152–154
  printing colored pages, 161
  removing page numbers, 158
  removing section breaks, 167
  setting page margins, 151–152
  setting page size, 149–150
  slicing documents into sections, 163–167

starting text on new pages, 158–159
  starting with different page numbers, 156–157
  using preset headers/footers, 170
page margins, setting, 151–152
page number field, adding, 271
page numbering
  about, 155
  adding automatic, 155–156
  adding in headers/footers, 171–172
  removing, 158
  with Roman numerals, 157
  starting with different, 156–157
Page Setup dialog box, 152–154, 166–167
page size, setting, 149–150
pages
  centering, 208–210
  coloring, 160
  deleting, 44–45
  numbering lines on, 244
  printing odd and even, 101
  printing on both sides of, 100–101
  printing ranges of, 100
  printing specific, 98–100
  splitting, 159
paper documents, 95–104
Paragraph dialog box, 123–124, 188
paragraph formatting
  about, 121
  alignment, 124–125
  commands for, 123–124
  hanging indents, 129–130
  indentation, 128–132
  indenting first lines, 128–129
  indenting paragraphs, 130
  justification, 124–125

Word. *See also specific topics*
  quitting, 17
  starting, 7–9
Word 2016 For Professionals For Dummies (Gookin), 3, 55, 57, 85, 109, 121, 210, 227, 243, 248, 254, 273, 338, 357
Word button, 19
word count, 271, 295–296

Word Count button, 296
WordArt, 255–256
WordArt button, 256
WordPerfect, 29
words
  deleting, 42–43
  finding, 52
  finding variations of, 53

wrapped images, 256
wrapping text around images, 257–258
writers, features for, 285–296

Z

zooming text, 15–16

About the Author

Dan Gookin has been writing about technology for nearly three decades. He combines his love of writing with his gizmo fascination to create books that are informative, entertaining, and not boring. Having written over 160 titles with 12 million copies in print translated into over 30 languages, Dan can attest that his method of crafting computer tomes seems to work.

Perhaps his most famous title is the original *DOS For Dummies*, published in 1991. It became the world's fastest-selling computer book, at one time moving more copies per week than the *New York Times* number-one bestseller (though, as a reference, it could not be listed on the Times' Best Sellers list). That book spawned the entire line of *For Dummies* books, which remains a publishing phenomenon to this day.

Dan's most popular titles include *PCs For Dummies, Laptops For Dummies,* and *Android Phones And Tablets For Dummies.* He also maintains the vast and helpful website www.wambooli.com.

Dan holds a degree in Communications/Visual Arts from the University of California, San Diego. He lives in the Pacific Northwest, where he enjoys spending time with his sons playing video games indoors while they enjoy the gentle woods of Idaho.

Publisher's Acknowledgments

Acquisitions Editor: Katie Mohr
Senior Project Editor: Paul Levesque
Copy Editor: Becky Whitney
Editorial Assistant: Matthew Lowe
Sr. Editorial Assistant: Cherie Case

Production Editor: G. Vasanth Koilraj
Cover Image: © elinedesignservices/iStockphoto